# THE MIDDLE EAST IN 2015

## The Impact of Regional Trends on U.S. Strategic Planning

*edited by* Judith S. Yaphe

Hobson Library
317586

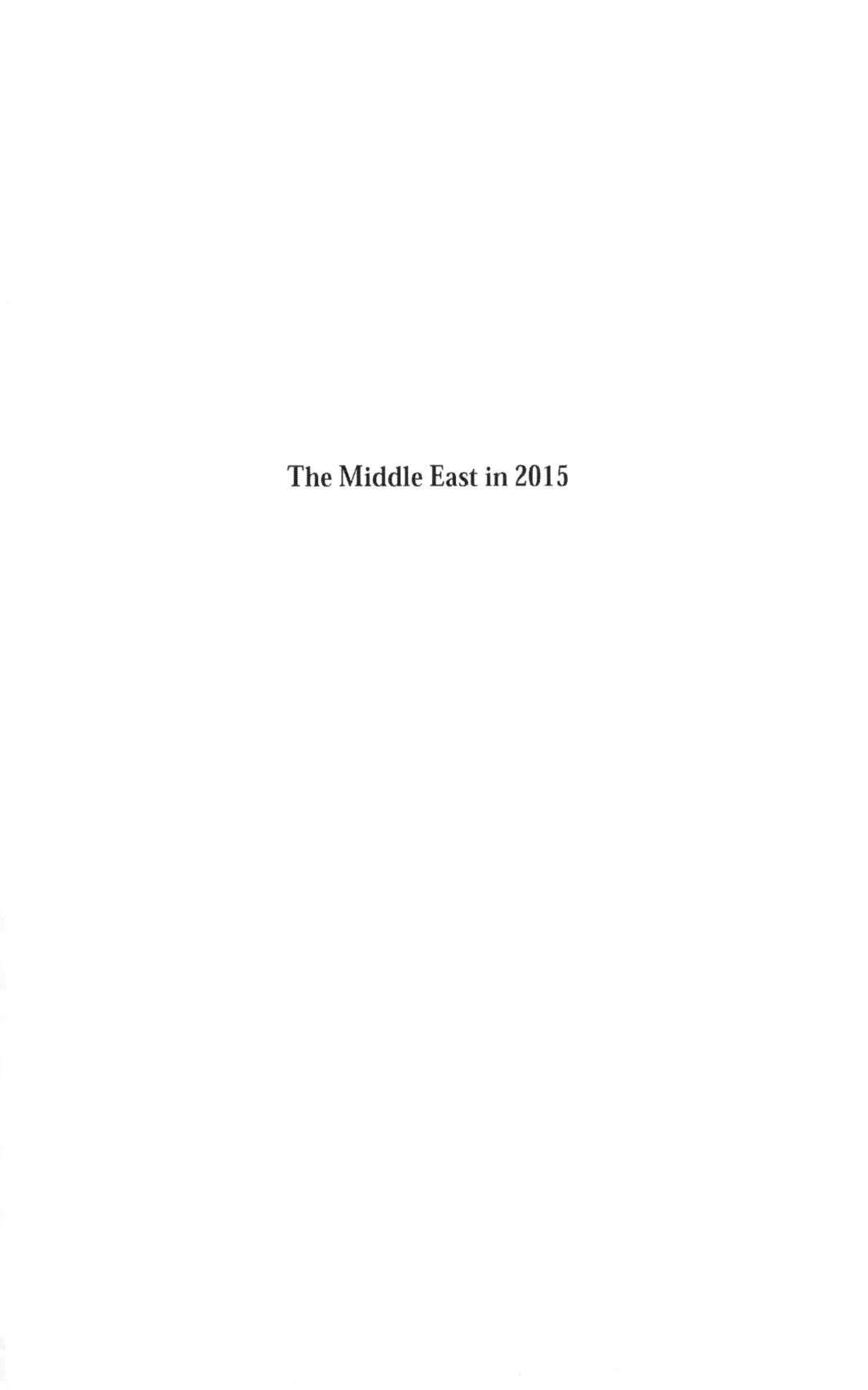

# The Middle East in 2015

# The Middle East in 2015:
## The Impact of Regional Trends on U.S. Strategic Planning

*edited by* Judith S. Yaphe

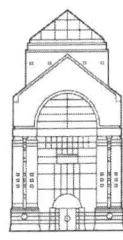

NATIONAL DEFENSE UNIVERSITY PRESS
WASHINGTON, D.C.
2002

The opinions, conclusions, and recommendations expressed or implied within are those of the contributors and do not necessarily reflect the views of the Department of Defense or any other agency of the Federal Government. This publication is cleared for public release; distribution unlimited.

Portions of this work may be quoted or reprinted without further permission, with credit to the Institute for National Strategic Studies. A courtesy copy of any reviews and tearsheets would be appreciated.

# Contents

Preface ......................................................................... ix

Chapter 1
The Middle East in 2015: An Overview ................ 3
Judith S. Yaphe

Chapter 2
Algeria: Can National Order Be Restored? ............ 15
Hugh Roberts

Chapter 3
Morocco: Will Tradition Protect the Monarchy? ......... 43
Azzedine Layachi

Chapter 4
Egypt: Could It Lead the Arab World? ..................... 59
Mamoun Fandy

Chapter 5
Israel: Reconciling Internal Disparities? ..................... 75
Kenneth W. Stein

Chapter 6
Palestine: Moving toward a Democratic State? ............ 97
Muhammad Muslih

Chapter 7
Iran: Can the Islamic Republic Survive? ..................... 119
    Mark J. Gasiorowski

Chapter 8
Iraq: Another Saddam on the Horizon? ..................... 143
    Adeed Dawisha *and* Judith S. Yaphe

Chapter 9
The Arab Gulf: Will Autocracy Define the
Social Contract in 2015? ............................................ 163
    F. Gregory Gause III *and* Jill Crystal

Chapter 10
Arms Control: In the Region's Future? ...................... 195
    Steven L. Spiegel

Chapter 11
Conclusion: Three Parts of the Whole ...................... 213
    Judith S. Yaphe

Postscript
Israel-Turkey: Strategic Relationship
or Temporary Alliance? ............................................. 231
    Alan Makovsky

About the Editor ....................................................... 237

# Preface

This volume was begun in 1999, when the National Intelligence Council asked the Institute for National Strategic Studies (INSS) at the National Defense University to examine change in the Middle East. At that time, little political change had occurred in the region in 30 years. In fact, the governments of the Middle East had shown a remarkable stability. Except for the 1979 Islamic re volution in Iran and a military coup in Sudan in 1989, the region had been stable. Most rulers had been in p lace for a gen eration—Syrian President Hafiz al-Asad since 1971, the Iraqi Ba'thists and Saddam Husayn since 1968, Jordanian King Hussein since 1952, Moroccan King Hassan since 1961, Omani Sultan Qaboos since 1970, and Libyan leader Muammar Qadhafi since 1969. The same families have ruled Saudi Arabia and the Gulf states for much of the 20 th century. Iran, the only country in the region to undergo a revolution in the past 25 years, passed power to new leaders through elections. Assassinations in Egypt and Israel brought in new leaders but did not change the basic political structure in those countries. With the exceptions of Qatar , Iran, Sudan, and Algeria, transfers of power were orderly and preordained by elections (in Israel) or family, tribal, or party consensus.

At the same time, the economies of the countries—including the oil-rich Persian Gulf states—have remained stagnant, and an unchanging trend in demographics—rapidly increasing populations, lowered mortality rates, growing unemployment, and insufficient job creation—seems poised to threaten stability . The spread of weapons of mass destruction, new security alliances, drugs, terrorism, and the increasing popularity of religiously defined activist movements, both Islamic and Jewish, raise questions about future challenges to internal and external regime security.

INSS held a series of conferences to examine the general political, economic, and social trends and to consider the range of issues affecting the region and U.S. policy. Conferences focused on the Maghreb states of Algeria, Morocco, and Libya; the Mashreq states of Egypt, Israel, Syria, the Palestine Authority, and Jordan; and the Khalij states of the Arabian or Persian Gulf, including Iraq, Iran, and Saudi Arabia. The current volume offers case studies presented during the conference series. We are grateful to the following scholars for their contributions: Ibrahim Karawan, University of Utah; Alan Richards, University of California at Santa Cruz; Steven Spiegel, University of California at Los Angeles; Henry Munson, University of Maine; Mamoun Fandy, Georgetown University; Hugh Roberts, London School of Economics; Azzedine Layachi, St. John's University; Dirk Vandervalle, Dartmouth University; Simon Serfaty, Center for Strategic and International Studies; Kenneth Stein, Emory University; Muhammad Muslih, Long Island University; Michael Fishbach, Randolph-Macon University; Murhaf Jouejati, the Middle East Institute; Alan Makovsky, the Washington Institute for Near East Studies; Jon Alterman, the U.S. Institute for Peace; Mark Gasiorowski, Louisiana State University; Adeed Dawisha, George Mason University; F. Gregory Gause, University of Vermont; Jill Crystal, Auburn University; and Neil Partrick, Royal United Services Institute, London. Without their diligent efforts, this study could not have been completed. Our thanks go as well to Ben Bonk, then National Intelligence Officer for the Near East and South Asia, for his support; Stephen Flanagan, Director of INSS, for his encouragement; and Mona Yacoubian for her help in preparing the chapters for publication.

We also acknowledge those who contributed to the production of this volume. The Publication Directorate at INSS and the staff of National Defense University Press—William Bode, George Maerz, Lisa Yambrick, and Jeffrey Smotherman—under the supervision of Robert Silano, Director of Publications, edited the manuscript and proofread the final pages. Jeffrey Smotherman also designed and composed all text. William Rawley of the Typography and Design Division of the U.S. Government Printing Office designed the cover.

As we prepared this draft, two topics arose that made prediction more difficult than it normally would be. These two issues—Syria after the death of Hafiz al-Asad and the Palestinian-Israeli *intifada*—made these chapters too current and complicated for our scholars to feel comfortable discussing. (A chapter on the shorter-term issues facing the Palestinians is included.) Yet it seemed unwise to hold up the study for real-time issues that may have unpredictable outcomes. And while the events of September 11 and the seeming inability or unwillingness of Israelis and Palestinians to halt the violence of their *intifada* appear daunting, by 2015 they most likely will have been overtaken by other equally dramatic events or, hopefully, resolved peacefully.

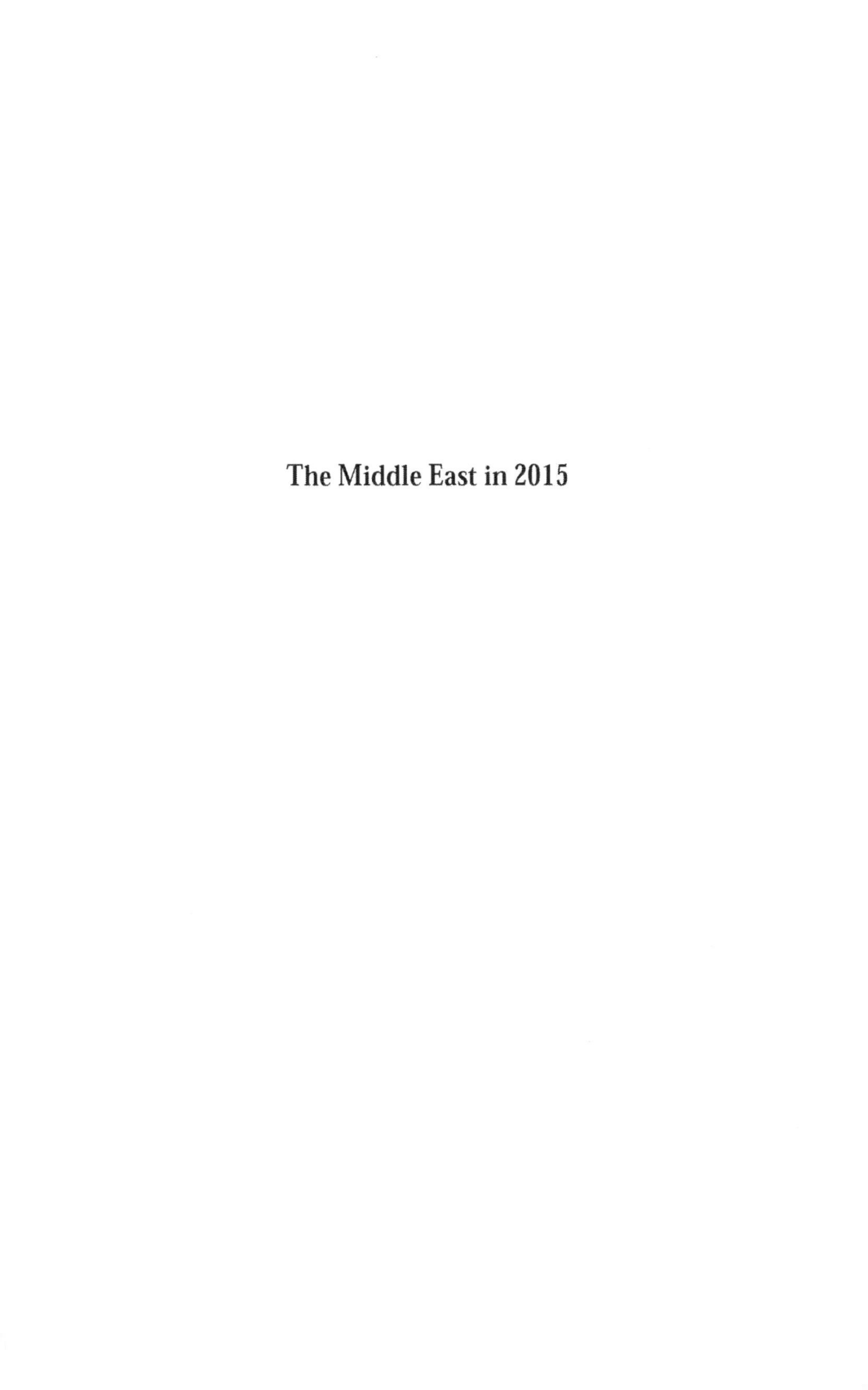

# The Middle East in 2015

Chapter 1

# The Middle East in 2015: An Overview

*Judith S. Yaphe*

In the year 2000, two stereotypes of a "typical" Middle Eastern country and government described the views that many Americans held of the Middle East: a smallish country rich in energy resources but with a small population base; or a lar gish country, mostly desert, with a large population but few natural resources. The ruler, over the age of 65 and in ill health, was a traditional male, the head of his tribe, party, or family who was "elected" by consensus. More than 50 percent of the population were under the age of 18, 25 to 30 percent were unemployed, and perhaps 40 percent were literate. Women constituted more than half of the school-age population, but their presence diminished in the higher grades. Nearly 80 percent of the population received religious education, many in state-funded Quran schools, but few graduated with the skills required for a highly technological job market. There were more satellite dishes than computers in the private homes of those who could afford them.

---

*Judith S. Yaphe is senior r esearch professor and Middle East pr oject director in the Institute for National Str ategic Studies at the National Defense University . Previously, she was a senior analyst on Middle Eastern and Persian Gulf issues in the Office of Near Eastern and South Asian Analysis, Directorate of Intelligence, CIA. Dr. Yaphe teaches Middle East r egional studies in the Industrial Colle ge of the Armed Forces and Goucher College.*

In the year between the conferences that form the basis of this study and publication, the few changes that have occurred, while dramatic in themselves, have so far had little impact on policymaking or society. President Hafiz al-Asad of Syria, King Hussein of Jordan, King Hassan of Morocco, and Amir Isa of Bahrain have died, and succession is in progress in Saudi Arabia, where an ailing King Fahd has turned over much of the daily running of the government to his successor, Crown Prince Abdallah. The rulers of the two countries with a real electoral process—Israel and Iran—have faced major challenges for supporting the peace process, in Israel's case, and for favoring reform, in Iran's case. High oil prices have rescued governments from looming budget shortfalls, but a dividend from peace, war, or new-found oil wealth has yet to trickle down to the broad base of society. Arms sales and the search to acquire advanced weapons systems continue apace, especially in Iran, Iraq, Libya, Syria, and Egypt.

What will the Middle East look like in 2015? New leaders will rule in most of the countries—except perhaps for Iraq—but the governments will almost certainly resemble those of 2000. They mostly will be hierarchical, autocratic, undemocratic or minimally so, and vaguely representational. More countries will have some form of elected representative assembly, but they also will retain a monarchical or autocratic form of government; an example would be the new "Kingdom" of Bahrain with an elected, representative national assembly. More important for policymakers are these issues: What will these societies look like in terms of demographic factors, economic conditions, threat perceptions, and security needs? What factors or factions might shape government decisionmaking—will popular opinion, economic conditions, or changes in strategic alliances be important? What key trends will shape this strategic part of the world?

## The Key Questions

With these issues in mind, INSS asked specialists in the government and academic communities to assess the current situation and speculate on the future for the region and the United States. The first goal was to identify medium- and long-term strengths and vulnerabilities of regional regimes. Factors to consider included political succession, demographic changes, Islamic activism, and the spread of weapons of mass destruction. The second goal was to assess the implications of those changes, trends, and issues for U.S. strategic interests and defense policy. Four key questions to address are:

*What are the key political changes that are likely to occur, and how could these affect American interests?* Examples include, b ut are not limited to, succession, generational change, factionalism, calls for political reform and transparency in government, demands for wider political participation versus adherence to traditional autocratic values and systems, the nature of the social contract between ruler and ruled, and defining the role of the military , party, or tribe in decisionmaking.

*What are the key economic changes that are likely to occur, and how could these affect American interests?* Examples include the impact of an uncertain oil market, unstable budgets, demographic trends, under-employment or unemployment, education, and role of the family or state as the safety net for society . Two fundamental questions emerge: Is the country part of the technological revolution, or is it a global loser? What is or will be the impact of the information revolution upon the country?

*How will issues important to the United States be viewed?* Is success or failure of the Middle East peace process key to relations with the United States? Are the proliferation of weapons of mass destruction, arms control, and terrorism important, or is the region straining to join the nuclear club and shelter so-called freedom fighters because not doing so would engender popular wrath?

*What could change these assumptions?* What seemingly improbable events or unpredictable behavior could alter our judgments on Middle Eastern politics, economics, or other key issues? Could current enemies become future allies? How would a change in regional strategic alliances affect regional power players and U.S. strategic planning? Will Europe be an important factor in determining American regional security policy?

Inherent in these questions is the need to identify potential threats to U.S. security interests. W ill our military presence be in greater or lesser demand, at greater or lesser risk? Can any proactive measures or policies be adopted to counter the existing or potential threats?

## Identifying Regional Trends

In looking for broader trends in the Middle East, conference participants noted several larger developments in political and economic thinking, some with views common to the region and the United States, others that were in sharp contrast to American perceptions.

*Political Trends: American Optimism versus Middle Eastern Fatalism.* As Ibrahim Karawan, an Egyptian scholar, noted, American political culture prefers optimism; it is based on a simple theory that things can always be made to work, and solutions can always be found. Not so in the Middle East, he asserted, where trends are more influenced by time and the quality of leadership. The more time passes, Karawan claimed, the less likely the trend. He gave two examples. The first is the apparent resurgence in Islamic activism. Islamic activism is not irrelevant, but neither is it a decisive trend. "Touristic" scholars equate beards on men and *hijab* (headscarves) on women with Islamic activism. Karawan predicted that no government would be overturned by an Islamist movement because opposing a government is much easier than becoming a government. The second false trend is resurgent Arabism. It too lacks the cohesion to overthrow governments or reorient regional policies in an Arabist direction. Islamic rhetoric can be compelling and preachers charismatic, but state interest is more important; the example offered by this scholar was Arab Syrian ties with Persian Iran.

Several trends are much more disturbing, according to Karawan. The first is globalization, a trend more feared than welcomed in the Middle East on the whole. Most Arabs see globalization as an American and Israeli conspiracy to marginalize them. It heightens their sense of vulnerability in an increasingly digital world. This scholar also asserted that resolution of the core issues between Israeli and Arab, whether Palestinian or Syrian, could not occur within the space of one American administration eager for peace.[1] Other political trends contributing to regional uncertainty are the increasing presence of unstable coalition governments (in Israel and Lebanon, for example); terrorism, with the targets shifting from U.S. Embassies to local economic and cultural symbols, such as corporations and movie theaters; and the spread of weapons of mass destruction.

The risk for the United States from these political trends lies in the explosive stratum of society that is young, semi-educated, unemployed, unskilled, and urban. Members of this stratum tend to be more politicized, articulate, and indignant than those in the mainstream. They are obsessed with social and economic justice and political reform. They are ready material for radical movements, Islamist or nationalist.

*Economic Trends: The Dismal Science Faces East.* Economists looking for trends in the Middle East during the next 15 years are as pessimistic as political analysts. The regional economic outlook, according to one professor, was "unpredictable," the nature of change "inconceivable."[2] Alan Richards, an economist and Middle East specialist, listed nine challenges that Middle Eastern governments would face regardless of the person in power, the range of responses pursued, or domestic tensions. The key, according to Richards, would be for governments to learn how to manage or cope with these unsolvable problems. The list of challenges includes restoring economic growth, restraining population expansion, providing jobs, alleviating poverty, coping with urbanization, saving water, obtaining food, halting environmental destruction, and attracting money for investment from foreign and domestic savers.

Some salient economic facts include per capita income in the Middle East, which has been stagnant for the past decade, oil prices, and demographics. An increase or decrease in oil prices, unless sustained over a long period of time, is unlikely to have a significant impact on the economic woes of any country. The problem lies in the demographics of the region. According to the World Bank, Middle Eastern countries have the highest population growth rate in the world. The average growth rate of 2.7 percent means that the population of a country, if unchecked, will double in 26 years.[3] By 2025, Richards projects that the population of the Middle East region will rise to 600 million from the current 300 million. Moreover, he speculates that the fertility rate will decline, especially as populations (particularly women) become better educated. But, he notes, the benefit is a distant one—the youth population bulge is now. The populations of most Middle Eastern countries, Israel included, are young, with the bulge in the 15- to 30-year-old group. Half of all Saudis, for example, are under the age of 15, and 65 percent of the Iranian population is under the age of 25. In Algeria, 70 percent of the population is under the age of 30. Unlike East Asia, where a rapid fertility decline was the main reason for increased savings and capital for economic growth, money that normally would be invested abroad or saved must be invested now in job creation. In Richards' calculation, few jobs plus high unemployment equals low wages and a politically volatile population.

Most of the problems outlined by economists are not regime threatening or dangerous. Governments have muddled through them

| Country | Population 1995 | Population 1999 | Population Growth (%) 1995 | Population Growth (%) 1999 | Gross Domestic Product (GDP) 1995 | Gross Domestic Product (GDP) 1999 | Annual GDP Growth (%) 1995 | Annual GDP Growth (%) 1999 | Unemployment (%)[1] 1999 | Total Fertility Rate 2000 |
|---|---|---|---|---|---|---|---|---|---|---|
| Algeria | 29,060,000 | 29,950,000 | 2 | 2 | 41,256,300,544 | 47,015,100,416 | 4 | 4 | 30 | 2.8 |
| Bahrain | | 634,137 | | 1.78 | | 8,600,000,000 | | 4 | 15[2] | 2.82 |
| Egypt | 58,180,000 | 62,429,600 | 2 | 2 | 60,159,201,280 | 92,412,600,320 | 5 | 6 | 11.8 | 3.15 |
| Iran | 58,954,000 | 62,977,200 | 2 | 2 | 89,980,002,304 | 101,073,002,496 | 3 | 2 | 25 | 2.2 |
| Iraq | 20,779,000 | 22,796,500 | 2 | 2 | – | – | – | – | – | 4.87 |
| Israel | 5,545,000 | 6,093,260 | 3 | 2 | 87,771,103,232 | 99,067,797,504 | 7 | 2 | 9.1 | 2.6 |
| Jordan | 4,195,000 | 4,692,630 | 3 | 3 | 6,507,990,016 | 7,616,370,176 | 4 | 1 | 15 | 3.44 |
| Kuwait | 1,585,000 | 1,924,400 | 5 | 3 | 26,558,300,160 | 29,571,999,744 | 1 | – | 1.8 | 3.26 |
| Lebanon | 4,005,000 | 4,271,230 | 2 | 1 | 11,118,499,840 | – | 6 | – | 18 | 2.08 |
| Libya | 4,967,000 | 5,419,430 | 2 | 2 | – | – | – | – | 30 | 3.71 |
| Morocco | 26,386,000 | 28,238,000 | 2 | 2 | 32,986,200,064 | 35,328,100,992 | -7 | 0 | 19 | 3.13 |
| Oman | 2,135,000 | 2,348,000 | 3 | 2 | 12,101,999,616 | – | 3 | – | – | 6.08 |
| Qatar | 655,000 | 757,190 | 7 | 2 | 8,137,909,760 | – | – | – | – | 3.25 |
| Saudi Arabia | 18,979,000 | 21,429,000 | 3 | 3 | 127,824,003,072 | – | 0 | – | – | 6.3 |
| Sudan | 26,617,000 | 28,993,300 | 2 | 2 | 7,194,379,776 | 19,379,599,360 | 25 | 4 | 30 | 4.06 |
| Syria | 14,112,000 | 15,652,800 | 3 | 2 | 16,548,299,776 | 21,187,899,392 | 7 | 5 | 13.5 | 2.04 |
| Tunisia | 8,957,500 | 9,456,660 | 2 | 1 | 17,987,000,320 | 188,374,007,808 | 2 | 6 | 16.5 | 2.16 |
| Turkey | 60,500,000 | 64,328,000 | 2 | 1 | 170,046,996,480 | 188,374,007,808 | 7 | 0 | 7.3 | 2.16 |
| West Bank/Gaza | 2,434,250 | 2,838,560 | 4 | 4 | 3,283,389,952 | 3,627,760,128 | -1 | 4 | 14.5 | 5.78[3] |
| Yemen | 15,250,000 | 17,047,600 | 3 | 3 | 4,014,370,048 | 6,768,940,032 | 8 | 2 | 30 | 7.05 |
| MENA | 269,572,000 | 290,860,000 | 3 | 2 | 506,310,000,640 | – | 2 | – | – | – |

Source: <http://devdata.worldbank.org>.

[1] Unemployment figures taken from *CIA World Factbook 2000*, accessed at <http://www.odci.gov/cia/publications/factbook>.
[2] 1998
[3] Total fertility rate for the West Bank is 5.02 percent, and Gaza is 6.55 percent, estimated for 2000.

before. Little attention is being paid to the endemic problems of alleviating poverty or curbing rapid urbanization. With the exceptions of Jordan, Morocco, and Tunisia, most Middle Eastern governments do not produce reliable data to measure growth rates or unemployment, especially by ethnic or regional sectors of the population. Does poverty matter *politically*? Yes, Richards says, if we consider that poverty delegitimizes a regime and that the semi-educated poor may have different intellectual and political responses to the question, Why are we poor?

The longer-term problems could prove more dangerous to regional governments. *Saving water* is already a serious problem in the Mashreq region of Israel, Syria, Jordan, and Palestine. Irreplaceable water tables are falling in the Gulf states, and Egypt, by 2015, will face a major water crisis. Richards notes five water-related issues:
- increasing scarcity
- poorer quality
- rising demand
- expensive recycling
- inadequate management.

*Obtaining food* is a growing problem in an area that is the world's least self-sufficient in food production. Except for the damage caused when Iraq set the oil fields of Kuwait on fire in 1991, little attention has been paid to *environmental destruction,* yet deforestation, soil erosion, and desertification are serious concerns as well.

*Religious Extremism: A Plague in Both Houses.* Repressive political conditions and the stagnant economy have fed a resurgence of religious and ethnic nationalism in the Middle East. Most Arab or Muslim countries have entrenched Islamist movements, legal and clandestine, while Jewish ultraorthodox movements in Israel are exerting wider influence on government policies and efforts to resume the peace process. Most governments are coping with the challenge from the extremists, but their methods—mostly repression, occasionally cooptation—could reap a bitter harvest.

In the year 2000, 20 years after the Islamic Revolution in Iran, movements representing religious activism had gained popularity in most countries of the Middle East—especially Lebanon, Algeria, Morocco, Jordan, the Arab states of the Gulf, and Egypt—but had not gained political power. Islamic activists—Muslims with a political agenda calling for rule under religious law in a more religious society—had gained supporters in their search for political reform.

Islamist movements became popular because they called for political accountability, social justice, rule by Islamic law, establishment of a just Islamic state, and elimination of foreign influence and interests (usually directed against the United States). The more extremist, or militant, Islamists believed terrorism and violence to be the only recourse and urged *jihad*, or holy war, to overthrow corrupt governments and establish a new Islamic order.

Governments blamed extremists for civil war in Algeria, antigovernment violence in Bahrain and Egypt, and threats to destroy the secular foundation of the state of Turkey. More moderate Islamists in Kuwait, Egypt, Lebanon, Morocco, Jordan, and Turkey sought power to shape the institutions of civil society, introduce Islamic law and education, and monitor regimes through legitimate means—legal political parties and elected national assemblies. In all these countries, Islamists running as parties or as individuals have won or been appointed to seats in elective and consultative assemblies and won municipal elections.

Although Islamist factions in the Middle East have different agendas and tactics, they agree on two issues. First, they reject peace with Israel, and they oppose the existence of the state because, they say, Jews cannot rule over the Islamic *'ummah* (community) or *waqf* (territory or wealth held in trust for the community). They view the Oslo Accords as a sell-out of Muslim rights to Jerusalem and its holy places, an act which, they argue, no Muslim or Palestinian has the right to do. They also share certain basic characteristics: they are grounded in local communities, providing religious, medical, educational, and social welfare benefits to those who fall outside the state social safety net. The second mutual concern of Islamist factions is ending sanctions against the Iraqi people, which are often described as a U.S. plot to weaken Iraq and, by extension, the Arabs.

Arab governments in the region have tried several tactics to counter the growth and influence of Islamist movements. The governments most successful in countering Islamic activism have been Jordan and Morocco, in part because their rulers both claim descent from the family of the Prophet Muhammad. All states use a mix of accommodation, repression, and political control to contain, if not eliminate, Islamist opposition elements:

- *Accommodation:* Most governments have tried to co-opt the Islamists' popularity by adopting some of their social programs and political goals. Mosques are built, public displays of piety encouraged, and Islamic justice is applied in criminal la w. In Egypt, Islamic scholars determine whether laws conform to Islamic standards. Support is given to beleaguered Muslims in Bosnia, Kashmir, and Central Asia, and all Muslim governments, including Saudi Arabia and T urkey, attend meetings of the Islamic Conference; the last was held in T ehran in December 1997. Moreover, many government leaders, including those in Saudi Arabia, have become increasingly critical of U.S. policies and actions in the region, ranging from criticism of perceived American unwillingness to punish Israel for obstructing the peace process to refusing to support U.S. military action or sanctions on Iraq.

- *Repression:* While most Muslim go vernments tolerate a limited level of personal piety and Islamic politics, they also deal harshly with those Islamist activists whom they view as threatening their control. Tunisia, Libya, Egypt, Algeria, Syria, Oman, Bahrain, and Saudi Arabia apply draconian tactics in dealing with imagined and real Islamist opponents. Those believed to be too public in their Islamic observance—wearing beard or veil—are watched closely and risk loss of career (especially in the military or civil services). Those suspected of membership in or supporting Islamist causes—either moderate or militant— are denied jobs and housing, arrested, interrogated, tried in military courts, and often condemned to exile or long prison terms. Membership in proscribed organizations, such as the Gama'at al-Islamiyyah in Egypt and the Armed Islamic Group in Algeria, can bring prison and even death sentences if implicated in organizational activities deemed terrorist.
- *Control:* Most go vernments limit access to the political process. Several pro-American governments that allow elections, parliaments, and a degree of transparency in government are finding that unrestrained democracy can work against their self-interest. Most countries ban political parties based on religion; Algeria and Turkey, for e xample, have cancelled or postponed elections; Jordan has gerrymandered electoral districts; and Egypt has conducted security sweeps and arrests of Muslim Brotherhood leaders before elections and made elective municipal offices appointive to keep Islamists out of office. The

regimes see these actions as internal matters and assume that they will have American support because of shared strategic interests and treaty commitments. Islamists regard the U.S. Government as hypocritical in not supporting their quest for traditional, basic American values of democracy, equality, and the application of constitutional safeguards. The United States asserts its right to meet with whomever it pleases but shies away from contacts with dissidents that might disrupt relations with regimes that support American policies.

The result of these policies of accommodation, repression, and control has been to limit the ability of many legitimate Islamist parties and politicians choosing to work within the system from acquiring political power or expanding their role in government.

Israelis generally identify political and religious extremism and terrorism with Arab Muslims within their borders and across their borders in the Occupied Territories and Lebanon. They tend to view Arab Muslims not only as a security risk but also as a source of cheap labor. Once, however, the Israeli government encouraged the rise of Islamic activism as a way to distract and divide Palestinians and weaken support for the Palestine Liberation Organization. Frightened now by the ability of Hizballah and Hamas to attack, Israel has concentrated its energies on identifying and eliminating these extremist threats. Until Baruch Goldstein murdered 29 Muslims worshipping in a mosque in Hebron in 1994 and a fanatical yeshiva student assassinated Prime Minister Yitzhaq Rabin in November 1995, Israelis saw no reason to worry about the violence inherent in Jewish extremist movements inside the country.

Current Israeli extremist factions use violence to defend Jewish "rights" to build in Arab East Jerusalem, expand settlements anywhere in Judaea and Samarria, settle in Arab-dominated Hebron—site of the Tomb of the Patriarchs—and close down sections of Jerusalem for proper (that is, Orthodox) religious observance of the Sabbath. A few— for example, adherents of the late Rabbi Meir Kahane, murdered by Muslim extremists in New York in 1990, and his militant Kach organization—demand the expulsion of all Arabs from Eretz Israel (the Land of Israel). While the majority of Israelis are secular, many support the preservationist objectives of the extremist factions because they feel unsafe in a small Israel, are deeply suspicious of Arabs, and mistrust political parties and the peace process.

Israel is a society in transition, and, as Kenneth Stein points out, the changes are profound. He describes Israeli Jewish society as divided by religious, ideological, economic, political, cultural, and ethnic cleavages. The divisions include those between the secular majority and the Orthodox religious minority, between the Likud-led political right and the Labor-dominated left, between Ashkenazim (Jews tracing their heritage to Europe) and Sephardim (Jews tracing their origins to the Middle East), and between the generations of Zionists and the new Russian immigrants, many of whom profess no interest in fighting for land or religion. The ability of the *haredim*, the ultrareligious, to influence government policy toward settlements as well as toward the definition of who is a Jew has shaken Israeli politics and disturbed its relations with overseas Jewry, most of whom fall outside the Orthodox camp.

The threat of war and early flush of success in the peace process kept many of the strains within Israeli society at bay. But in the past several years, the character of Israeli politics and society, if not the basic Zionist vision that guided much of Israeli policy through its first 50 years, has changed. The growth of extremism owes more to the decline of external threats than to economic conditions, since the Israeli economy has improved over the past decade. Yet when Israel faces serious security threats on its borders, few Israelis would risk condemnation by challenging government policies on national defense or security issues.

## Formidable Challenges

This chapter has defined some of the key challenges facing the Middle East region as a whole. In varying degrees, most of the governments face demands for political reform, transparency and accountability, and wider popular participation, although this does not always translate to support for Western-style democracy and elections. They face profound economic woes, whether they are oil-rich or people-rich—the two do not appear concurrent except in Iran and Iraq. In all, the populations are burgeoning even though fertility rates for women have been falling. A semieducated generation—that is, literate with advanced degrees but little technical training—has grown up in virtual isolation from Western or foreign contact. Schooled in their home countries, they study religious sciences and law but lack the technical skills and, in some areas, the ambition or drive—what American historians once described as the Protestant work ethic in accounting for the rapid industrialization of the West—to enter the 21$^{st}$-century job market in their own countries.

The generation gaining power and influence today has several characteristics that will be key in defining the generation coming of age in 2015. They have not experienced war or revolution. They did not fight in the Arab-Israeli wars and have only seen the Palestinian *intifada*, with its stone throwers, on television. Most have known only one ruler or—as in Syria, Morocco, Jordan, and Bahrain—change of ruler but not of government. Iraqis know only Saddam Husayn, war, and sanctions. Iranians, for the most part, never knew the Shah, and memories of the revolution are growing dim. What does remain is a sense of transition to a post-revolution style of rule versus strict conformity to revolutionary ideals—no one in Iran appears to be talking (openly, at least) of returning to secular rule. The rising generation in the oil-rich Gulf States does not remember a time of poverty, before oil, before a state-supported welfare system that guaranteed all citizens free health care, education, and a general sense of well-being.

What will the generation coming of age in 2015 resemble? The following chapters are case studies of several countries, chosen in shaping U.S. policy in the region. The choices are not intended to be inclusive or to suggest that those countries not represented are unimportant. The case studies are followed by a comparative examination of the three regions that comprise the Middle East for purposes of this study: the *Maghreb*, or North Africa; the *Mashreq*, or Levant area; and the *Khalij*, or Gulf area.

## Notes

[1] At the time of the conferences in 1999 and 2000, negotiations were still deemed possible between Syria and Israel, the Israeli-Palestinian track had not yet collapsed, and the events of September 11, 2001, were unimagined.

[2] Alan Richards, "Economic Challenges and Potential Policy Responses in the Middle East: Implications for U.S. Interests," unpublished paper prepared for the Conference on the Middle East in 2015 (Washington, DC, November 5, 1999).

[3] Rates are considerably higher in the Palestine Authority, among religious Jews in Israel, and in Yemen, where the average growth rate is closer to 7 percent.

Chapter 2
# Algeria: Can National Order Be Restored?

*Hugh Roberts*

The question "Where is Algeria going?" has been a hardy perennial of academic and political discussion of Algerian affairs ever since the late President Mohammed Boudiaf first raised it in 1964.[1] Since we are today considering this question again, it is worth reflecting that many if not most of the answers given to it over the last 36 years—and especially over the last decade—have turned out to be mistaken, sometimes badly so.

Algeria has not become a second Iran, nor a second Sudan, nor a second Afghanistan, nor any other kind of Islamic republic, however much it may have given an impression of heading in each of these directions at one moment or another . Nor has Algeria actually ended up emulating the T urkish model or e ven the Chilean model, both of which ha ve been freely b ut misleadingly in voked by insiders in Algiers as guides to foreign observers trying to get their bearings in the Algerian labyrinth.

---

*Hugh Roberts is senior research fellow at the Development Studies Institute, London School of Economics and Political Science. A specialist on Algerian politics and history, he was pr eviously a lecturer at the Univer sity of East Anglia and a research fellow at the University of Sussex. His most recent publication is "The International Gallery and the Extr avasation of Factional Conflict in Algeria" in* The Cambridge Review of International Affairs *(1998). He is currently working on a study of the Algerian state.*

If a lesson can be drawn from these observations, it is that Algeria's evolution has not so far involved as marked a tendency to approximate that of other, more clear-cut, and accordingly better understood cases as many observers have been inclined to suppose. A prudent observer thus may assume that Algeria's evolution over the next 15 years is likely to remain the product of a specifically Algerian mode of development and that the most likely lines of development and the main alternative scenario may best be identified by taking proper account of the particular features of the Algerian political economy.

In this context, however, defining and identifying trends is one thing, but predicting future developments is quite another. A brief backward glance should be enough to establish the truth of this. For who could have deduced from even the most careful and sensitive analysis of Algerian economic and political trends in 1975 that contested elections in which an Islamist party would score a landslide victory at the expense of the National Liberation Front (FLN) would take place 15 years later? Whatever trends are discernible today are unlikely to disclose where Algeria will be by 2015. At most, they can help us to discount certain possibilities as unlikely to occur and anticipate others as being in the cards.

## Trends to Anticipate

*Social and Economic Change.* One of the most important and clearly discernible trends is *demographic*. Algeria's population now stands at 31 million, having tripled since independence in 1962. The annual growth rate has slowed appreciably from its high point of 3.2 percent in the 1970s to about 2.2 percent currently. On this basis, the population will have risen to about 40 million by 2015.

*Unemployment* is the second trend. The Algerian unemployment rate is officially evaluated at some 28 to 30 percent of the workforce, but the true figure is probably well above this. The economy is not growing at a rate capable of keeping unemployment at this level, let alone reducing it. On the contrary, structural adjustment measures over the past few years have aggravated the unemployment problem, and no real evidence exists that enough new jobs are being created to compensate for this. The problem of mass unemployment undoubtedly has been one of the premises of the social unrest and political instability of the last 12 years, and it is likely to become appreciably worse over the next 15 years as a result of demographic growth alone.

*Urbanization* is the third key social trend. Before independence, Algeria's population was predominantly rural throughout its history. Since 1962, however, a massive rural exodus and corresponding swelling of Algeria's cities and towns has occurred. The urban population now accounts for about 55 percent of the total. If the trend of the past 40 years continues, some 65 percent of the population will be urban by 2015. The social and political implications of this are enormous, considering that Algeria's urban infrastructure was established by the French colonial authorities for a far smaller urban population (well under one million) of the European settler community. Far too little has been done to adapt this infrastructure to meet the strains it now carries, notably with respect to water supply and sewage disposal systems, electricity supply, transport, and housing—let alone provision of other urban services and facilities, especially cultural amenities. It was the populations of Algeria's main towns (Algiers, Blida, Oran, Annaba, and Mostaghanem) that rioted in October 1988; the social base of the Islamic Salvation Front (FIS) was a massively urban one.

Algeria's *dependence on hydrocarbons* is the fourth trend. Reliance on revenues from the export of oil and gas and derivatives—which account for more than 50 percent of government revenues and more than 95 percent of export earnings—has been accentuated over the last 20 years, and especially over the last decade. In the 1980s, the regime of President Chadli Bendjadid abandoned the ambitious state-led industrialization strategy of the 1970s but did not replace it with any alternative strategy for promoting the development of non-hydrocarbons production. Since 1991, the regime has been banking on boosting hydrocarbons revenues through injections of foreign capital via partnerships with the major international oil companies to enable it to live with, if not reduce, its huge burden of foreign debt (now about $35 billion). As a result, the rentier aspect of the Algerian economy has been aggravated, while manufacturing outside the hydrocarbons sector continues to stagnate if not regress.

The fifth key trend is *transition to a market economy*. The Algerian political economy has been undergoing a substantial change toward a market economy ever since the abandonment of socialist economics was broached in the early 1980s. The radical changes proposed by the Reformer wing of the FLN led by Prime Minister Mouloud Hamrouche in 1989–1991 provoked stiff resistance from powerful vested interests, but they were never fully reversed. Since the August 1993 decision to reschedule the debt, successive governments have accepted and implemented the structural adjustment measures mandated by the International Monetary Fund (IMF). The main changes to date have been the opening up of the economy and measures to integrate it into the world economy. Algerian elites have accepted globalization as an ineluctable reality and have sought to adapt to it.

The hydrocarbons sector has been opened to foreign capital investment on a large scale while preserving the government position as sole Algerian operator. Other substantive moves toward private enterprise, however, have been broadly limited to agriculture (where a substantial but incomplete retreat from collective and state ownership has been undertaken since the early 1980s), the service sector (including transport), and the import trade. Attempts to develop private banking are just beginning—five private banks have been established—but Algeria's private banking sector is still very much in an embryonic stage; further development in this direction reasonably can be expected over the next 15 years.

The liberalization of foreign trade has been far from complete. The end of the formal state monopoly has not given rise to genuinely free enterprise so much as to an oligopolistic situation in which powerful factions in the regime control access to the Algerian market for many foreign goods (especially mass consumption goods). As such, market shares are a function of political considerations rather than the unfettered play of market forces. A definite tendency toward a Mafia-style economy involving both a great deal of unregulated or illicit trading and widespread protection rackets is discernible and undoubtedly is an important factor in the violence that has been occurring over the last 10 years.

Privatization of state property has been proceeding slowly and unevenly, especially in the manufacturing sector. One reason for the visible diffidence of the regime has been the opposition of the General Union of Algerian Workers to forms of privatization that threaten workers' livelihoods. This opposition is soundly based on experiences that the government cannot afford to ignore. Secondly, the political management of the privatization process is itself a major bone of contention between the regime factions, a factor that accounts for much of the delay that has occurred. Third is the considerable difficulty of attracting private capital to invest in or buy state enterprises, given the continuing weakness of the Algerian entrepreneurial class and its reluctance to invest domestically, particularly in the manufacturing sector. Both the political situation and the availability of competing investment opportunities abroad and in other, more profitable sectors of the Algerian economy are critical disincentives, impeding the sale of state enterprises. The result is that privatization has been occurring around the edges of the public sector. However, this slow progress cannot realistically be blamed on the government alone, and this process can be expected to continue for the foreseeable future.

*Cultural Change.* In the linguistic sphere, complications arise from the dichotomy between *francisants* (Algerians educated in French) and *arabisants* (Algerians educated in Arabic). They intersect with a third category, Berber speakers, who number between 20 and 25 percent of the total, and a fourth category, those who have acquired a mastery of English. Population growth alone has ensured that the first three categories have grown in absolute terms, while all four in fact are continuing to grow. The strategic importance of the hydrocarbons sector and its deepening relationships with North American and other Anglo partners (such as British Petroleum) are encouraging the growth of English among Algerian technocrats who work in this sector, but the pre-eminence of *francisants* in the non-hydrocarbons sectors of the economy (outside small trade and agriculture) tends to inhibit the growth of the English-speaking element.

The intense friction that characterizes relations between *francisants* and *arabisants* is linked to the competition for political office and state sector employment and to the fact that these linguistic orientations are the vectors of opposed ideological orientations (to the secular West, to the Arabo-Islamic East) as well. These antagonisms are unlikely to diminish in the foreseeable future, especially if the regime continues its policy of deliberately exacerbating these tensions as part of a divide-and-rule strategy.

The question of Berber culture and identity is another important issue. Two trends can be identified. The first is for an identity-based preoccupation with the Berber language (*thamazighth*) to expand beyond its original base in the Kabyle population (by far the largest of Algeria's Berberophone populations, numbering some four million today) to the other Berber-speaking populations: the Ishenwiyen west of Algiers, the Shawiyya (Chaouia) of the southeast (who have been largely resistant to it until now), the Mzabis of the northern Sahara, the populations of other Saharan oases (the Ouargla district, the Oued Ghir around Touggourt), and the Tuareg of the far south.

The second trend points in the opposite direction, however, because it is for the Kabyles themselves to lose interest in specifically Berberist themes, for two main reasons. In so far as Kabyle Berberism has resisted government-promoted Arabization, it may prove to be broadly limited to the generation that has had difficulty adapting. The children of this generation may be able to cope reasonably well with the challenge of learning Arabic and may consequently be less inclined to invest in language-based forms of opposition politics in the future. This is especially true if the government maintains its firm refusal to concede to the Berberist demand for official and national status for *thamazighth*. Also, evidence suggests that the Kabyle population has become disenchanted with the Berberist movement. Although the two main Kabyle parties have invested heavily in the language issue, and each received half of the 14 seats in the National Assembly allocated to the *wilaya* (administrative region) of Tizi Ouzou in June 1997, they only polled 39 percent of the *wilaya*'s electorate. Moreover, turnout was a mere 51.6 percent. The outcome was similar in the *wilaya* of Bejaia, where the Berberist parties polled less that 40 percent of the vote and shared 10 seats. Moreover, during the 1999 presidential election campaign, the warm welcome given at Tizi Ouzou to non-Kabyle candidates (including even the notoriously pro-Arabic Dr. Taleb Ibrahimi[2]) testifies to the beginning of a recovery in Kabylia of an interest in wider, national, political issues at the expense of the language-fixated identity politics in which they have been virtually ghettoized for the last decade or more. [3]

Religion plays a role in cultural change in Algeria. The traumatic events of the last decade have left Algerian Islam in a state of profound subjective and organizational confusion. The eruption of the radical Islamist movement from the political fringe to center stage in 1989–1992 under the auspices of the FIS involved a mutation of the Islamist movement itself. Its leadership passed from the men of religion—whether drawn from the older generation of the *'ulama* who were veterans of Islamic reform movements (*islah*) of the 1930s and 1940s, or from the younger generation of the Islamic *da'wa* (the proselytizing mission) inspired by Middle Eastern examples (for example,the Egyptian clerics Sayyids Qotb and Kishk, and Iran's Ayatollah Khomeini)—to the political activists drawn from and oriented by the very different traditions of Algerian revolutionary populism. [4] Thus, the rise of the FIS tended to consummate the eclipse of an older tradition that had been the mainstream of Algerian Islam from the 1930s to the end of the 1970s.

At the same time, the state itself provided evidence of this same eclipse through the re gime's increasingly explicit cultivation of the old Sufi brotherhoods—the *turuq*. The example was set by none other than President Chadli himself from the early 1980s onward and was followed by Prime Minister Mould Hamrouche in the first half of 1991 in the run-up to the le gislative elections then scheduled for that summer . The continued propensity of the regime to indulge and seek support from the *turuq* is evidenced by the uncritical coverage that the national press provided their activities in palpable contrast to the tone of press coverage in the 1960s and 1970s and the choice of the current minister of religious affairs, who reportedly is closely linked to the big *turuq* of western Algeria.

With the political defeat of the FIS, the military defeat of the mainstream of the Islamic rebellion, and the reduction of the Badisiyyan tradition to minority opposition status in the person of Dr . Ahmed Taleb Ibrahim and his supporters, Algerian Islam is in greater disarray in terms of organization and leadership than at any point since the 1920s, if not earlier.

It does not follo w, however, that religious belief is in decline. While the evidence suggests that the appeal of radical Islamist ideas has receded so far as the general public is concerned, this decline concerns the political projects of the Islamists, not religious belief itself. Moreover, given the v alue of religion (Islam in particular) as an instrument for the promotion of civic virtues and maintenance of social control, and the fact that the combined pressures of demographic growth and urbanization are liable to exacerbate greatly the problems of social control in Algeria' s teeming cities o ver the ne xt 15 years, a recovery of the Badisiyyan tradition is possible. The recovery could take the form of a development from below against the prevailing powers or of a reversion by the authorities to the religious policy of the Boumediène era. The former possibility is perhaps foreshadowed by the emer gence of Sheikh Abdallah Djaballah' s National Reform Movement (*Mouvement de Reforme National* [MRN], or in Arabic

*Harakat al-Islah al-Wataniyya*). Future developments in this respect, however, are likely to depend on developments in the outside world, particularly the Middle East.

Globalization is also affecting Algeria. The country is getting online. Many of its newspapers (such as *El Moudjahid, El Watan, La Tribune, Liberté, Le Matin, Le Soir , Le Quotidien d'Oran, and El Khabar*) can already be read on the Internet. The number of Web sites dealing with Algeria also is proliferating, including those established by Algerian political parties (such as the FIS, the Socialist Forces Front [FFS], and the Rally for Culture and Democracy [RCD]) as well as by the Algerian government. Ordinary Algerians in the Internet cafés that have opened in Algiers and other big towns also are beginning to access these and other sites to enlarge their sources of information and (perhaps) their mental horizons.

This development could work to the benefit of opposition currents in Algeria. The access that Algerians have enjoyed through satellite dishes to foreign television programs for at least the last decade has apparently not subverted regime propaganda. Rather, it has merely aggravated ordinary Algerians' sense of deprivation when confronted with the evidence of Western living standards and provoked their support for the Islamist movement when confronted with the evidence of contemporary Western morals. Access to the Internet, on the other hand, is liable to undermine official discourse and especially the official version of what is going on, to the extent that opposition tendencies can put alternative versions into circulation via the Internet.

The prototype here, perhaps, is the Web site of a group that presents itself as an organization of dissident officers of the Algerian army, the so-called Algerian Free Officers' Movement. This group has posted numerous dossiers about some of the darkest aspects of the last decade, challenging head-on the official version of events (such as the assassination of Mohamed Boudiaf). The site features detailed allegations about corruption in the army high command, which reportedly has caused consternation in high places in Algiers. [5]

*Political Succession.* Under the constitution promulgated in 1996, Algeria's current president, Abdelaziz Bouteflika, is limited to serving two 5-year terms. His current term began in April 1999 and continues to April 2004. If he completes this and is re-elected, he will serve until April 2009, at which time he will be 72 years old. Between now and 2015, therefore, barring a constitutional change to permit more than two 5-years terms or to lengthen the term (for example, to 7 years, à la française), a presidential succession will take place. While it should occur by 2009, it could well take place earlier than this. Bouteflika's immediate predecessor, Liamine Zeroual, did not e ven complete his first term but stood down rather than accept his de facto subordination to the army commanders. Bouteflika may not fare better than Zeroual in this respect. He has already manifested a restive disinclination to be the mere puppet of the army leadership.

Succession in the army is equally significant. The most powerful figures in the Algerian armed forces—for example, Chief of the General Staff Lieutenant General Mohammed Lamari, *Direction des Renseignements et de la Sécurité* head Major-General Mohamed Mediène, and Commander of the Gendarmerie Nationale Major-General Tayeb Derradji—are likely to retire within the ne xt several years. These changes may be problematic, because the Algerian army has been living through an incomplete command succession since the retirement of Major-General Khaled Nezzar as Defense Minister in July 1993. Despite possessing considerable support within the officer corps, his successor, Liamine Zeroual, w as unable to e xercise all of his notional prerogatives as defense minister even with the reinforcement of his constitutional prerogatives as president of the Republic. In this respect, Bouteflika is even more poorly placed to exercise these prerogatives, since he has had little personal following within the army at any stage. This suggests that major changes in the military hierarchy are no longer subject to authoritative arbitration and decisionmaking at the level of either the defense ministry or the presidenc y. For as long as the alliance of Mohammed Lamari and Mohamed Mediène remains in effect, changes in the leadership of the armed forces can be expected to be secured by their joint agreement, but how matters will be handled when the y themselves bow out is entirely unclear . Such changes are unlikely to be managed without difficulty or without substantial political fallout.

Political successions will also occur in Algeria' s various political parties. The General Secretary of the FLN, Dr . Boualem Benhamouda, born in 1933, is likely to be replaced in the next few years. His counterpart in the other re gime-sponsored party, the Democratic National Rally (RND), Ahmed Ouyahia, is a much younger man who probably will remain an important player over the next 10 to 15 years. In any case, leadership changes in these parties are unlikely to be politically problematic unless they are linked to disputes over the succession in the army hierarchy.

Succession problems will certainly confront the Algerian opposition as well. A question mark hangs over Hocine Aït Ahmed, the leader of one of the most substantial opposition parties, the FFS. Born in 1926, he withdrew from the presidential election campaign in April 1999 following a minor heart attack. Matters are probably different with the RCD, the main FFS rival for the Kabyle constituency. Its leader, Saïd Sadi, is a youthful 54 and can be expected to lead his party for at least the next decade.

The question arises whether the Islamist parties will survive the disappearance of their founders. All depend to a great extent on the stature and charisma of their respective leaders, and it is by no means evident that they are replaceable. Flux in the party-political sphere can be expected over the next 15 years. The leader of the Movement of Society for Peace (MSP), Sheikh Mahfoud Nahnah, is 60 and may give way to a younger colleague between now and 2015. The new Islamist parties could also face leadership changes—*Wafa* founder Ahmed Taleb Ibrahimi is 70, while the heads of the other legal Islamist parties, the *Nahda* Movement and the National Reform Movement, are younger men who probably will figure in the political scene for the foreseeable future.

*Generational Change.* The question of generational change is conceptually distinct from that of political succession but is liable to be intimately linked to it in practice. And whether political succession takes place in respect of a particular leadership position, generational change will occur in any case and is bound to have political implications.

The next 15 years will see the coming of age of the generation born in the 1990s and the takeover of positions of economic and cultural as well as political and administrative responsibility by the generation born between 1970 and 1980. By 2015, Algeria will be largely run by 45-year-olds who graduated from universities in the 1990s and whose heads are full of the notions of the free market, the Internet, and globalization. They will have no memory of the nationalist and anti-imperialist era of Boumediène's socialist revolution and New International Economic Order of the 1970s. This new generation will be ruling a country whose 20-year-olds were born in the 1990s—the era of intense violence and terror and sharply reduced socioeconomic expectations.

What of the presidency? Will Bouteflika's successor come from the wartime FLN? Bouteflika himself was seen as the Benjamin of the "Oujda group," the coterie in the w artime FLN that came to po wer in the 1960s in the w ake of Houari Boumediène's General Staff. His immediate predecessor as president, Liamine Zeroual, was born in 1941, making him almost as young as one could be and still claim a measure of historical re volutionary legitimacy. Within the front rank of the Algerian political class, only Mouloud Hamrouche is younger than Zeroual (by 2 years) and can claim both the status of *ancien moudjahid* (veteran of the liberation war) and experience of high political office. Hamrouche also was the only presidential candidate apart from Bouteflika last April with both these credentials.

If the Hamrouche option is not e xercised, however, the next president of Algeria very possibly will come from the post-war generation. As such, he will lack any personal claim to historical legitimacy, a point that may count in his f avor with the military decisionmakers, who clearly prefer malleable presidents. It may , however, simultaneously reduce his usefulness as a source of le gitimation of the military-based power structure in the eyes of the Algerian public. The point is that the advent of the post-war generation at this level will, all things being equal, tend to reinforce the trend of weakening the presidency in relation to other power centers within the executive of the state—a trend observable since the 1978 death of Boumediène and greatly accentuated since Chadli's fall.

The same process will apply to the armed forces themselves. The departure of the last cohort of officers who served in the wartime *Armée de Libération Nationale* (ALN) and the advent of the post-ALN generation to the command of the National People's Army (ANP) will reinforce the trend toward delegitimatizing the political power of the military. Whether new sources of le gitimacy can be found to substitute for historical-revolutionary legitimacy remains to be seen.

The current ANP leadership appears to be banking on the combination of two elements to fill the legitimacy gap that is opening up. The first, *technical expertise and the ethic of pr ofessionalism*, may be enough to justify promotion of individual officers to command posts within the military sphere but will fall short of legitimating the ANP commanders' collective pretensions to political power outside this sphere. The second, *ideological correctness*, is the declared adher-ence of officers of the new generation to "republican" values. This latter phrase is code in Algerian political terminology for the modernist outlook, hostility to Islamism, and (formal) commitment to (formal) political pluralism. It is not obvious that these elements will prove sufficient, and it may be that the army commanders will seek to secure and exploit other sources of legitimation, notably in their dealings with Western (French and American) counterparts.

At the level of the political class, the advent of the first age cohort of the post-war generation is well under way. This cohort already supplies the leaders of the RND (Ahmed Ouyahia), the RCD (Saïd Sadi), *En Nahda* (Lahbib Adami), and the Algerian Renewal Party (Noureddine Boukrouh), all of which parties are present within Bouteflika's coalition government. Former Prime Minister Ahmed Benbitour also belongs to this new generation, as does the leader of the small but combative opposition Workers Party, Louisa Hanoune.

The advent of this generation will tend to confirm the dependence of civilian political figures on either technocratic bases of legitimacy or ideological ones, in both cases supplemented by external endorsement (for example, endorsement of claims to technical competence by international financial institutions, of "democratic" or "modernist" credentials by spokesmen for Western governments, human rights nongovernmental organizations, and media commentary). This dependence will grow at the expense of a national—let alone a nationalist—political vision and the capacity to obtain a genuine national popular following. This trend could, therefore, entail a significant and potentially dangerous aggravation of regionalism as the principal internal mobilizer of popular political support.

Since 1989, political opposition to the regime has been of two main kinds:
- *Programmatic opposition*, which has opposed the regime in the name of certain definite political changes that have been canvassed in opposition to the form of government in force
- *Participationist opposition*, which has criticized the regime on the basis of arguments from cultural legitimacy, while in effect negotiating the terms of a bargain by which the brand of opposition in question, representing one or another fraction of an essentially middle-class constituency and conveying cultural rather than political demands, might accept co-optation by the regime.

The main leaders of programmatic opposition to the new post-1989 order have all been of the revolutionary generation: Aït Ahmed (FFS), Ahmed Ben Bella (Movement for Democracy in Algeria), Abdelhamid Mehri (FLN qua opposition party 1992 –1996), Abassi Madani (FIS), Dr. Ahmed Taleb Ibrahimi (*Wafa*), and the late Kasdi Merbah (Algerian Movement for Justice and Development, 1990– 1993). Also included in this category are the various leaders of the Communist tradition in Algerian politics—Sadek Hadjerès, Abdelhamid Benzine, and even El Hachemi Cherif, the present leader of the small but vociferous Democratic and Social Movement. All three took part in the nationalist movement and the national liberation w ar. The same applies to those individuals who have represented principled and implicitly programmatic opposition to the political status quo without acting in the framework of opposition parties, notably Abdennour Ali Y ahia and Hocine Zahouane of the Algerian League for the Defense of Human Rights (LADDH) and Khatib Y oucef and Mouloud Hamrouche, both of whom ran as independents in the 1999 presidential elections but did so on implicitly programmatic platforms of some kind.

The evidence of a strong link between the capacity to offer programmatic opposition to the regime and possession of historical legitimacy arising out of personal participation in the national revolution is striking. It follows that the passing of this generation from the political scene will blunt the thrust of political opposition, since future opposition leaders will possess neither revolutionary nationalist legitimacy nor the ex-insiders' knowledge of the nature of the power structure they oppose.

This trend accordingly implies the eventually definitive ascendancy of participationist opposition of the Sadi-Nahnah-Adami-Boukrouh variety over the programmatic opposition of the Abassi-Aït Ahmed-Mehri-Taleb-Kasdi variety. In this conte xt, the destruction of the FIS in volved the dismantling of the main party frame work, offering a brand of programmatic opposition in which the post-war generation—personified not only by the radical Ali Benhadj but also by the more pragmatic figures of the late Abdelkader Hachani and Rabah Kebir—was inclined to participate in large numbers. Of the political parties still operating within the law led by elements of the post-war generation, only those led by Louisa Hanoune and Abdallah Djaballah continue to oppose the political status quo. The T rotskyist birthmarks of the former and the Islamist birthmarks of the latter—to say nothing of regime hostility and harassment—are likely to limit their capacity for political expansion. Prospects for vigorous constitutional opposition politics of the programmatic variety are, on current trends, depressingly dim.

## Problems of the Algerian Polity

### Pluralism without Enfranchisement

The Algerian polity is characterized by an extremely limited form of pluralism managed and manipulated by an executive dominated by the military. This form of pluralism is limited in six ways.

*The state of emergency* in force since February 1992 places severe restrictions on the exercise of normal democratic political rights, notably the right to hold public meetings and especially marches and demonstrations.

*Only political parties representing essentially middle-class constituencies are allowed* in addition to the regime-sponsored RND and FLN. The FIS has had no successor as a populist party speaking for and mobilizing the enthusiastic support of the urban poor, the *mustadh'afin* (the weak, the wretched of the earth). Turnout in elections in 1997 and 1999 confirm that the mass of ordinary people have no party to vote for and do not vote.

*Only parties whose opposition expresses a willingness to participate in government are allowed to prosper.* Participationist parties outside the fold of the FLN-RND tandem are accepted. Parties with a principled programmatic opposition to the regime may be able to remain legal but are subject to endless harassment and occasional destabilization. Apart from the FIS, two other cases testify eloquently to this unwritten rule. The first is that of the FLN under Abdelhamid Mehri; it was a genuine source of opposition to the regime, a state of affairs that the government eventually found intolerable and ended by engineering Mehri's overthrow and replacement by the reliably docile Boualem Benhamouda. The second is that of *En Nahda*. Founded in 1990 by Sheikh Abdallah Djaballah as an opposition party, it polled only 150,000 votes in the first round of the legislative elections in December 1991. In the legislative elections of 1997, however, its vote rocketed to over 900,000, and it won 34 seats. This success was short-lived; like the FIS in 1991, it was the prelude to the party's destabilization. Within a few months, the party split into two camps, those loyal to Djaballah and those supporting the new General Secretary, Lahbib Adami, who had been elected to the National Assembly in the *wilaya* of Khenchela and who happened to be the brother of Mohamed Adami, minister of justice at the time. At issue in the dispute was precisely the question of whether the party should persist in programmatic opposition (Djaballah's view) or negotiate its participation in a coalition government (Adami's proposal). The Adami camp won the battle for control of the party, and Djaballah was forced to quit the party he had founded and to found the MRN.

*Legislative weakness hinders the operation of pluralism.* Draft bills voted by the elected lower house, the National Assembly, require the approval of a three-quarters majority of the upper house, the Council of the Nation, to become law. A third of the 144 members of the Council of the Nation are presidential appointees; the remaining two-thirds (96) are indirectly elected from among the members of municipal and regional assemblies in each of the 48 administrative regions. Because 80 of the 96 elected in 1997 were RND members, the Council of the Nation is massively dominated by regime placemen.

Despite these safeguards, the regime has allowed the Parliament (both houses taken together) very little independent initiative. Members of the Council of Ministers do not owe their mandates to the Parliament and are not substantively answerable to it, although they may be questioned by it. Members of the National Assembly who are given ministerial portfolios vacate their assembly seats on assuming ministerial office. The initiative in matters of constitutional reform remains in practice a monopoly of the president of the Republic. As a result, the legislature is widely regarded either as a stepping-stone to executive power or as a platform on which to launch rhetorical attacks on the regime.

Apart from members affiliated with the minority opposition parties, who take the latter view of their possibilities, members of the two houses tend to view their position as one of two things. It can be a launching pad for ministerial ambitions to the extent that it enables members to bring themselves to the attention of the power brokers within the regime, or a base from which to maintain and cultivate clienteles given the opportunities their position affords them for preferential access to and influence with the executive via party colleagues in government office. The two houses qua deliberative assemblies actually function much more as a consultative body than a legislature worthy of the name. As such, the Parliament has failed comprehensively to amount to a significant center of political power outside the executive of the state. Consequently, the notional party-political game conducted within it has proved quite unable to eclipse or supersede the factional struggle conducted within the executive, which remains the political game that really matters and the real motor of political change (at the level of both policy and personnel). Thus, the weakness of the Parliament entails the chronic weakness of the political parties.

*The parties are mainly based on alternative conceptions of identity (the orthodox nationalist conception of Arabo-Muslim Algeria, Islamist conceptions, the Berberist conception, and so forth) and accor dingly rooted in the cultur al sphere.* As a result, these parties ha ve little or nothing to say about issues arising in other spheres, notably social and economic policy and foreign polic y. They have neither the capacity nor the inclination to de vise and canvass alternative policy proposals concerning these matters. This not only limits their appeal to the Algerian electorate but also inhibits them from pressuring the government and holding it accountable for its conduct, let alone from constituting serious alternatives to the government in office.

*The practice of fraudulent elections à la Naegelen* limits the character and significance of political pluralism in Algeria. [6] While concrete evidence of fraud is hard to come by, and some of the claims concerning fraud made by party leaders following the legislative elections in 1997 and by opposition candidates after the presidential election in 1999 may have been exaggerated, little doubt remains that serious frauds were perpetrated in all three elections (legislative, regional, and municipal) held in 1997. [7] In part, this may be seen as the consequence of the re gime's decision to sponsor a ne w party, the RND, as the principal standard-bearer of the state in the electoral arena, relegating the old FLN to a secondary role. The RND is based very heavily on the administration, as its leadership (Ahmed Ouyahia, Abdelkader Bensalah) testifies. It lacks any clear basis of popular appeal and accordingly has relied heavily on administrative measures to secure electoral victory. Its privileged relations with the state administration ha ve made it natural that the latter should manage matters in its fa vor.

A fundamental corollary of this state of affairs is that changes in party electoral fortunes cannot be assumed to be the reflection of any real movements in public opinion. Between June 1997 and October 1997, the RND vote rose from 3.53 million to 4.97 million and the FLN from 1.49 million to 1.69 million, while the MSP vote fell from 1.55 million to 1.2 million. The other opposition parties ( *En Nahda*, FFS, RCD) suffered similar abrupt declines in their votes and corresponding falls in their tallies of seats won. Genuine gains or losses of popular support cannot satisfactorily explain these changes in electoral fortunes. They almost certainly can be explained as the outcomes of decisions taken by the power brokers in the regime and registered in terms of fluctuating vote tallies thanks to administrative measures to "correct" (falsify) the actual results of the election.

The advent of pluralism in the party-political sphere has not enfranchised the Algerian people substanti vely. No e vidence indicates that Algerian public opinion counts for more in national political life in the era of formal pluralism than it did in the era of formal monoliths. When the actual policies of the government are borne in mind, there are clear grounds for the view that it actually counts for less. It is a system of pluralism without enfranchisement. This severely limited formal pluralism may be enough to secure international approval and legitimation for the re gime. However, it cannot secure internal le gitimation on democratic grounds beyond the restricted middle-class circles that are represented after a fashion in the political process through the medium of the participationist parties. It is not at all obvious that this system can evolve toward a more substantial kind of political pluralism. However, it exacerbates a ke y problem of the Algerian polity , namely the chronic weakness of the presidency of the Republic, and thereby contributes to the perpetuation of the impasse in which the Algerian state as a whole is stuck.

### *The Powerless Presidency*

In January 1992, President Chadli Bendjedid was forced out of office despite the fact that he had 2 years of his third 5-year term to run and that he was willing to cohabit with the predominantly FIS government that was in prospect. Moreo ver, the FIS w as willing to cohabit with him. This event revealed the primacy of the armed forces over the executive as a whole and that of the army commanders over the president, the formal ape x of the ex ecutive, in particular. Both aspects of this military primacy have been affirmed repeatedly over the last 10 years, as the f ates of Mohammed Boudiaf and Liamine Zeroual testify .

At issue is the ability of the president to fulfill the function of arbiter of the political game. This requires him to arbitrate the competing claims of the various factions within the power structure and of the various policy options being canvassed—notably in respect of issues of economic policy, but also of the internal political situation as a whole. Algeria's first three presidents (Ben Bella, Boumediène, and Chadli) all possessed this power of arbitration, if in varying degrees. Since the events of early 1992, the army commanders, and not the presidents, possess this power. They collectively and informally arbitrate both the factional competition and the policy debate. The president and his supporters are merely one faction among others.

Like Zeroual in November 1995, Bouteflika in April 1999 sought to stand above the party. He has been unable, however, to sustain this posture in the matter of choosing his government and has been forced to allow the parties that "supported" his candidacy to share in ministerial portfolios. As he himself complained in October 1999, *"je suis obligé d'aller vers un mosaïque qui ne me convient pas."* The fact that these parties are all linked in some way to the military decisionmakers indicates that the army commanders instrumentalize the players in the game of formal party pluralism to encircle the president. Insofar as the resolution of Algeria's chronic political crisis requires decisive action by an authoritative head of state—that is, by a president able to exercise his constitutional prerogatives to the full—the continuing structural weakness of the presidency means that no resolution of the conflict is in prospect.

### *Violence without End?*

That the Algerian people are exhausted by the violence of the last 8 years and passionately want peace cannot be doubted. But what does it signify? This popular attitude was already evident in November 1995, when the Algerians voted massively to give Liamine Zeroual a mandate to sort things out. Despite Zeroual's best efforts, this mandate counted for little. The violence occurs independently of the popular will, and the popular will cannot end it.

Abdelaziz Bouteflika has mobilized popular support in endorsement of his approach—the referendum in September 1999 invited the electorate to approve or disapprove nothing more precise than *"la démarche du Président"*—but his election promise to "put the fire out" may turn out to be equally vain. He did not light the fire, and he may not have any control over the forces that have kept it alight.

The number of alleged terrorists who have taken advantage of the clemency provisions of the July 1999 Civil Concord Law is not very impressive. Since these provisions appear to apply only to those who do not have blood on their hands, its applicability to the elements that really matter is not obvious. These include the forces of the Islamic Salvation Army ( *Armée Islamique du Salut*, or AIS) of Mezrag Madani and Ahmed Benaïcha, and several other smaller groups that associate themselves with the AIS and reportedly have negotiated comparable understandings with the Algerian army commanders. If we assume that a formula will be found to complete the provisional deal between the army and the AIS and others, and so put a definitive end to the latter's activities, this will still lea ve the rump of the Armed Islamic Group ( *Le Groupe Islamique Armé*, or GIA) of Antar Zouabri and Hassan Hattab's Salafi Group for Preaching and Combat ( *Groupe Salafiste pour la Prédication et le Combat*, or GSPC) to be reckoned with.

The violence has now lasted for longer than did the war of national liberation. The longer it has gone on, the less it has had to do with the notional political objectives of the initiators of the rebellion—indeed, the less it has appeared to be oriented by intelligible political purposes of any kind. The aim of establishing an Islamic state by force of arms, which oriented the Algerian Islamic Movement ( *Mouvement Islamique Algérien*, MIA) of Abdelkader Chebouti in 1992–1993, gave way from mid-1994 onw ard to the more modest objecti ve of the MIA's successor, the AIS, of forcing the re gime to relegalize the FIS. The GIA at first shared the MIA objective and approach, but after its leader's capture in 1992, it adopted a different orientation—the immediate and coercive re-Islamization of the populations of the areas it controlled. This strategy pitted it not only against the people, particularly non-Muslims, rather than the regime, but also against the MIA and subsequently the AIS.

The GIA reorientation toward a strategy that tended to let the regime off the hook while queering the pitch for (if not actively combating) the rival armed movements likely owed much to manipulation by the Algerian intelligence services. In the process, ho wever, GIA activities have become politically aimless and increasingly indistinguishable from banditry, the organized preying on passing traffic, and racketeering. More politically minded elements of the GIA have split from it as the extent of regime manipulation and its deviation from original purposes have become clear. Generally, the extreme fragmentation of the armed movements, which the regime has clearly encouraged, has made it harder , if not impossible, to end the violence. Considering the extreme economic hardship that more of the population now endures (especially the mass unemployment afflicting young men), and the absence of any effective political representation of the poorer strata of the population, the premise of endless violence exists. In addition, the existence of some 300,000 armed men enrolled in various auxiliary forces (the communal guards, the patriot militias, or groups of legitimate defense) further militates against an end to the violence, since demobilizing these forces in the foreseeable future is not a given.

The regime offers little evidence of having a serious will to end the violence, as distinct from reducing it to tolerable levels. The violence serves to justify the annual renewal of the state of emergency, and the regime has an interest in maintaining the restrictions on opposition political activities that the state of emergency authorizes.

## Possible Futures

The overall impression of the political situation in Algeria in recent years is one of *immobilisme*. No decisive movement in any direction has occurred. Indeed, political forces proposing decisive action have uniformly been blocked (for example, the FLN reformers), if not destroyed (the FIS, Boudiaf, Kasdi Merbah). All evidence suggests that this is a state with a very weak impulse for reform in which proposals for substantial, as distinct from cosmetic, change almost in variably are vetoed.

The scenarios that follow offer alternative predictions to clarify the main available options. Fourteen years ago, I suggested that, confronted with the challenge of radical Islamism, the two clear-cut options open to the Algerian state were either to reinforce society's capacity to resist the Islamists by fostering the development of civil society and democratizing the state or to crush the Islamist movement by state terror. Each option threatened vested interests.[8] I accordingly expressed the view that the Algerian elite would fudge the issue, which is what it has done. And I expect that the political condition of Algeria in 2015 will similarly be the product of a fudge that combines certain features of several lines of development.

The common premise of the following scenarios is that something, somewhere, will have to give at some point. The combined effect of continued population growth, continuing if not increasing mass unemployment, recurrent violence and insecurity, the urgent need to promote substantial economic growth in non-hydrocarbons production, and the equally pressing need to address effectively the problem of Algeria's massive foreign debt burden could constitute the basis for a more or less radical departure from the political status quo. What forms might this take?

*The military faces up to its responsibilities.* If the chronic weakness of the presidency is accepted as a major impediment to the decisive resolution of Algeria's numerous problems, the army commanders may eventually decide that they must reempower the presidency by replicating the only way it has been done before: a military take-over *à la Boumediène*. Boumediène was a strong president because he brought to the office the power he already possessed as Defense Minister and Chief of the Armed Forces. Few observers doubt that the Army Chief of Staff, Lieutenant General Mohamed Lamari, is the single most powerful figure in Algeria. Were he to assume the presidency, the conflict between the army and the presidency that has bedeviled Algeria since 1992 would be resolved—at least temporarily and possibly for long enough for some of the major problems listed above to be addressed.

In evaluating the probability of this scenario, numerous factors militate against an outright *coup d'état*, not least the attitude of Algeria's foreign partners (France, the European Union, the United States), whom the Algerians know they must humor. But the reempowerment of the presidency through the accession of the most powerful military figure need not take the form of a flagrantly unconstitutional *coup de force*. It could be managed more subtly than that—for example, in the manner in which Philippe Pétain or Charles de Gaulle assumed power in France while formally respecting the constitutional proprieties. A variant of this scenario is that a major figure commanding the allegiance of Lamari and the other army commanders assumes the presidency; a possible candidate is the former Defense Minister, retired Major General Khaled Nezzar.

*Some civilians are allowed to come into their own.* The defeat of the Zeroual-Betchine tandem may have marked the wider defeat of the last faction in the officer corps directly linked to and legitimated by the heroic *maquisard* traditions of the ALN. The defeat of this faction would also give rise to the ascendancy of the rival faction of former French army officers who rallied to the ALN late in the war but saw little or no action inside the country. The victory of the latter f action may signify an irremediable loss of political legitimacy for the ANP as a whole and the corresponding reduction in the medium and longer term of its corporate political ambitions. In short, the rise of a new caste of military professionals may be accompanied by their realization that they have to arrange a transfer of some power to the civilian wing of the political class.

If we further assume that the new military caste will not share power with any body of civilians whose political legitimacy outweighs its own, we must conclude that any civilians thus empowered will belong to the post-war generation and will lack historic nationalist credentials, popular followings, or serious representative status in respect of public opinion. This scenario in volves a qualified transfer of po wer to the technocrat generation personified most notably by former Prime Minister Ahmed Ouyahia. His special status as Minister of State as well as Minister of Justice emphasizes his superior position in the pecking order after the prime minister. From the army's point of vie w, Ouyahia is a safe pair of hands, a docile executant of the army commanders' instructions as well as those of the IMF, a product of the diplomatic corps with practical e xperience in conducting Algerian foreign polic y, and a competent technocrat whose handling of structural adjustment is regarded as a success, irrespective of the social cost.

A corollary of the Ouyahia option for the post-Bouteflika presidency would be that the army would, at long last, allow a civilian president to enjoy the organized support of a nation-wide party-political base, since Ouyahia is the general secretary of the RND. This could be acceptable to the army commanders, precisely because the RND itself lacks legitimacy—as its dependence on electoral fraud suggests. Thus, the Ouyahia option might be a neat way of reempowering the presidency to some extent while preserving the decencies of civilian rule and formal party-pluralism. A virtue would no doubt also be made of the fact that he would be the first Kabyle to hold presidential office.

Rather than entailing a radical departure from the status quo, this scenario arguably would amount to a significant improvement of it to the extent that it would end the colossal waste of political energy that has been expended in the army-presidency rivalry over the last decade. It would also permit a recovery in coherence at the top. As such, it is a formula that might enable the Algerian state to address some of the accumulating social and economic problems. While coherent and competent technocratic government will not resolve them, it may be able to mitig ate them effectively, at least as long as the oil price holds up.

*Toward a State Bound by Law* . Algeria has been subject to ar - bitrary rule since 1962. The demand for a state bound by law ( *un état de droit*) has become the common coin of political discourse. All six of the presidential candidates running against Bouteflika in April 1999 paid lip service to it. At least two of them, Hocine Aït Ahmed and Mouloud Hamrouche, presented themselves as consistent crusaders for this cause. But what do they mean by it?

The striking thing about the current condition of Algerian politics is that no one has made any precise proposals with a view to promoting tangible change in this direction. Y et the main conditions of Algeria becoming a state bound by law are not at all mysterious. Given that the Islamist v ersion of this idea—a state bound by God' s law, the *Shari'a*, and presumably subject to authoritative supervision by the *'ulama*—is ruled out, the realization of this ideal requires, first and foremost, that the judiciary and the legislature both acquire a substantial measure of autonomy from the executive. At present, they are both massively dependent upon and dominated by the executive, which is in turn subject to the hegemony of the army—which manipulates the political parties to ensure that the conditions of its hegemony are reproduced within the legislature itself.

Given the extent to which the army has managed to stitch everything up, the failure of even opposition figures to challenge the status quo in the name of law-bound government by anything other than the vaguest and most inconsequential rhetoric—almost certainly meaningless as far as Algerian public opinion is concerned—probably translates into a fundamental pessimism on their part. It also indicates the mental limitations of opposition currents in Algeria and particularly the absence of the philosophical bearings that are required to orient a substantial movement for liberal political reform.

Will internal social and economic change o ver the next 15 years help remedy this? The probable answer is that it will do so only to the extent that it helps reinforce the fledgling class of Algerian entrepreneurs in the non-hydrocarbons sectors of productive economic activity. If there is a potentially influential section of the society with a fundamental interest in the advent of the rule of law, it is this. The absence of a stable and reliable politico-juridical framework that guarantees contracts and protects private property is arguably the single most important factor impeding productive enterprise in Algeria. The need to cover for the multiple kinds of political risk that must be run in the Kafkaesque universe of the unreformed Algerian state depresses the propensity to take economic risks—that is, to invest capital in productive ventures where immediate returns are not expected. At present, however, this social interest is profoundly disorganized. Algeria's employers are represented (or misrepresented) by a plethora of different organizations, and to date various attempts to unify them have come to nothing.

This scenario accordingly seems to have only one factor in its favor: namely, the need for the Algerian economy to enjoy a massive expansion in non-hydrocarbons production over the next 15 years if it is to stay abreast of accumulating social demands for jobs, goods, and services. Unless this objective finds articulation at the political level, however, it is unlikely to give rise to the benign and entirely desirable line of development in question.

A second factor that might push things in this direction is the state's need for increased sources of revenue, a need that might develop rapidly in the event of a collapse of the world oil price. A state decision to supplement revenues from hydrocarbon exports by increasing domestic taxation might eventually entail a substantive empowering of the national parliament. This might give the middle classes a qualitatively enhanced interest in the activities and behavior of the legislature, and, accordingly, an interest in elections to this legislature being free of fraud.

*The Resurgence of Populism.* The destruction of the FIS dismantled the sole truly populist party in Algeria. The result has been the eclipse of Algerian populism, a development that most of the protagonists as well as observers of Algerian politics today regard as definitive. There are at least two reasons to believe they are deluding themselves:

- *The populist tradition constituted the Algerian state*. Messali Hadj's *Étoile Nord-Africaine* and its successor, the *Parti du Peuple Algérien* (PPA), its legal front, the *Mouvement pour Le Triomphe des Libertés Démocratiques* (MTLD), and the FLN, an offshoot of the PPA-MTLD, originally canvassed the separatist idea. States do not long outlive the traditions to which they owe their foundation, and some elements of the Algerian political class must be expected to be aware of this.

• *Projected demographic growth over the next 15 years, together with the trend to urbanization, will expand the natural constituency of populist politics: the urban poor* . This constituency is no longer represented politically and appears to be well aware of that fact, as is suggested by its failure to vote in 1997 as well as 1999. The urban poor probably cannot be kept unrepresented indefinitely.

How would the regime handle a revival of populism? Repression can, of course, work up to a point and for a time. But continuous repression of embryonic forms of populist politics could stimulate the development of the human rights movement, which, however weak, already enjoys enough international support to oblige the regime to tolerate it. A question worth asking here is whether, in the light of the disastrous consequences of the FIS adventure, a second wave of urban-based populist politics can develop that draws the lessons of the past and accordingly manages to avoid stigmatization as ideologically regressive and to enlist the support of part of the Western-oriented middle class.

*Political Regression.* The events of the past decade have placed immense strains on Algeria's national unity. In addition to the bitterness occasioned by the violence itself, the rise of identity-based politics (such as Islamism and Berberism) have undermined the previous orthodox nationalist conception of Arabo-Muslim Algeria and thus put the common national identity of Algerians in question. At the same time, the decline of the capacity of the state at the national level to cater to, or even interest itself in, the day-to-day concerns of ordinary Algerians has aggravate the centrifugal impulses in the body politic. In this context, calls made in recent years for a federal constitution (which I believe would be a disaster for the country, a mere prelude to its Balkanization) can be interpreted as the expression of an understandable growth of interest in a surrogate for progressive political reform at the center, given the grounds for despairing of a revival of purposeful and effective government from Algiers.

In addition, the extent to which the violence of the last 8 years has involved the militarization of Algerian politics should not be underestimated. Considering the fragmentation of the Islamist movement, the exacerbation of regionalism within the regime and its facade parties, the growth of virtual warlordism at the local level in many areas as a byproduct of the re gime's reliance on the auxiliary militias, and the persistence of important zones of insecurity in numerous parts of the country, there is e vidence to support a most pessimistic assessment of the real underlying trend of events.

This trend is to ward the definitive disruption of Algeria' s development as a nation-state and the revival of forms of organization, solidarity, loyalty, and identity characteristic of the pre-colonial era. This is, of course, only one trend among several, and others can reasonably be expected to counter it. But this trend exists; the government itself is exacerbating it through the application of the structural adjustment program. The unemployment of thousands of Algerian workers and the impoverishment of important sections of the middle classes are propelling hundreds of thousands of Algerians into sociological limbo and undoing very rapidly a crucial aspect of the national development of the first three decades of independence, namely the constitution of national society through the formation across the country of modern social classes.

The Algerian nation-state is young and fragile and has been gravely destabilized and badly damaged. It will not survive indefinitely unless the current political and socioeconomic disarray is brought to an end and a modern national order that—whether democratic or not—is legitimate in the eyes of the Algerian people is restored. The next 15 years may be decisive in this fundamental respect.

## Notes

[1] Mohammed Boudiaf, *Ou Va L'Algérie?* (Paris: Librairie L'Étoile, 1964).

[2] Dr. Taleb Ibrahimi is the son of the late Sheikh Bachir El Ibrahimi, the companion of Ben Badis who succeeded him in 1940 and led the Association of the 'Ulama from 1940 to 1951 and from 1962 to 1965.

[3] Information obtained during author visit to Tizi Ouzou, April 14–15, 1999.

[4] For a fuller discussion of this point, see Hugh Roberts, "From Radical Mission to Equivocal Ambition: The Expansion and Manipulation of Algerian Islamism, 1979–1992, in Martin E. Marty and R. Scott Applebyeds., *Accounting for Fundamentalisms: The Dynamic Character of Movements* (Chicago: University of Chicago Press, 1994), 428–489, and Hugh Roberts, "Doctrinaire Economics and Political Opportunism in the Strategy of Algerian Islamism," in John Ruedy, ed., *Islamism and Secularism in North Africa* (New York: St. Martin's Press, 1994), 123–147.

[5] See *Le Monde*, November 26, 1999.

[6] Marcel-Edmond Naegelen achieved lasting notoriety when, as governor-general of Algeria, he oversaw the comprehensive rigging of elections in 1948, 1951, and 1953 at the expense of the nationalist parties.

[7] Hugh Roberts, "Algeria's Contested Elections," *Middle East Report* 209, no. 28 (Winter 1998), 21–24.

[8] Hugh Roberts, "The Embattled Arians of Algiers: Radical Islamism and the Dilemma of Algerian Nationalism," in *Third World Quarterly* 10, no. 2 (April 1988), 556–589.

*This chapter is based on a paper that was presented at a conference on* The Middle East in Transition: The Maghreb , *which was held at the Institute for National Strategic Studies, National Defense University, Washington, DC, on January 7, 2000.*

Chapter 3
# Morocco: Will Tradition Protect the Monarchy?

*Azzedine Layachi*

Morocco is in a period of prolonged political and economic transition. Two key events mark political change: the accession to the throne of King Mohammed VI and the control of the government by a reformist, opposition coalition led by the Socialist P arty. The main impetus for ongoing economic change is the go vernment's economic liberalization program. This chapter examines the nature of transition in Morocco and identifies possible future trends and their significance for U.S. foreign polic y. An adequate and useful identif ication of these future trends must rest on an objective assessment of the political, economic, and social conditions that pre vail in Morocco today.

## A Time of Transition

*The Political Scene.* To what extent do political changes in Morocco represent a departure from past policies and practices? This

---

*Azzedine Layachi is associate professor of politics at Saint John's University and adjunct associate professor at New York University. His publications include* Economic Crisis and Political Change in North Africa *(1998),* State, Society and Liberalization in Morocco: the Limits of Associative Life *(1998),* Civil Society and Democratization in Morocco *(1995), and* The United States and North Africa: A Cognitive Approach to Foreign Policy *(1990), as well as chapters and articles on political change and policy options in Mor occo and Algeria.*

question is at the heart of a current debate in Morocco itself. [1] The accession of King Mohammed VI and the empowerment of the Socialist Party—significant developments in their own right—occurred soon after important institutional reforms had been introduced; these reforms were designed to encourage power sharing between elected officials and the king. The effort was especially important in a traditional society and culture where rule by a king is legitimized by hereditary right and his claim to descent from the family of the Prophet Muhammad. For some Moroccans, the more open ruling style of Mohammed VI, in stark contrast to that of his late father, King Hassan II, is reason enough to be optimistic about the future. For others, however, King Mohammed's actions and speeches since his accession have merely reaffirmed the central role of the monarchy in Morocco as one of unrestrained power.

As analysts attempt to predict the future of Morocco under Mohammed VI, many have focused on the differences between this monarch and his father. To his admirers, King Hassan was the only person capable of insuring Moroccan stability. Hassan is credited with the consolidation of the country's independence, the re-establishment of its territorial integrity (against French and Spanish ambitions and by reclaiming the Western Sahara), and the preservation of the monarchical regime in a relatively hostile environment. On the international scene, Hassan kept the country within the non-aligned movement while skillfully leaning toward the West during the Cold War. He also played an active yet discreet role in the peace process between Arabs and Israelis.

To his critics, King Hassan became an anachronism in an era of global democratization. He ruled Morocco for 38 years with absolute power, constantly harassing and persecuting all opposition, both leftists and Islamists. Many opposition leaders (and often their families too) were jailed, tortured, killed, or forced into exile abroad. During his reign, and especially since the late 1970s, disparities in income grew: poverty spread among the general population while an elite group, with connections to the monarchy, was allowed to amass wealth, privileges, and power. Meanwhile, political repression became the hallmark of Hassan's Morocco. In Casablanca in June 1981, in Marrakech and Tétouan in January 1984, and in Fès and Tangier in December 1990, popular riots were brutally suppressed.

By the mid 1990s, the political situation in Morocco had become untenable and unjustifiable. International pressures, domestic malaise, and ailing health forced King Hassan to agree to limited political reforms near the end of his reign. The reforms included a constitutional amendment that allowed for the direct election of all members of the Chamber of Representatives and the creation of an upper house of Parliament. Municipal and parliamentary elections were held in late 1997, effectively ending the political crisis that had prevailed since the debacle of the 1993 elections, which excluded the opposition from real participation in the political process. [2] In February 1998, Hassan appointed as prime minister the Socialist opposition leader Abderrahmane Youssoufi, but without granting him real po wer. As monarch, Hassan, who is legally above all criticism and accountability, maintained total control o ver what were considered national so vereignty sectors: defense, interior , justice, and foreign polic y.[3] His son inherited a country still in need of the kinds of political and economic reforms that would allow Morocco to compete in a 21 $^{st}$-century global environment.

*Economic Conditions.* As the first North African country to engage in structural adjustment in 1983, Morocco has witnessed a major overhaul of its economy. At the macro-economic le vel, reforms stabilized a faltering economy and began the long restructuring process, notably through pri vatization and stringent f iscal policies. However, success at the macro-level did not improve living conditions for most people. Over the years, a growing number of people joined the burgeoning ranks of the unemployed. Some were unable to find work, some were laid off, others could not enter the job market with a first job. As the state be gan its economic retreat, man y of the urban poor lost access to public services because of lack of funds.

In a September 1999 report, a Moroccan think tank, Le Centre Marocain de Conjoncture (CMC), painted a grim picture of the country' s economic situation. Economic growth—less than 1 percent in 1999 and 6.3 percent in 1998—remained highly dependent on agricultural production, which itself was directly affected by a recurring drought. Agriculture employed 50 percent of the workforce and contributed 17 percent of the gross domestic product (GDP). [4] On the other hand, the International Monetary Fund (IMF) praised Morocco for stabilizing and liberalizing its economy , for disciplined b udgeting, and for prudent monetary and exchange rate policies, which helped lower inflation, rebuild foreign exchange reserves, and reduce the external debt. However, the IMF also indicated that the economy needs higher gro wth rates, more structural reforms, a reduction in the state wage bill (the administration, which employs 750,000 people, consumes 11.5 percent of the GDP), and reduced food subsidies. [5]

Foreign aid has shrunk over the years, and the little foreign assistance that Morocco has received has been tied to the conditions of economic liberalization and improved human rights. However, in 1999, the World Bank pledged to double its annual aid to $450 million. Earlier, in 1996, France and Spain decided to assist Morocco by using debt swaps. France agreed to convert $120 million dollars (out of $4.8 billion dollars) into investment projects in Morocco and canceled $80 million in debt. Spain decided to convert $520 million dollars of the $1.3 billion it was owed by Morocco. The country's foreign debt of $18 billion represented 39 percent of the GDP. It is serviced with 22 percent of export earnings and uses up about one third of the state budget. Only 15 percent was left for investment.[6]

In 1996, the European Union (EU) and Morocco signed an Association Agreement aimed at establishing free trade between the EU and Morocco by 2010. The European Union also signed a fisheries accord, but it was short-lived primarily because it disadvantaged the Moroccan fishing industry and because the EU refused to agree to Morocco's demand that European restrictions on its fruit and vegetable exports be lifted. The commitment of the European Union to several projects in preparation for the free trade zone of 2010 carries the condition that Morocco's economy attain European economic standards. The country also must curtail drug trafficking and illegal migration to Europe substantially.

Direct foreign investment (DFI) has thus far fallen short of expectations for many reasons, notably the better business climate and profit opportunities found elsewhere in the world. In 1998, foreign investment fell by 50 percent compared to total DFI in North Africa the previous year. However, in the same year, Morocco netted the second highest value of foreign investment in the Arab world. It attracted $500 million out of $3.1 billion total DFI in the Arab world, second only to Egypt and ahead of Saudi Arabia, Tunisia, and Libya.

Revenues from tourism along with remittances from Moroccan expatriates working abroad have grown in the last 2 years. The number of tourists increased by 18 percent in the first 10 months of 1999 (more than 2 million tourists visited the kingdom), while remittances increased by 6.6 percent, totaling approximately $2 billion. On the negative side, Morocco's oil import bill rose by 40 percent in 1999 ($580 million) as a result of both price hikes and a 22 percent increase in the volume of oil imports.

*Socioeconomic Issues.* While macro-economic indicators reflect a mixed picture of improvement and shortfalls, domestic socioeconomic conditions give rise to serious concern. External constraints—such as economic conditions and practices, as well as inadequate public services—have combined to produce a precarious socioeconomic situation in Morocco, whose young king inherits a country in need of major urgent changes to diffuse an explosive situation and to allow Morocco to adapt adequately to globalization. Similar to most developing countries, Morocco is not ready yet to meet such challenges.

Morocco's population in 2000 stands at 30 million and is growing at a yearly rate of 1.89 percent. More than 50 percent are under the age of 30; more than 40 percent are less than 20 years old. It is this youth bulge (those between 15 and 40) that comprises the majority of those who have been bypassed by economic development and are dangerously marginalized. Approximately 20 percent of Morocco's population (6 million) live in poverty today; 10 percent are in sheer misery; and 30 percent, mostly the young and elderly, are officially classified as "vulnerable"; 56 percent are illiterate; and only 18 percent of women know how to read and write. Unemployment hovers around 25 percent, although the official figures for 1999 put the rate at 12.9 percent. Those figures also indicate that unemployment was 37.7 percent among people aged between 15 and 34 years. The unemployment rates are even higher in rural areas. Job creation has not been able to keep up with demand. Nearly 300,000 university graduates are without jobs (23.5 percent of the unemployed hold high school and university diplomas).[7]

Income disparities have worsened in recent years. The gaps between higher and lower incomes as well as between rural and urban incomes are immense. Among the rural population, 63 percent have no running water, 87 percent are without electricity, 93 percent have no access to health services, and 65 percent are illiterate. The health system, which receives only 1 percent of GDP, is deteriorating. Statistical social data released in December 1999, stimulated the following commentary in the weekly *Vie Economique*:

> The current social situation carries heavy threats. The social dialogue is out of order, the social indices are deteriorating, the country

has two million new poor people since 1991. In the prevalent depression, there is a wait-and-see attitude in the political and business spheres. The government is attacked from all sides (this is too easy, given the conjuncture) while the country needs a wake-up call in order to deal with a worrisome economic and social situation. The Moroccans do not live better than eight years ago: their living standard fell by 1.9 percent in eight years. The numbers speak for themselves. Read on! F ortunately, the politicians ha ve come back to a discourse of appeasement.[8]

## Near-Term Trends

The serious nature of Morocco' s social and economic problems, combined with the demands of international institutions and W estern governments—mainly the European Union—constitute a sizeable challenge that the country will have great difficulty meeting in the near future. The difficulty will lie, in part, on Morocco' s limited institutional and financial means and, in part, on the restrictions that admission into the EU free-trade zone could place on native craft industries, labor migration to Europe, and the removal of tariffs, a source of revenue for the poorer Arab countries seeking admission into EU economic graces. The IMF demands may help improve the overall situation in the long run, but in the short term, they are likely to increase social tensions because of their negative social impact. The country will continue to have great difficulty in reducing po verty and unemployment, increasing literac y, and dampening mounting social pressures. [9]

The coalition government led by the Popular Union of Socialist Forces (USFP), appointed in 1998, is caught between trying to meet the socioeconomic needs noted above and the demands of international financial institutions. The government also faces resistance from right-wing opposition elements and a number of self-serving interests in the bureaucracy as well as in pri vate sectors of the economy . To its credit, the government has realized some modest economic gains, including an increase of 6.2 percent in state income, increased tourism revenue, a rise of 10 percent in exports, an increase of 7.8 percent in domestic investment, a 20 percent rise in stock market earnings, and a 6.6 percent increase in e xpatriate remittances. Moreo ver, the b udget deficit was cut, foreign exchange reserves reached a record level, and inflation appeared to be under control.

To build on these gains, the government must undertake a multitude of domestic reforms that would guarantee steady economic growth and a minimum of social services for the needy and vulnerable. The areas that need urgent attention include poverty, illiteracy, health, and justice. The government also must find a long-term solution to the Moroccan economy's deep dependency on rain-fed agriculture to eliminate wide economic fluctuations related to local climate patterns and one vital resource: rain.

*Prospects for Stagnation or Change.* Despite the hope engendered by a new young king and an opposition-led government, genuine political change in Morocco is illusive. The government remains weak due to King Mohammed's unyielding control over critical issues, such as the Western Sahara, structural adjustment, and relations with the European Union. Moreover, the King retains control over cabinet nominations, specifically those for interior, justice, and foreign affairs. Further, elements within the regime as well as some business interests have been actively resisting change while the majority of the population has grown impatient with the slow pace of government action. The removal of the powerful Minister of Interior, Driss Basri, from government in November 1999, where he had served for 20 years, was a key event, but his replacement, Ahmed Midaoui, was still appointed by the king, not the prime minister.

*The Islamist Opposition.* As a result of their political exclusion and the neutralization of the left through repression and cooptation, the Islamists have in recent years increased their popularity and ability to challenge the government. Their success lies in confronting social issues. Their activism in schools and universities has become more overt. Two Islamist groups, in fact, dominate the Moroccan scene: al-Adl wa al-Ihsan (Justice and Charity Organization [JCO]), led by Abdeslam Yacine, and al-Islah wa al-Tawheed (Reform and Unity Movement), led by Abdelilah Benkirane. The JCO is the more popular of the two and was genuinely feared by the late king. It is banned, and Yacine remains under house arrest. Al-Islah wa al-Tawheed was allowed to place five of its militants in Parliament in 1997 as members of the Party of Justice and Development (formerly known as the Popular Constitutional and Democratic Movement).

As the Islamist challenge sharpens, King Mohammed will have a choice to make: either include more of the moderates among the Islamists in government or revert to the repressive measures used by his father. Continuing social and economic exclusion and hardship may mobilize more people under the religious banner. The urban, educated, and unemployed youth—marginalized by lack of power, status, and jobs—could add their voices to the Islamists to demand accountable and transparent governance; they may even look for more extreme changes.

Even though the Islamists present themselves as the only real opposition to the government, their leadership is unlikely to resort to violence to further its cause. Having witnessed the loss of popular support when Islamist factions turned to violence in Algeria, Tunisia, and Egypt, Morocco's religious militants are more likely to use political action to enhance their position. For example, they likely will exploit any political opening offered by King Mohammed to impose themselves gradually as a legal and respectable political force.

However, if the socioeconomic situation remains stagnant and if the outlets for political dissent remain limited, the radical opposition may venture into bolder challenges. The new king seems to be aware of this danger and has quickly initiated a crusade against poverty. He acknowledges that this phenomenon constitutes a serious obstacle to development. He also certainly is cognizant of the fact that Islamic militants find fertile recruiting ground among the poor by providing services in areas where the government is unable or unwilling to do so.

*The Need for Reform.* Morocco's political and economic development stands to gain from serious and profound reform in three areas: equitable distribution of economic opportunities, which needs to be fair and mindful of the need to integrate youth; fair administration, which needs to simplify procedures and be more accessible to people and business; and establishment of the rule of law, which needs to be just and transparent.

In addition, corruption is so entrenched in the bureaucracy that it has become institutionalized. Corruption must be contained if not eliminated, especially when it distorts major development policies and diverts badly needed resources at the highest levels. Action in this area has been promised, but too little has been done so far. In most areas, there is an urgent need for transparency, which has been a key political theme in Morocco in the last 2 years. The huge profit made from the 1999 sale of the Moroccan mobile telecommunication network to foreign investors was mostly credited to the transparency of the negotiations.[10]

At the political level, a meaningful change would have to include real empowerment of a duly elected government and parliament and a monarch confined to a limited constitutional role. Greater press freedoms and the young king's more open ruling style ideally will contribute to greater transparency. Despite Morocco's history, rituals, and client-patron networks, a new political and institutional order can be negotiated on the basis of a consensus that produces a reformed monarchy and country run by accountable elected officials. But will King Mohammed agree to this and not be concerned about losing his grip on the society his father left him? It is too early to tell.

## Long-Term Domestic Trends

*Economic Prospects.* Morocco's economic situation is grim but not hopeless. The country has the potential to integrate into the global economy better, particularly the European economy. Its geographic location, notably its proximity to Europe and its longstanding tradition as a bridge to Africa and the Middle East, is an important asset, as is Morocco's valuable tourism industry. Morocco also is endowed with rich fishing waters and an agricultural sector with strong export potential.

Morocco has long desired membership in the European Union, but the best deal it could get was a 1996 Free Trade Association Agreement. In preparation for the coming into force of the agreement in 2010, Morocco has received some European assistance. European aid, however, has been channeled largely through technical assistance programs and social safety net projects designed to reduce inequalities in living conditions among those in rural areas, particularly in the impoverished northern Rif region.

While the EU Free Trade Agreement provides some clear benefits to Morocco, it also presents some significant challenges. The risk is that the arrangement with the EU will benefit Europe more than Morocco by opening Morocco to European business and the dumping of cheaper European goods while European markets remain restricted to Moroccan industries and labor, its chief export. But it may not bring the longed-for investment that Morocco seeks from Europe. European aid remains far lower and slower than promised. Rabat also remains concerned that Morocco could be a net loser in the long term if its role in the Association remains limited to providing cheap labor to foreign investors and a consumer mark et for European products. In its current form, the Agreement provides European businesses greater access to Moroccan markets than it allows Moroccan goods in European markets. At the same time, reforms needed to help make the M oroccan economy competitive could result in labor layoffs and the shutdown of inefficient state enterprises. It is important to note that because Morocco's trade relations with Europe already account for 60 percent of all its foreign trade, a much closer association with the European economies will make it more vulnerable to a recession in Europe and to major shifts in EU economic policies. Colloquially stated, if Europe sneezes, Morocco will catch cold.

The same potential for benefits and risks for Morocco exists with American initiatives to promote the establishment of a Maghreb economic union closely associated with the United States. While the prospect for such a cooperative relationship among Maghreb states is remote in the near term, it could offer a lateral opening in the long term that would allow Rabat to negotiate better deals with its trans-Atlantic and trans-Mediterranean partners.

Europe has its own concerns as it enters into economic agreements with Morocco and other states in the region—Egypt, Jordan, Israel, Mauritania, and T unisia. A serious economic or political crisis in Morocco or any of the North African states could lead not only to domestic instability but also to an increase in the wave of illegal immigration to Western Europe. Also, a crisis could e xport militant Islamist fervor and violence to the Arab communities in Europe.

*Political Changes.* Over the next several years, opposition groups are likely to increase pressure for meaningful political change. Both secular and religious opposition parties will exploit the transition to a new monarch, who is viewed as being more open to change, and demand substantive institutional and political reforms. Specif ically, they may push for constitutional and electoral reforms that devolve greater power to elected officials. King Mohammed may be pressed to grant some concessions in this area if the social and economic crisis persists.

A generational change also is likely to occur among the political elite, most notably among the leaders of the established parties. The "old timers" have become too close to the establishment and increasingly isolated from their popular base. These party leaders are largely vested in the status quo and therefore cannot be expected to push for real change. In the absence of a shift in power from the older to the younger generation, the latter will grow more alienated and may turn to more violent, destabilizing forms of opposition if they feel there are no other outlets.

Immediately following his accession to the throne, King Mohammed undertook personnel changes in the palace by bringing in younger advisers to replace several senior officials from his father's administration. The most notable change was that of Interior Minister Driss Basri, who had served since 1979. This trend is likely to continue. If, in the future, there is any major reshuffling of the government—including a change of prime minister—the king may draw from the pool of young politicians and technocrats.

The Islamists could take advantage of mounting pressures for change and ask for adequate and full recognition as a representative political force. The Islamist strategy is to exploit the weakness and unpopularity of the traditional opposition, which now controls a government that they perceive to be impotent and unresponsive. The king may look for ways to include more moderate Islamists in the political process. However, his attitude and policy toward the most radical among them may well be the same as his father's response. Following the publication of a prominent Islamist's letter demanding that King Mohammed return funds deposited in foreign bank accounts to Moroccan banks, the new interior minister moved to ban the sale of all the newspapers that carried the letter. The letter, reminiscent of a similar missive sent to King Hassan in 1974 by the same Islamist, stimulated the same old reflex of state censorship.

*Military Trends.* The future role of the military is difficult to predict. Since the coup attempts of 1970 and 1971 against King Hassan, the military has been watched closely by the paramilitary corps known as the gendarmerie, which is headed by General Housni Benslimane. No army movements escape the watchful eye of the gendarmerie. Even when military exercises are conducted, the gendarmerie counts all munitions and reports on their usage. King Hassan combined his tight control over military activities with a deeply entrenched patronage system that enriched senior officers. Hassan also turned a blind eye to corruption and drug trafficking within the military. As a result, many senior officers accumulated substantial wealth in real estate, agriculture, and industry. They are opposed, therefore, to any change in the status quo. However, contrary to his father, Mohammed appears willing to make changes in this area. He may have to force some senior officers into retirement. Otherwise, there is some risk that dissatisfied young officers, who have not benefited from the many perks enjoyed by their commanding officers, may take matters into their own hands. [11]

This problem of the military could be compounded by the eventual resolution of the Western Sahara question. Any resolution would prompt the issue of reintegrating many of the troops, who are quartered in the disputed territory, back into society, unless they become mobilized again for the reintegration of the territories that are still under Spanish control. These are the "plazas de soberania," or the five places of sovereignty that are located on and off the coast of Morocco: the coastal enclaves of Ceuta and Melilla, which Morocco contests, as well as the islands of Penon de Alhucemas, Penon de Velez de la Gomera, and Islas Chafarinas.

## Longer-Term Foreign Policy Trends

Several issues, some of which impact directly on Moroccan security, are under scrutiny. One of the most important foreign policy preoccupations for Morocco is that of securing international support for its claim to the Western Sahara, a territory that Morocco annexed after Spain withdrew from it in 1974. Morocco has repeatedly postponed a proposed United Nations referendum for allegedly technical reasons (non-agreement to the list of eligible voters). Likely, the Moroccans will continue to use this tactic in the hope that the international community will finally accept a *fait accompli*. To avoid potentially destabilizing unrest, the United States should urge Morocco to agree to hold a referendum sooner rather than later. A resolution to this long-festering conflict would also reduce the possibility of an escalation in tension with Morocco's regional rival, Algeria.

*The Middle East Peace Process.* The peace process was an important issue for King Hassan, who played a key role in supporting it and as Chairman of the Jerusalem Committee of the Organization of Islamic Conference (OIC). It will continue to be important to Morocco under King Mohammed. The new king, however, lacks the clout, influence, and experience of his father and is not likely to exert as much influence as his father. However, because of the special relationship that his father built with some Israeli leaders, Morocco likely will remain an important player among Arab states not on the front line of the conflict. While members of the political elite have in the past supported the king's Middle East polic y, including contacts with Israeli political figures, there is still resistance among the masses to such policy and contacts, especially where Islamist sentiment is strong. Such resistance may become more vocal if the newly found relative freedom of expression is maintained, and if U.S. policy and Israeli actions appear to be detrimental to Arab and Palestinian interests.

*Sanctions against Iraq.* As with most Arab countries, the UN-imposed sanctions against Iraq are highly unpopular in Morocco. While the official position on this issue has been moderate, several Moroccan associations and parties have not hesitated to condemn the sanctions whenever they have a chance. Spontaneous demonstrations in support of the Iraqi people have taken place in recent years, and the government has made no effort to prohibit them. Many Moroccans hold the United States and Great Britain responsible for the persistence of sanctions and suffering of the Iraqi people long after the end of the war in 1991. The United States needs to be mindful of domestic reactions in Morocco to some of its foreign policy actions in the Arab and Muslim world; otherwise, it may put the Moroccan regime in the odd position of having either to side with the street or repress it in order to side with the United States.

Morocco supports policies of nonproliferation and control of weapons of mass destruction. It is a signatory of the Non-Proliferation Treaty and the Comprehensi ve Nuclear Test Ban Treaty. In addition, it hosts an International Monitory Station, which verifies compliance. Rabat, however, keeps its options open re garding future arms and security arrangements, notably because of the potential for armed conflict or spillover violence from Algeria.

*Trends in Relations with the United States.* The United States closely follows the interests of its European allies in defining its security interests and military presence in the W estern Mediterranean. It is in U.S. and EU interests that Morocco succeeds in overhauling its economy and having a sustained and healthy growth rate. American economic interests in Morocco are still small, b ut increased American in vestments may be profitable to American in vestors and may also gi ve the United States additional political leverage.

Perhaps the greatest threat to regional stability in the Maghreb emanates from the economic duress and resulting deterioration of the region's social fabric. The United States can help Morocco weather its current difficulties through giving economic assistance, opening

U.S. markets to more Moroccan products, and encouraging American investment there. The American approach to the Maghreb may best serve American interests if undertaken with a regional view. The Maghreb states are sensitive to preferential relations between any one of them and the United States. The Eizenstat Initiative for the creation of a common Maghreb market was welcomed by Algeria, Morocco, and Tunisia, but the United States must realize that economic integration in the Maghreb cannot take place before major political issues are settled among the Maghreb states, mainly Algeria and Morocco. Therefore, the United States may use the little diplomatic leverage it has, but also its greater economic influence, to propel the Maghrebis toward resolving the most pressing issues, such as resolving the Western Sahara dispute and resuming the construction of the Arab Maghreb Union.

*Relations with Europe.* A major conflict or crisis in North Africa constitutes an important concern for the Europeans, particularly France and Spain. From a European perspective, any serious crisis in Morocco could lead to domestic instability, which in turn could increase the wave of illegal immigration to Europe. America's North Atlantic Treaty Organization (NATO) allies fear such a possibility and have contingency plans in case such a crisis arises. For their part, the Maghreb states are concerned that some Europeans would consider the possible use of NATO forces for crisis intervention in the Maghreb should the situation warrant it. [12] The Maghreb states also would not welcome a similar action by the United States. Some European governments, most notably France, are concerned about the potential U.S. inroad in the Maghreb, but such concern remains minimal for now because the European presence in North Africa is dominant, especially in Morocco and Tunisia.

## Notes

[1] See the debate among Moroccan intellectuals on this question in "Des intellectuels se prononcent sur l'avenir de la transition," *La Vie économique*, no. 4048 (December 31, 1999–January 6, 2000).

[2] At that time, the opposition block *Koutla* denounced what it perceived as electoral manipulations by the administration in the interest of pro-monarchical groups *Koutla* refused to participate in any government, in spite of King Hassan's eagerness to see it participate in a government set up by him.

[3] Ignacio Ramonet, "Où va le Maroc?" *Le Monde diplomatique*, August 1999.
[4] "CMC to See the Moroccan 2000 GDP Growth at 8.4%," *The North Africa Journal* 68 (November 11, 1999), accessed at <http://wwwnorth-africa.com>.
[5] "IMF: Morocco Economy Growing 'Below Potential,'" Reuters, April 1, 1999.
[6] "Morocco foreign debt down 6.7 pct to $18 bln," Reuters (Rabat), October 27, 1999.
[7] Centre d'Etudes et de Recherches Démographiques (CERED), *Populations Vulnérables: Profil Socio-Demographique et Repartition Spatiale*(Rabat, Morocco: CERED, 1997), 253. See also *La Vie économique* (Morocco), January 15, 1999.
[8] Mohammed Moujahid, "En huit ans 2 millions de pauvres!" *La Vie économique*, December 17–23, 1999.
[9] On June 3, 1999, some 300 Moroccan farmers stoned the motorcade of Interior Minister Driss Basri and other senior officials to protest the seizure of land in the 1970s to build the upper class residential area of Hay Riad, Rabat. Many of the farmers lived in unbuilt areas of the residential neighborhood and rejected orders to evacuate. See "Morocco Denies Farmers Stoned Ministers' Cars," Reuters (Rabat) June 3, 1999.
[10] In August 1999, Morocco raised $1.1 billion from the sale of a GSM mobile phone license. The total fiscal impact of the GSM phone license on fiscal revenues, including future taxes, could reach between $2 and $3.5 billion by 2008.
[11] On the issue of corruption in the military see Jean-Pierre Tuquoi, "Des officiers marocains dénoncent la corruption qui sévit dans l'armée," *Le Monde*, December 10, 1999.
[12] In 1960, the United States and Morocco signed a secret agreement in which the United States promised to come to the rescue of the monarchy if it were endangered in exchange for American access to Moroccan military facilities in a crisis.

---

*This chapter is based on a paper that was presented at a conference on* The Middle East in Transition: The Maghreb *, which was held at the Institute for National Strategic Studies, National Defense University, Washington, DC, on January 7, 2000.*

Chapter 4
# Egypt: Could It Lead the Arab World?

*Mamoun Fandy*

Egypt and the United States reestablished formal diplomatic relations more than 25 years ago. In that time the relationship has matured, shaped by mutual interests in regional security and stability. Egypt was the first nation to sign a peace agreement with Israel and one of the first Arab states to join the anti-Saddam Husayn coalition orchestrated by America in 1990 after Iraq in vaded and occupied Kuwait. The Egypt-U.S. relationship has required careful and skillful management as new and complex regional and domestic challenges have emerged. Despite occasional strains, the history of cooperation between the two countries has been closely connected with the mutually shared goal of bringing lasting peace to the Middle East. The enduring commitment of both parties to this objective is impressive, even when the going has not been smooth. Cairo has not been as cooperative as Washington might have desired on some issues (for example, influencing the Palestinians toward accepting a peace agreement with Israel), while Cairo has criticized the seeming refusal of the

---

*Mamoun Fandy is professor of politics at the Near-East South Asia Center for Strategic Studies at the National Defense Univer sity. His research focus is the politics of North Africa and the Arabian Gulf. His most recent publication is* Saudi Arabia and the Politics of Dissent *(1999). Dr. Fandy is preparing two studies for publication,* Kuwait and a New Concept of International Politics *and* Egypt: An Old Society and a New Modern State.

United States to demand the kinds of compliance of Israel that it demands of the Arabs (for example, Iraqi compliance with United Nations [UN] resolutions and Israel's nuclear capability). Yet the relationship endures to the benefit of both countries.

This chapter examines several trends in Egypt's domestic and security views and gauges their impact on both Egypt and its relations with the United States by 2015. It concludes with an examination of areas of cooperation and divergence and offers an assessment of the implications of all these factors for the future of Egypt-U.S. relations. What are and what will be the issues of concern for both countries? Identifying Egypt's domestic challenges and assessing the government's responses to these challenges is a good way to answer this question. A review of the historical importance of the Egypt-U.S. relationship indicates the reasons that Egypt has been and remains an important American ally.

## Domestic Trends and Government Responses

Egyptian domestic trends can be distilled into three key challenges for the stability of the political order, and all threaten Egyptian internal stability in varying degrees:
- capacity to transform the economy into one that is competitive in the new global economy
- ability to control the Islamist challenge
- willingness to ensure that the military retains a fully professional role and does not raise the prospect of a military coup.

*The Egyptian Economy.* To judge the trends and performance of the Egyptian economy, we must consider the traditional indicators, such as demographics, gross domestic product (GDP), and unemployment rates. We also should consider the inflation rate and evaluate external viability based on the stability of the exchange rate and level of international reserves.

Egypt has made significant economic progress since it embarked on a wide-scale economic reform program in 1991. In the first phase of the program, emphasis was placed on achieving macro-economic stability in a noninflationary environment and stabilizing the exchange rate of the Egyptian pound. In the second phase, the economy moved toward designing and implementing a wide range of policies aimed at achieving growth and increasing private investment. On the growth front, GDP grew 4.2 percent from 1990 to 1998, according to World Bank statistics.[1] The GDP growth rate was negative in 1990, an estimated -3.2 percent. It has since progressed steadily from weak growth (approximately 1.6 percent in 1993) to stronger growth (ranging from 5–6 percent between 1997 and 2000). At the same time, Egypt managed to curb inflation from a rate of 21.1 percent in 1992 to 3.7 percent in 1999.[2]

An influx of direct foreign investment, which grew from $598 billion in 1993 to $1.076 trillion in 1998, helped stimulate Egypt's economic growth.[3] This in turn helped increase foreign exchange reserves, which has signaled the stability of the Egyptian currency and helped attract more foreign investment. As for the unemployment rate, Egypt has managed to reduce the rate from a high of 11.3 percent in 1995 to 8 percent in 1999.

*Demographic Trends and Economic Growth.* Despite a lower unemployment rate, the composition of the Egyptian unemployed remains a troubling problem. In 2000, most of Egypt's unemployed university graduates had few prospects for employment. They are ready recruits for Egypt's radical Islamist factions. While the government has blunted the radical Islamist trend, root causes such as poverty, especially in Upper Egypt, remain a cause for official worry. It is not sufficient merely to reduce the overall number of the unemployed without addressing their place in the local political and economic map. Egyptian policymakers must pay particular attention to sectoral unemployment (that is, university graduates and those in regions outside Cairo) when devising job creation schemes. Otherwise, Egypt's service sector-led growth, especially in tourism, could suffer a significant setback, as it did in 1997 when an extremist Islamist faction attacked foreign tourists at Luxor. Working-class Egyptians were hurt the most, however, as tourism and foreign investment fell, and Egyptians were killed along with Western tourists.

Complicating this picture even further are rumors associated with the new business environment in Egypt. Some analysts question the stability of private investment in the wake of an enormous expansion in private credit, raising concern about the viability of investment projects and the abilities of borrowers to pay back debt in case of default. While some level of concern can be ascribed to unsubstantiated rumors, the Egyptian government should seize this opportunity to draw lessons from the Asian economic crisis. Government regulations should be established to streamline the expansion of private credit, while ensuring the soundness of investment and the feasibility to pay back private loans.

The bulk of Egypt's economic growth has been achieved in the service sector. While many regional economies have managed to sustain growth over time in the service sector, the Egyptian economy, with its diverse resources and human capital, has established more diversified growth. To sustain this growth, new foreign capital and the growth of private investment should be directed to productive enterprises that seek to establish Egypt's comparative advantage among industrial countries.

Economic and political stability in Egypt serves the strategic interest of the United States. An economically strong Egypt can be a bulwark against extremism and a source of internal stability. It also enhances regional stability. It is in the mutual interest of both countries to have a serious and open dialogue about economic and strategic issues. Currently, however, the Egypt-U.S. economic dialogue is not properly focused. The American government has criticized Egypt for its inability to implement International Monetary Fund (IMF) recommendations, particularly regarding privatization and economic restructuring. Egyptian officials, however, see the United States as insensitive to larger political implications and risks if Egypt were to implement the IMF reform agenda.[4] For them, the stakes go well beyond that agenda. They weigh the pace and substance of economic reform against the short-term risk of increased unemployment and the longer-term risk of political instability. The political cost of privatization would be high for Egypt if it were to result in increased unemployment, which is a key contributing factor to political instability and risks political dislocation. In their view, the Egypt-U.S. dialogue should look beyond the issue of economic reform and take the interests of both countries into consideration.

*The Islamists.* When addressing the question of the Islamists in Egypt, a frequent oversight on the part of policy analysts and scholars is the tendency to examine the issue as a contemporary problem and thus to overlook the root causes of violence. Historically, Islamic resistance existed in Egypt long before the rise of the Muslim Brotherhood in 1929. Moreover, it has always been closely associated with certain geographical patterns. For example, examination of the list of assassins of the late President Anwar Sadat reveals that the violence was connected with southern (Upper) Egypt. [5] Since the 17th century, Islamic activists from Upper Egypt have challenged the political, economic, and cultural dominance of Cairo and northern Egypt. Numerous uprisings occurred in the southern province of Qena in the 1820s. In 1867, southern Egyptians attacked tourist boats on the Nile, prompting Ismail Pasha to send troops to southern Egypt to eradicate three villages near Qena.

One reason for the pattern of violence then, as now, is the unbalanced economic development of the country. Most development programs have focused on the northern region of the country. While Cairo has received the lion's share of funds, the south has been neglected consistently. Gamal Abd al-Nasser attempted to devote special attention to development in Upper Egypt by initiating programs associated with building the Aswan High Dam and sugar factories. However, these efforts led to the creation of a small oasis of industrialization in the south, which was soon taken over by management and even workers from the north.

The Cairo government failed to understand the root causes of Islamist activities until the campaign of violence from 1990 to 1995. By 1997, the government had managed to eradicate numerous Islamist extremist cells. The reduction in violence and the victory of the government over extremist forces came as a result of three factors:

- The government did not waver in conducting a decisive campaign against the radical military wing of the movement. In spite of the criticism surrounding human rights violations, the government persisted in its efforts and succeeded in achieving its objective.
- The Islamists lost considerable public support when they massacred tourists in Luxor in 1997. The nature and scale of the massacres turned the whole country against them.
- The president's support for major development projects in Upper Egypt is almost certainly the primary factor behind the government's success against the Islamist extremists. Especially important were the Toshka Canal Project near Aswan and the encouragement of business investment in the southern region. For the first time in their history, southern Egyptians saw themselves as part of the country—and only then did the violence subside.

However, loyalty in the southern pro vinces is limited to the president himself rather than to a specific government institution. For the government strategy to succeed, it must transform a personal loyalty to the president into a loyalty to the political order in general and institutionalize popular participation. The government should help the south move away from traditional loyalties such as tribal affiliation, which is frequently exploited by demagogues. The unwritten social contract in the south needs to be renegotiated. The ruling party must create a power base for itself away from the tribe and tribal chiefs, which cannot be done without a presidential decree. If the south is neglected again, the same problem will arise. It is not enough to treat the symptom of the violence without addressing the root cause of it.

*Trends in the Egyptian Military*. Since 1971, the Egyptian military has moved away from Nasser's legacy of heavy-handed involvement in civil affairs toward a more professional role and mission, which includes defending Egypt against its foreign enemies and contributing to internal and re gional stability. In the January 1977 bread riots, the military mobilized in the streets, restored order, and then returned to its barracks. During the police mutiny of 1986, the army was called in to restore order a second time, and it did so, returning once again to its barracks. The military's professional and dignified conduct during these episodes underscores the perception that the military has no ambition of taking over Egypt during periods of turmoil.

Except for the 1960s in volvement in the Yemen civil war and the crossing of the Suez Canal, which triggered the 1973 Arab-Israeli war, the Egyptian military has refrained from in volvement abroad unless a vital national interest is at stake. One future exception to this non-interventionist policy could be Sudan. Cairo has accused Khartoum of aiding anti-government Egyptian militants and of responsibility for the assassination attempt against Hosni Mubarak in 1995. The Egyptian military could become involved in Sudan if it vie wed its role as necessary to preserving Egyptian security and re gional stability.

In its internal role, as well as for its "success" in 1973, the Egyptian military won the confidence of most Egyptians as a trusted institution with the single mission of defending Egypt's national interest. Reversing the Nasserist tendenc y, both Sadat and Mubarak w orked hard to de-politicize the military. By so doing, the y neutralized the threat of a military coup d'etat. No Egyptian today anticipates a military takeover, even under the se verest of circumstances. This is, to a large extent, the result of the Sadat and Mubarak policy toward the military. In addition, Egypt has a mechanism for the peaceful transfer of power in case of trouble; the speaker of the parliament becomes the president for 60 days, after which the parliament selects a candidate for the presidency.

This does not mean that the Egyptian military can be ignored in the formulation of national policies or that its role is minimal. On the contrary, the military has occasional veto power in policy areas that affect its personnel. The Egyptian military is estimated to have around 400,000 professional soldiers,[6] far more than in the past. An even greater number of Egyptians depend on the military institution for employment and social welfare benefits. Egypt's military plays a significant role in domestic projects as well. For example, it participates in civilian industrial and agricultural projects, the building of roads and schools, and the installation of telephone lines.

Any political change that might happen in Egypt is likely to be the result of a civilian-military coalition. However, given the complexity and competition between various branches of the Egyptian armed forces, it would be difficult, but not impossible, to initiate a coup, which would probably require communication with a number of senior generals.

## Current Trends in Egypt-U.S. Relations

Whether at times of turmoil or peace, Egypt has remained a keystone state in the strategy of great powers seeking entry into the Middle East, North Africa, or Africa in general. Egypt's cultural role, its geographic location, and large population have made it indispensable to any great power seeking influence in this complex region. The United States is no exception. Egypt is the linchpin that connects the Arab *Mashreq* (Syria, Palestine, Lebanon, and Iraq) with the *Maghreb* states (Tunisia, Algeria, and Morocco). As the second Gulf War demonstrated, Egypt's role in regional security is central to U.S. security arrangements in the region.

Egypt may not have a great deal of hard power (for example, natural resources and technology), but it has an unlimited reservoir of much-needed soft power (such as cultural influence). Egypt's history and cultural legacy resonate throughout the Arab world and beyond. Through the al-Azhar Mosque and University, Cairo long ago established a leading role in the Arab and Muslim world as the source of learning, religious studies, law, and moral guidance. Teachers and scholars trained in Egyptian schools—and thus versed in Egyptian ideologies of Arab nationalism or Islamic renaissance—have staffed most of the educational institutions and ministries of the Gulf states and influenced whole generations of students.

The United States, by contrast, has a great deal of hard po wer, which is needed and, at the same time, resented in the Muslim and Arab world. For America to be accepted, it has to rely heavily on Cairo's ability to mark et the positive aspects of the U.S. role in the Arab and Muslim world. In the same way that Cairo is capable of promoting American interests in the region, it is also capable of hindering these interests. Egypt' s soft power, though implicitly understood, has been given little attention in the context of the bilateral relations of the two countries.

*Egypt-U.S. Relations in a Re gional Context.* Clearly, the region has changed since the second Gulf W ar and the Madrid Peace Conference. If the Arab states, including Syria, and the Palestinians conclude peace deals with Israel, more changes are likely to occur and a new map of the Middle East will emerge. But who will draw this new map, and on what basis? Gi ven its history, geography, cultural legacy, and prominent leadership role, Egypt is likely to be a co-architect of this ne w regional order, preferably with the United States. Egypt has proven capable of accommodating change and sometimes anticipating it, especially when it opted in 1973 for an alliance with the United States at the expense of the former Soviet Union. Nonetheless, it is important to consider how Egypt and America have cooperated or differed over various regional issues to make a wise assessment about the future relationship between the two countries and about the basic characteristics of a ne w regional order.

Regionally, Egypt and the United States ha ve cooperated effectively in strategic military matters by coordinating efforts to bring about a lasting peace in the region and by fighting terrorism. Despite success in these areas, Egypt and America have encountered policy differences on several key issues, such as sanctions on Iraq, the conflict in Sudan (and Sudan' s apparent support for terrorism), and constructive engagement with Libya. Reviewing the areas of mutual interest and the points of divergence should shed light on the future direction of bilateral relations.

*Points of Cooperation.* Several issues signify the positive relationship between Cairo and Washington. These include regional stability and the role of the military, the Middle East peace process, and countering terrorism.

*Military Cooperation.* The Egyptian military shares many of the objectives and mission goals of the U.S. military. In fact, one could argue that Egyptian and U.S. military relations are the strongest component of the relationship between the two countries. As the primary beneficiary of U.S. aid, the Egyptian military is perhaps the most pro-American segment of Egyptian society. The Egyptian military receives nearly two-thirds of the $2.1 billion in U.S. annual aid to Egypt. The United States continues to be the primary source of military aid and weapons to Egypt and has played a key role in the modernization of the Egyptian military, both in terms of weaponry and organization. Over the past 15 years, the United States has provided Egypt with nearly $20 billion for force modernization. Furthermore, the United States and Egypt have cooperated in regular joint military exercises, such as BRIGHT STAR. The success of these efforts was demonstrated during Operation *Desert Storm.* Not only was access to Egypt critical for U.S. military transport to the Gulf, but it also reflected a high level of coordination and compatibility between Egyptian and American forces.

Although military cooperation between Egypt and the United States has resulted in the fulfillment of mutually shared interests, more can be done to ensure that this relationship is maximized. During his visits to Washington, President Mubarak regularly appeals for parity in aid between Egypt and Israel. The United States has substantially contributed to the military industry in Israel, which has become a formidable force both in sophistication and in the variety of the weapons and technologies that it produces. The advanced military industry of Israel allows it far greater freedom of action than Egypt, which must rely on outside aid for weapons. The military and technology imbalance between Egypt and Israel contributes to the sense of inequity and to the possibility of regional insecurity over the long term.

If a post-peace Middle East order is to be defined in terms of security arrangements, then the question of Egyptian and Arab insecurities must be addressed. Egypt worries about Israel's strategic edge over neighboring states. In an interview last year, then Minister of Foreign Affairs Amre Mousa made it clear that "security is indivisible."[7]

By this statement, he meant that the Arabs cannot live with Israel as the sole nuclear power in the region. The proliferation issue, which is also a high priority on the U.S. agenda, is a major issue for Cairo, which has called on Israel to abide by UN resolutions on weapons of mass destruction and for the re gion to be declared a nuclear -free zone. Israel's nuclear power status will contribute to a new arms race as other countries in the region—most notably Iraq and Iran—struggle to compete with Israel's military superiority.

*Arab-Israeli Peace Negotiations.* As the first Arab country to initiate and sign a peace treaty with Israel, Egypt has had a direct interest in guiding other Arab states down the same path. Indeed, Anwar Sadat's bold decision to opt for peace with Israel came at considerable cost. The 10-year boycott of Egypt by the Arab states had serious ramifications for the Egyptian economy, the welfare of the Egyptian people, and the image of Egyptians in the Arab w orld. However, spurred by a confidence in its social cohesion, strong cultural identity, and the belief in its destin y to lead the re gion, Egypt's leaders at the time calculated that they could gradually regain their preeminent status in the Arab world. Some 20 years later, history appears to ha ve proved them right. Egypt is more prosperous today than it was before peace with Israel, its standard of li ving is higher, and its military is stronger .

In spite of the price that Egypt paid for peace with Israel, some critics fault the peace agreement between Egypt and Israel, calling it a *cold peace*.[8] While there have been few trade ventures or diplomatic contacts other than the exchange of ambassadors, this cold peace paved the way for gradual acceptance of Israel by the larger Arab world. These critics do not realize that Egypt would have been more isolated and less instrumental in con vincing other Arab states to follow suit if it had adopted a more embracing approach to peace. The fact that most Arab states had opened a dialogue with Israel by the late 1990s testifies to the inherent soundness of the Egyptian strategy. It illustrates, moreo ver, that the Arab w orld continues to take its cues from Cairo and that Egypt' s sense of the pulse of the Arab w orld is more or less on target.

Among the re gion's leaders, President Mubarak is one of the most sympathetic to the concerns of both America and Israel. In fact, Mubarak has faced criticism for being too eager to accommodate American interests. U.S. pressure, therefore, on Mubarak to deliver everything on the wish list of American foreign policymakers is counterproductive.

Instead of blaming the Egyptian leaders, the United States should judge them by their actions and the risks that they have taken. Egypt has staked out for itself an important role by attempting to rebuild shaken Arab confidence and to prevent any further deterioration that could potentially lead to new eruptions of violence in the region. When Egypt advised Yasir Arafat to proceed carefully in his ne gotiations with Israel, the ultimate objective was to ensure that Arafat could sell the agreement to the Palestinian people without risking his own demise. Egypt has long recognized that the alternative to Arafat is violence. No other Palestinian leader can deliver peace with Israel. Hence, in this and other endeavors, the overriding objective for Egypt has been to build a slow but durable peace instead of a hastily conceived formula that would not last.

Despite the impasse in Israeli-Arab relations caused by the renewal of the *intifada* in September 2000, at some point regional peace talks may resume. Egypt would be called upon to take a leadership role among the states bordering Israel to bring other Arab states on the path toward normalization with Israel. Or Egypt may be called upon to help initiate a new regional security organization that includes Arab states and Israel. Some in Egypt support normal relations with Israel, given that Israel accepts being a "normal" state (that is, a state willing to be part of the region with no explicit advantage in weapons or other issues). If the United States wants a partner to create such a regional order, Egypt is ideal.

*Countering Terrorism.* Egypt has not w avered in its commitment to combat terrorism, both domestically and re gionally. In 1996, Egypt and the United States co-hosted the Summit of the Peace Makers at Sharm al-Sheikh in the wake of terrorist attacks against Israel. The summit helped assure the Israeli people that Egypt does not tolerate random violence against innocent people. While Egypt has worked hard to crack down on terrorism in the region, it does not always share American views on the issue. For example, Egypt includes Israeli attacks on any targets in Lebanon as terrorism, while the United States prefers to restrict the definition of international terrorism to attacks on non-military targets. Nonetheless, for the last 10 years, President Mubarak has advocated a global conference on terrorism. [9] His intention is to steer the debate away from mere cultural linkages that connect Islam to terrorism to a more pragmatic approach that addresses the underlying causes of this global phenomenon. Better intelligence coordination and support for economic development projects, job creation, and assistance programs that would deny these organizations a recruitment base are also important components in the battle against terrorism.

*Points of Difference.* Although Egypt and the United States share a commitment to stability and to the territorial integrity of all states in the region, they differ on how to ensure this objective, especially regarding Sudan and Iraq. For example, in May 2000, Egypt and Libya established a joint initiative for reconciliation among the various factions involved in the longstanding civil war in Sudan. From the Egyptian perspective, partnering with Libya does not conflict with Egypt's ongoing commitment to combat terrorism. Rather, the initiative can be viewed as a policy of pragmatic engagement. Egypt is not promoting Libya by giving it a role in Sudan; rather, it does not want to appear in the region as acting on behalf of the United States. Toward off this potential criticism, Egypt looked to the nemesis of the United States, Libya, as a partner. No one in the Arab world would claim that Libya is cooperating with the United States in Sudan.

Cairo's strategic interest in Sudan also must be taken into consideration. If there were any place in the world where President Mubarak may decide to commit Egyptian troops to battle with the full support of his people, it would be Sudan. Furthermore, Cairo's view that the Sudanese problem is a political problem rather than an ethnic or a religious one is important for the stability of Africa as a whole.

Iraq is another area of disagreement between Egypt and the United States. While both countries agree that Iraq must implement UN Security Council resolutions, especially those related to weapons inspection, Egypt remains sensitive to popular criticism regarding the human cost of sanctions on the Iraqi people. Cairo and Washington do not agree on how to resolve the issue of Saddam's rule. If America believes that Iraq will not comply with sanctions while Saddam rules, Cairo wonders how to preserve Iraq's territorial integrity without Saddam.

The United States should not ignore Egypt's regional concerns. In fact, if Egypt is to be a partner in shaping the new regional security order, it should be encouraged to take a leading role in fashioning a post-Saddam Iraq, an Iraq that is forward looking and also part of the Arab world. An Egyptian role in Iraq could be more useful than the various disjointed initiatives proposed by Congress. U.S. engagement of the Iraqi opposition certainly contributes to an erosion of the political capital of these groups. But Egypt's domestic circumstances may not allow it to play such an ambitious leading role in fashioning a new order in the Middle East.

## Future Trends in Egypt-U.S. Relations

Despite its domestic challenges, Egypt will continue to play a pivotal role in promoting re gional stability, shaping Arab and Muslim public opinion and policies, and, in the process, furthering American interests. For these reasons, the Egypt-U.S. relationship will continue to be an important element in the foreign policies of both countries and in the economic future of Egypt. Because of the need for mutual assistance and shared interests, problems in the bilateral relationship will need to be addressed as they arise.

In 2015, both countries will still have differences on specific policy issues. These may still include the peace process (or whatever has replaced it), Iraq, or regional alliances (something akin to the Israel-Turkey military cooperation which the Arabs claim threatens them). Cairo and Washington may agree on what to do about Sudan, Libya, or nuclear weapons proliferation. Whatever the issues, both governments need to ha ve a better appreciation of the other's style of diplomacy and the factors that impact on foreign policy decisionmaking. In particular, the United States will need to be more sympathetic to Egypt's efforts to reconcile its complex position—as a leader in the Arab world, as an important Muslim country, and as an African country—with its desire to preserve its special relationship with the United States.

The lack of a coherent U.S. policy toward Egypt will continue to add to the confusion. Aside from W ashington's interest in the role of Egypt as a facilitator in the peace process, American policy toward Egypt consists primarily of a series of disjointed initiatives on areas of common concern. Too often, the public polic y atmosphere surrounding these issues has been characterized by emotionalism and driven by media campaigns rather than strategic thinking about where the relationship is heading and what can be realistically accomplished. This is true in the American media and the Arab media as well. The United States cannot call for freedom of the press and civil liberties and, at the same time, complain about the Egyptian media displeasure with U.S. policies in the region.

With the exception of the Pentagon, man y in the United States, especially in Congress, fail to appreciate Egypt's role in adv ancing

American interests in the region. Others assume that whatever Egypt does for the United States is compensated by American military and economic aid. However, this military and economic aid to Egypt is both a source of support for a strong relationship and a source of tension for the Egyptians. Although Egyptians would like the support to continue, they do not want to be dependent on the United States, nor do they want to be perceived as having compromised their independence. [10]

The issue goes beyond dependence and sovereignty, however. It will continue to include a vision of a peaceful Middle East with Egypt as America's partner. The sense of partnership between Egypt and the United States will become more important if and when Palestinian-Israeli tensions flare. The key questions will become these: Can America determine its relationship with Egypt *independent* of its relations with Israel? Must *one* dictate the other? To many Egyptians, the relationship has been viewed in the United States through an Israeli lens. Egyptians would like to change this perspective and have America consider what Egypt can offer to enhance U.S. global and regional strategic interests.

A careful review of Egyptian foreign policy under President Mubarak reveals that Egypt has taken a new turn, one that emphasizes pragmatism and economic prosperity over the ideological style of politics that had dominated Egypt's foreign policy agenda previously. One reason for this success may lie in the quality of leadership contributing to foreign policy formulation. The pragmatic approach was evident in Sadat's decision to expel Soviet advisers in 1973. Despite this pragmatic bent, Egypt's foreign policy will continue to be sensitive to its image in the Arab world, the Muslim world, and in Africa. Since coming to power upon Sadat's assassination in 1981, Mubarak has skillfully managed a strong Egyptian presence in these circles, while maintaining close ties to the United States and protecting Egyptian-Israeli peace.

Assuming that by 2015 we will have achieved a post-peace environment, Egyptians and Americans may be free from the dissonance caused by their shared need to support Palestinians on the one hand and Israel on the other. Both countries may then be able to engage each other on broader fronts, including a new strategic dialogue. The twin pillars of economic and strategic interests could provide the basis for a more serious partnership in keeping with the new regional priorities. The Gore-Mubarak initiative of September 1994, which aimed at expanding U.S. economic growth opportunities in Egypt and at building mutually beneficial economic and commercial ties between the two countries, could serv e as a model. [11] Specifically, the initiative promotes economic growth and job creation in Egypt with the ultimate goal of achieving sustainable economic growth. In this vein, the initiative addresses numerous related issues, such as education and the environment.

Those who advocate liberal economics should keep in mind that a liberal political culture is necessary for liberal economics to take hold. Yet a critical shortf all in the Egypt-U.S. relationship is that, despite the long years, it has remained a relationship between the elites of both countries and has not yet acquired a rooted popularity in either society. For a stronger relationship to flourish, the United States must go beyond the elite level to a broader cultural relationship that capitalizes on Egypt's position as a cultural leader in the re gion. Thus f ar, Egyptian-American cultural relations are limited. T o strengthen these ties, the two countries should establish a new cultural commission analogous to the Gore-Mubarak economic initiative to promote cultural understanding. Cooperation should focus on promoting American cultural values through Egyptian public institutions. The approach should look beyond Cairo to the rest of Egypt, where most Egyptians live. Ordinary Egyptians should benefit from Egyptian-American cultural exchanges, in particular, because they constitute the pool from which the Islamists recruit their supporters.

Whether the American vision of the Middle East focuses on a regional security-based order, a political order with normalization with Israel as its centerpiece, or a re gional economic order, Egypt will play an important role. The United States should not allow parochial interests to define its relationship with Egypt. Rather, the United States should take a broad-based approach to its ties with Egypt, focusing equally on all aspects of the relationship—political, economic, and cultural. If America skews its relationship with Egypt by allowing more parochial interests to define it, then the United States could lose not just Egypt but its relative position in the greater Middle East.

## Notes

[1] World Bank, *World Development Indicators* (Washington, DC, 1999).

[2] International Monetary Fund, *World Economic Outlook*, October 1999, accessed at <http://imf.org/external/pubs/ft/weo/1999/02/index.htm>.

[3] Ibid.

[4] In 1977, riots erupted in Cairo when the Egyptian government cut the bread subsidy and raised prices to meet IMF requirements. When, instead of increasing prices, the government gradually shrank the size of the loaves, the policy succeeded.

[5] Mamoun Fandy, "Egypt's Islamic Group: Regional Revenge?" *Middle East Journal* 48, no. 4 (Winter 1994).

[6] Arms Control and Disarmament Agency, *World Military Expenditures and Arms Transfers 1998* (Washington, DC, 1999).

[7] Amre Mousa, interview in *Al-Hayat*, February 4, 2000.

[8] Hilal Khashan, "The New Arab Cold War," *World Affairs* 159, no. 4 (Spring 1997).

[9] *Al-Ahram*, February 14, 2000, 5.

[10] Mamoun Fandy, "U.S. Policy Towards Egypt," Hearing before Committee on International Relations, Washington, DC, April 10, 1997.

[11] U.S.-Egypt Partnership, *Economic Growth and Development*, accessed at <http://www.usis.egnet.net/usegypt>.

---

*This chapter is based on a paper that was presented at a conference on* The Middle East in Transition: The Maghreb, *which was held at the Institute for National Strategic Studies, National Defense University, Washington, DC, on January 7, 2000.*

Chapter 5
# Israel: Reconciling Internal Disparities?

## *Kenneth W. Stein*

For the next decade, Israel probably will remain the most militarily powerful and economically dominant non-oil power in the Middle East. While Israel's neighbors—Syria, Jordan, the P alestinians, Egypt, and Saudi Arabia—will experience a series of national leadership changes, none of these successions, indi vidually or collecti vely, is likely to threaten Israel' s well-being or bring about another Middle Eastern war. Regional powers' acquisition or production of weapons of mass destruction (whether chemical, biological, or nuclear) and the requisite delivery systems will pose the primary threat to Israeli security .[1] Political and economic turmoil that may cause unrest in surrounding Arab states and among Palestinians will have a marginal impact on Israel's economy but not on its e xistence. Israel's bipartisan foreign polic y will remain focused on creating, sustaining, and broadening relationships with contiguous neighbors while trying to generate deeper interstate relationships with noncontiguous Arab and Muslim states. Most Arab states will continue to believe that Israel is not making concessions to

---

*Kenneth W. Stein is William E. Schatten professor of contemporary Middle Eastern history and Israeli studies at Emory University. He is the author of* Making Peace Between Arabs and Israelis: Lessons from Fifty Y ears of Negotiating Experience *(with Ambassador Samuel W. Lewis) (1991) and* Heroic Diplomacy: Sadat, Kissinger, Carter, Begin and the Quest for Arab-Israeli Peace *(1999).*

the Arab side quickly enough and will try to find ways to slow or halt aspects of normalization with Israel. At the same time, Israel's participation in globalization in its many forms will mak e it an object of en vy and fear to its neighbors. Israel's economic growth also will distance it from its neighbors, generating further imbalances in gross national and gross domestic products. Israel will further expand its markets into Southern and Central Asia and sustain its trading relationships with Europe and the United States.

The irony for Israel is that as it seeks diplomatic normalization in the region and expands its trade areas—thereby enhancing its national strength and security—enormous pressures are building within the country to resolve myriad domestic problems. As Israel enters its second 50 years, areas of domestic distress could be as troublesome and contentious to Israelis as were their earlier fears about their hostile Arab neighbors. Israelis, while possessing the intellectual ability , technology, and resources to identify their domestic problems, are nonetheless endlessly embroiled in protracted debates about how to resolve them. Over the next two decades, Israel is not likely to become any more efficient in resolving key internal and external issues than it was in the first half-century of its existence. Cleavages in Israeli society are profound and deep. A split between the left and right over how to deal with the Arabs hampers Israel politically . The Ashkenazi-Sephardi division is profound, while the ultra-Orthodox–secular gap seems almost unbridgeable. Israeli Jews and Israeli Arabs are growing farther apart, especially as Palestinian statehood is debated and the current wave of Israeli-Palestinian confrontation continues. Both events have prompted previously unraised questions about Israeli Arab loyalty to the state.

Finally, Israel's recently re vised election system encourages division between the prime minister and the parliament. The procedure of casting separate ballots for both creates parallel lines of political legitimacy to both. W ith a parliament already fragmented and acting in a highly developed, contentious political culture, a prime minister cannot lead or take initiative except on very basic national consensus issues like the country's security. The downfall of Israel's last two prime ministers (Benjamin Netanyahu in 1999 and Ehud Barak in 2001) occurred because both negotiated agreements with the Palestinians to which the Israeli parliament vigorously dissented, causing the marginal coalition governments to fall. With five prime ministers in little more than 5 years (November 1995 to February 2001), no stability in governance is achievable until the election system is changed. Without such a change, plans and actions to implement reform on the domestic agenda will remain paralyzed.

Furthermore, Israelis will tackle tough domestic issues and underlying social cleavages only if their lifestyles are immediately threatened. A wise Israeli leader would focus on resolving those issues that benefit most elements of society: reducing unemployment, improving transportation, protecting the environment, and assuring water supplies. Meanwhile, Israelis are seeking a sense of belonging that goes beyond an identity articulated by partisan or ethnic politics. They are in the midst of defining a national cultural identity that is Israeli but not Zionist, contemporary but linked to the Jewish past, Jewish but not prescriptive, identifiable but not ideological. This definitional process will be achieved neither easily nor quickly. Israelis understand that they need to define themselves by who they are or want to be rather than by what someone else tells them they are not. Israel remains, as it has since birth, in a struggle to make its immigrant melange into a workable mosaic. The definition that Israelis choose for themselves will be neither homogeneous nor static. They are a post-emancipation people living in the most powerful country in the Middle East, but they remain people bound to their geographic origins and Diaspora past who have yet to become comfortable with the role that Jews play in a Jewish state. Israelis, even in the midst of or despite a negotiating process, have security fears that remain indelibly imprinted on their national character. These fears will not dissipate simply because peace treaties are signed between the state of Israel and its Syrian, Lebanese, or Palestinian neighbors. Moreover, the renewed *intifada* with the Palestinians reinforces Israelis' unwillingness to trust fully their neighbors, a distrust that will linger even if peace comes tomorrow.

## Israel's Middle Eastern Environment

For much of its history, Israel has been able to make decisions free of Arab pressure because of individual Arab states' weakness and inter-Arab disunity. Arab succession issues only add to Israel's relative freedom to make national decisions without constraints imposed by Arab neighbors. Certainly, the succession process in several neighboring Arab states will influence the nature of Israel's relationship with those countries, but barring radical shifts among the frontline states away from a negotiated settlement and toward conflict, Israel will withstand the various political ripples from the succession shocks.

*Seeking Trends in Israel's Relations with Arab Neighbors.* Until the events that began the latest *intifada* in September 2000, most Israelis assumed that an Arab-Israeli negotiating process would transform the conflict into a series of disconnected and inconsistent relationships to accompany Israel's military and economic superiority. The Israeli public is as interested in foreign policy as the American public appears disinterested. On matters of national security, the Israeli population is split into thirds; one-third are hawks who do not trust the Arabs, one-third are doves who do not trust the Arabs, and one-third are in the middle, neither hawks nor doves, neither trusting nor distrusting the Arabs.[2] Within various ethnic and religious groups, one can find both hawks and doves. The extreme center in Israel likely will be where future Israeli political campaigns will be fought, even with the emergence of Russian Jewish, Israeli Arab, and Sephardi voting blocs. In any event, security matters were of primary concern in the February 2000 election and will remain the paramount issue for the foreseeable future.

According to a Gallup Poll released in November 1999, "It was already clear that national priorities as perceived by the public had undergone a transformation and social and economic affairs had taken the place of the diplomatic-security complex."[3] At that time, Israelis seemed to have internalized an accommodation with the Palestinians that included, if necessary, the establishment of a Palestinian state. They also appeared to feel more confident about their personal and national security. Since 1987, Israelis have slowly accepted the notion that a Palestinian state will come into being by 2004. When the 1999 Israeli election campaign began, support for the Oslo Accords was close to 70 percent among Jewish Israelis. Eighty percent reported enhanced feelings of personal security since the beginning of the peace process; two-thirds thought that most Palestinians wanted peace. In January 2001—4 months after the *intifada* began— two-thirds of the Israeli Jewish public still deeply favored a negotiated peace process. One month later, almost two-thirds of the Israeli Jewish public voted for Ariel Sharon. Israelis were not suddenly opposed to reaching agreements with their Arab neighbors, but they declined to have former Prime Minister Barak steward that process. Just as it had done before the May 1996 elections, Palestinian Arab violence prior to the 2001 elections greatly influenced the Israeli public to put the brakes on the negotiating process, as distinguished from breaking it off.

The earlier Gallup Poll also revealed that greater portions of Israelis were pessimistic for the long term. While two-thirds of Israeli Jews thought that the chances of peace would be sustained between 1999 and 2002, almost half thought that the probability of war between Israel and an Arab state in that period was high nonetheless. Fifty-four percent thought that the Golan Heights would be returned to Syria within 10 years. When asked in May 1998 about the next 50 years, two-thirds of the Israeli public believed that a Palestinian state and an Israeli state would be coexisting. Equally important, the same number were sure that the state of Israel would exist in 2048, but significantly, one-quarter of Jewish Israelis polled said the state of Israel would not be in existence in 50 years! [4]

Several factors—an inability to end the violent confrontation that began in September 2000, a return to a prolonged stagnation in the Palestinian-Israeli track, a break in Egyptian-Israeli or Jordanian-Israeli diplomatic relations—will cause U.S. foreign policymakers to yearn for the difficult days of the May 1996–May 1999 period. A complete breakdown of the peace process negotiations will force Israel to seek reassurance of American friendship and commitment to its security. This will make diplomatic life very difficult for the Department of State in particular and parts of the Executive branch in general, as officials find themselves trying to shape a policy that retains the U.S. role as an honest broker and preserves interests in the Arab world while protecting America's special relationship with Israel. Israel's advantage now, as it has been since the Johnson administration, is its influence on Capitol Hill. When the President is even slightly antithetical to Israel, the American Jewish community digs in, as they will again in such a scenario, defending Israeli security and national interests. The European Union (EU) will continue to be a diplomatic skirmish zone between Israel and the Arabs, particularly the Palestinians. Yet nothing indicates that the EU will supplant U.S. dominance of the peace process.

For Israelis, signing the Oslo Accords meant more than just recognizing that a portion of historic Palestine would be physically shared with the Palestinians. Israeli acceptance indicated an agreement to launch the Palestinian issue toward resolution and find ways to use recognition of the Palestine Liberation Organization (PLO) and Palestinian aspirations to open doors to Muslim and Arab states, both close and afar. Once Arafat made recognition of Israel acceptable, other Arab and Muslim states found it increasingly difficult not to follow in both official and unofficial fashion. Seven years after the Oslo Accords were signed, Israel had some contacts or relations with every Arab state except Iraq and Libya. Most of these ties were suspended when fighting broke out in September 2000 between the Israeli Defense Forces and Palestinian stone-throw ers. If Israeli-Palestinian negotiations resume, Israel will try to rebuild bridges to these countries. Its leaders understand that a diplomatic and an economic price will be paid if stagnation in the negotiating process sets in as it did from 1996 to 1999 and in late 2000.

The task for Israeli leaders, then, will be to renew positive relations primarily with Egypt, Jordan, Syria, Lebanon, and the Palestinians, and to widen contacts with Arab and Muslim states beyond the contiguous territorial ring. They will at the same time need to focus increasingly on managing the domestic and cultural issues that dominate Israel's national agenda if their resolution pro ves impossible.

*The Palestinian-Israeli Track.* In the September 1999 Sharm el-Sheikh Agreement, Israeli and Palestinian negotiators agreed that a framework for final status talks would be established by February 2000. One year after that deadline and several months into violent confrontation with the P alestinians, the difficult issues—Jerusalem, water, borders, settlements, refugees' right of return, and the nature of the Palestinian entity/state—remain highly unlikely to be resolved in neatly arranged negotiating packages in the near term. Some probably will be partially negotiated, while others are intentionally postponed or linked to a future timeframe because of the dual problems of sensitivity and complexity.

Also likely is that Palestinians will be dissatisfied because of what is not achieved. If that is the unfolding scenario—as appears to be the case—then ho w will the v ariety of Palestinian v oices in the W est Bank, Gaza, and East Jerusalem respond to unfulfilled expectations about the final status deliberations? And how might the United States respond to the jagged edges strewn on the road of another incomplete Palestinian-Israeli understanding? Core Palestinian negotiating objectives will not be met because Israeli leaders will make the ultimate decisions. Israelis will decide *without outside pressures* about what to relinquish, how fast, and under what conditions.

Water issues will be continuously monitored by joint Palestinian and Israeli committees, but Israel will not relinquish final control of water access to any joint body. Finally, while the populations will be politically separated, economic necessity will demand that at least one-third of the Palestinian labor force continue to work within Israeli borders. Implementation of proposed conclusions for all the final status issues will require coordination by both sides with the assistance of the United States.

What cannot be excluded is the possibility of Arafat's death before the implementation of final status negotiations. The scramble to succeed him may immediately influence the substance and pace of the negotiations. Those competing for his mantle are likely to want to show to the Palestinian public their unwavering commitment to core Palestinian positions. This, in turn, might cause a hardening of Palestinian negotiating positions and perhaps severely slow down the activities of the various final status committees. Progress (or lack of it) on the Syrian-Israeli front is not likely to impede implementation of Palestinian-Israeli understandings.

Nothing—not Arafat's longevity, the activation of a Syrian-Israeli track, or the American election cycle—will eliminate the need to provide economic assistance and investment capital from private and public sources for the Palestinian entity or state. Palestinian job creation, systematic dismantling of the refugee camps, and economic development can only support an unfolding agreement. In carrying out a Palestinian-Israeli agreement, constant care must be paid to how the final status issues affect the territorial integrity and economic well-being of Jordan. Therefore, Jordan will have to play some active, but not central, part in structuring industrial zones and trade agreements and in receiving its own basket of assistance.

## Negative Domestic Trends

The bad feelings present between Egyptians and Israelis before the Camp David talks did not vanish the day after the accords were signed. Many of those feelings have not dissipated in two decades. Israeli governments have long engaged in preemptive actions sometimes called "creating new facts," especially when trying to justify land seizures or settlement expansion in the name of "never again" putting Jewish lives in harms' way.[5] Moreover, since the Egyptian-Israeli Treaty, Israeli governments have believed that *force majeure* would change political realities on the ground. Examples abound: the 1981 bombing of an Iraqi reactor, the 1982 invasion of Lebanon, the bombing of the PLO Tunis headquarters, and the building of settlements in the territories despite commitments in negotiations.

Absent a significant external threat, Israelis in the last decade of the 20th century reevaluated their identity and the value of their national institutions. The collectivity that generated a national communal drive to establish Zionism's success is being replaced by individualism. Patriotism has not diminished, but allegiance to the Zionist ethos is under intense scrutiny. Time is now available to discuss previously existing issues and problems that were displaced by more pressing security matters. National institutions, political practices, perceived ethnic harmony, the role of religion, and economic sacrifice—all of which were present during the state's formation and early years—are under microscopic scrutiny. These often debated and highly volatile issues now include protecting citizens' rights, writing a constitution, defining the nature of the political system, electoral reform, the future composition and mission of the Israeli Defense Forces, glaring economic disparities, the secular educational system, ethnic cleavages, and resource scarcity.

A cursory review of topics covered in opinion pieces in Israeli national newspapers today would reveal increasing discussion of internal issues related to governance, the education system, poverty, unemployment, the environment, ethnic disputes, and transportation needs. These topics share the national debate about the pace and nature of the Arab-Israeli peace process. All the domestic issues are straining Israel's social fabric. Some of these issues and problems are solvable, while others are too complicated to tackle. Collectively, they affect the national psyche by causing dissatisfaction with the national leadership. None of these issues is so severe that it will generate major or prolonged civil disturbance. When taken together, however, they weigh heavily on the political agenda of any prime minister and Israeli government. Security issues are paramount, but Israeli leaders already are being held accountable for not doing more to tackle topics of lifestyle, governance, and ethnic interactions.

Characterizing a national mood, especially in as diverse a society as Israel's, is a dangerous endeavor. With that caveat, it is reasonable to state that a negative dynamism exists in Israel today. This sentiment is not all encompassing; it is internalized while Israelis go about their daily business. Israelis possess extraordinary levels of higher education, but they lack the political will or courage to confront the bureaucratic forces that shape and can obstruct their national agenda. Some noteworthy issues—air pollution, waste management, massive traffic congestion, inter-urban transportation system development, uncontrollable urban sprawl, ecological and environmental issues, and water scarcity—are not immediate threats to Israel's existence. However, they need national attention as urgently as do the religious-secular divide, ethnic friction, the vitality of national institutions, and governance.

Compounding the difficulty in resolving domestic issues, Israeli society is moving from a commitment to the national collectivity (*bisvilaynu*, or "for us") to a focus on the individual (*bishvili*, or "for me"). Israel's national expenditures on security and military requirements still dominate the annual budget and will remain high as long as Israel is in transition from a full conflict with regional governments to a series of uneven relationships. The move to lower expenditures on security requirements has not yet evolved, while public demand to resolve problems on the domestic agenda is intensifying. The slow shift to greater spending on the domestic agenda has not halted the intense competition between ethnic and special interest groups for greater allocations from the national budget. Competing interests were jostling for their piece of what could become a peace dividend, however elusive. In other words, even if Israeli leaders demonstrate political will, the country's collective ability to solve domestic issues will be severely retarded by financial constraints and unrealistic expectations, even despite an economy running at almost full throttle.

## *Economy: Powerhouse with Inequities*

Israel's gross domestic product (GDP) is close to $100 billion, and per capita GDP is close to $17,000. For comparative purposes, Israel's per capita GDP in 1972 was $3,200. *The Economist* ranks Israel sixth in the world of emerging economies.[6] In another comparison, the current per capita GDP for Palestinians living in the West Bank or Gaza Strip is less than half of what it was for Israelis in

1972. Furthermore, in 1998, donors promised the Palestinian Authority approximately $800 million in economic assistance. In the same year, more than $600 million was invested in Israel in venture capital funds alone.[7]

Israel's economy has the capacity to sustain annual growth rates between 3 and 5 percent. The continued influx of Jewish immigrants from the former Soviet Union will, as it has in the previous 15 years, inject into Israel streams of educated manpower necessary to maintain growth in various sectors, especially in the burgeoning high-tech sector. Any substantial cuts in subsidies to religious sectors of Israeli society will force these elements to become more engaged in the productive economy of the country and perhaps focused in the high-tech sector.

In the 1990s, Israel became a world leader in high-tech research industries. Venture capital investments in Israeli high-tech industries reached a record $301 million in the third quarter of 1999.[8] The proliferation of high-tech industries and the concentration of a large amount of research power generate economic activity in other areas as well, such as services, finance, real estate, and conventional industries. Economic experts believe that should the negotiating process be concluded successfully, Israel could become one of the economic hubs of the Middle East. Its geographic location at the crossroads of the Middle East could transform this country into a gateway to a large area of vast economic potential stretching from Central Asia to the Mediterranean and Africa. Overseas investors could continue to find business opportunities based on its advanced technology and wide industrial financial and commercial base, the government privatization program, and laws for capital investment that have been on the books for 40 years.[9] Israeli economic prosperity, including that stimulated by international investment, will be affected by Israeli-Palestinian violence. The *intifada* has hurt Israeli export trade.

However strong the Israeli economy is, the gap between rich and poor is ever widening. Pockets of poverty exist, particularly among the Sephardim, ultra-Orthodox, and Israeli Arab communities. According to *Ma'ariv* in November 1999, "The illusion that the former [Sephardim] would grow out of poverty in two generations has been refuted ... the ultra-Orthodox leadership must find gainful employment ... and Israeli Arabs have suffered from years of discrimination and isolation and now constitute both a social and national powder keg."[10]

A Gallup Poll from late 1999 sho wed that Israel's economy is the Achilles' heel of all Israeli prime ministers and that Barak was losing national support in large part because of his lack of attention to socio-economic issues.[11]

## Israel's Domestic Wars

*Ethnic Cleavages.* The face of Israel is changing. Descendants from the Ashkenazi (European-origin) generations that founded the state are a shrinking minority . In summer 1998, Dan Meridor , a Likud Knesset member, remarked that Israelis were faced with "the challenge of reconciling cultural individualism and pluralism within an Israeli democracy dominated by a Je wish majority." Today, Israel's population includes five million Jews and one million Israeli Arabs. Israeli Arabs comprise 16 percent of the population today and will be almost one-third of the population in 20 years. Jews from the former Soviet Union are 20 percent of the population and in 20 years will be a quarter of the total. More than half of Israel' s Jewish population has its roots in an Oriental or Sephardi background; in 20 years, this figure will expand to almost 60 percent.

From its founding in 1948, Israel has been a country of immigrants, and it remains so today . Half of the e xceptionally young population of 6.1 million Israelis was born elsewhere. [12] Israel has absorbed all but approximately 15 percent of Jews who lived in other Middle Eastern countries (Oriental/Sephardi origin), while 85 percent of Jews in Diaspora remain in Eastern Europe (Ashkenazi origin). The flow of Jews from the former Soviet Union is likely to continue at least for the next several years, prolonging the problems inherent in immigrant absorption. The paradox for Israel is that while it enjoys a political system that encourages democratic values, most immigrants come from illiberal backgrounds in which the state often provided broad social and economic protection or from countries in which leaders were historically more authoritarian. Such political backgrounds raise expectations for what government can and should do, and immigrants with such histories at times give blind, if not uncritical, support to political leaders, especially those who combine religious fervor with promised delivery of political services.

In its early years, Israel was based on a sense of community and consensus shaped by its overwhelming need for security for the Jewish people. Today, Israel's younger Je wish population has less historical connection to the state's roots. Qualities of commitment, dedication, improvisation, and heroism, which were prevalent in earlier Israeli generations, are not as evident in current Israeli society. Israelis under 40 did not f ight in any of the country's major wars and instead did their military service in the Occupied T erritories. Granddaughters and grandsons of Israel's founders, while proud Israelis, have less of an emotional connection to Zionism and more to Israeli nationalism. Half of Israel's Jewish population has no direct personal link to the state's active struggle with its Arab neighbors. Furthermore, the Americanization of Israeli culture has contributed to putting McDonalds before Maimonides, Michael Jordan attire ahead of Jewish practice, and indi vidualism ahead of the community .

*Political Parties and Special Privile ges.* The ideological domination enjoyed by the two largest Zionist blocs that founded the state of Israel has dissipated noticeably over the past few years. In its place, new parties are emerging that reflect specific styles of preferred political cum social life—Shinui/Meretz or Shas/United T orah Judaism. In a sense, the Likud Party in the late 1990s was similar to the Republican Party in the United States in the late 1980s: both lost the presence of a clear-cut adversary around which a foreign policy platform could be predicated, defended, and exploited for allegiance and votes.

Other trends in Israeli elections are e vident. Voters opposed to special privileges, especially those for the ultra-Orthodox, have filled the vacuum created by the ideological demise of the major parties. Parties such as Meretz, Shinui, and One Israel voiced fierce opposition to religious coercion, demanding instead the protection of individual rights. The majority of secular Israelis welcomed, for example, Ehud Barak's pledge—unfulfilled—in the 1999 campaign that yeshi va (religious school) students would be subject to the military draft like all other segments of Israeli Je wish society. A majority of Israeli v oters increasingly view national elections as a referendum on individual politicians. Personalities matter in Israeli voting preferences. But popular opinion is not always steadfast. Israeli political history is fraught with examples of yesterday's resigned or defeated politician returning at some future point in another guise (for e xample, Moshe Dayan, Y itzhaq Rabin, and Ariel Sharon).

Moreover, voting behavior and election results reflect fragmented interests. For example, in the 1999 election, 31 parties ran on specific parochial issues. By forming the One Israel P arty, Barak and his strategists captured the essence of the Israeli public's longing to be a more unified society. Barak echoed the values of the early Zionist generation in calling for more equitable distribution of the national budget. The quest for a collective identity, however, came up against the downward spiral of sectoral and fractious interest groups. Shas won 17 seats, the third largest result for any party. Its growing strength reflected voter interest in the domestic services it provides. The parliament elected in 1999—the 15th Knesset—had more factions than its predecessor, making it even more difficult to institute electoral reform or consensus on peace process issues. Sharon's election in 2001 reflected Israeli desires for a more unified country and a national unity government.

The overarching proviso guiding Israeli voters, of course, is that nothing shall be done that may prejudice Israeli national or political security. The Israeli voter who did not support the Oslo process in the 1996 election, which included a commitment to share the land of Israel with the Palestinians, understood that the major political party candidates—Netanyahu, Yitzhaq Mordechai, and Barak—held similar political views toward the Palestinians and campaigned on separation of the populations. This is Sharon's position, too.

The Israeli military will continue to provide a fertile pool of potential candidates for entry into Israeli politics. Former generals Yitzhak Mordechai and Amnon Shahak left the military to join the newly formed Center Party. Other prominent military leaders who became successful candidates include Moshe Dayan, Yitzhaq Rabin, Ha'im Bar-Lev, Sharon, and Barak. The Israeli public willingly accepts career military officers into politics, in part because they have not been tarnished by the typical verbal rancor characteristic of the Israeli political system. Former generals will play instrumental leadership roles in Israel's national governance in 2015 and beyond.

*The Religious Parties.* Israelis are striving to find ways to relate differently to their institutions and to one another. Whether the institutions are out of touch with the reality of the new millennium or groups within Israel believe that their special privileges are being jeopardized, there is unrest. Special interests want to protect their privileges and sinecures, underprivileged sectors want their part of the economic pie, and the disenfranchised demand a voice in the political system. Israelis of every political ilk want their priorities met, and they all seem to be making demands of their government simultaneously. In the process of protecting interests and seeking to wrest privileges from others, civility is rare. Voices are raised, epithets are hurled, disdain between societal elements prevails, and threats of varying dimensions are heard.

The conflicts between religious and secular elements of Israel's Jewish population underscore the prevalence of the ferment in Israeli society. In early 1999, 200,000 ultra-Orthodox Jews (*haredim*) protested against Supreme Court rulings viewed as hostile to their way of life. Nearby, 50,000 secular Israelis organized a counter-demonstration. One of the issues concerned extending the law allowing military exemptions for students in the yeshivas. The rate of religious exemptions historically was about 4 percent of the annual number of enlistments. In 1998, the rate doubled to 8.2 percent. Over the last decade, the number of enlistments each year grew by an aggregate total of 50 percent, but the number of exemptions increased by 350 percent. For secular Israelis whose children complete their compulsory military service, the outrage is palpable. On the other hand, the *haredim* complain that the Israeli Defense Forces have a permissive atmosphere that, in their view, jeopardizes the beliefs of religious soldiers. The rabbis protest deviations from Jewish dietary laws and desecration of the Sabbath and of God's name caused by male and female soldiers serving in the same unit. [13]

The Likud-religious party alliance, built to protect their mutual interest in preventing territorial withdrawals from Judaea and Samaria, clearly invigorated religious party leaders after the June 1967 war. It led them and certain Orthodox rabbis to believe that not only could they wield religious influence in Israel but also could they alter temporal institutions as well. That the religious parties were able to direct hundreds of millions of shekels for religious schools and their religious networks only convinced Orthodox religious leaders that their views and privileges were untouchable. Some rabbis became intoxicated with their newfound power and influence. In the last quarter of the 20th century, the religious parties drifted more to the right on the Israeli political spectrum, widening the gap between religious and secular Israelis and narrowing the political distance between the religious Zionist and ultra-Orthodox parties.

The ultra-Orthodox have become more nationalist, while the religious Zionists have become more extremist in their religious observance. Both disdain secular rule and secular judgments handed down by the courts. Distinguishing between the chief rabbis, who are products of religious Zionist training, and the rabbis of the ultra-Orthodox parties (Agudat Israel, Degel Hatorah, or Shas), who question the authority of both the Zionist state and its Chief Rabbinate, has become increasingly difficult. These leaders will inevitably rebel against any loss of privilege and threaten to bolt coalition governments, especially when their access to the government purse and special privileges is threatened. They will seek and create political alliances with whomever can promise them greater access to funds at the municipal or national political level.

The strength of ultra-Orthodox parties in Israel probably will increase, barring constitutional changes that would otherwise diminish the influence of smaller parties upon coalition formation. For example, a pronounced increase in the threshold percentage to obtain representation in the Knesset—from the present 1.5 percent to 5 percent, for example—would severely diminish the influence of the smaller parties in general and smaller religious parties in particular . However, the demographics are such that the v oter base of the *haredi* parties is very young; they have a critical mass of voters coming of age in the next 20 years who have grown up with the idea of active participation in the political process. The ultra-Orthodox parties are politically savvy and cognizant of their ability to affect policy within the democratic process. They possess a focused ideological mandate and agenda and a well-honed mobilization machine. Controversy only serv es to increase their v oter base. Thus, United T orah Judaism, Aguda, and De gel HaTorah are poised to e xpand their influence, singly or in combination.

Public support for the National Religious Party (NRP) is likely to diminish in future elections. Its constituents—settlers and traditional religious Zionists—are wholly disaf fected by the party' s inability to articulate key issues effectively in recent years. Those who are serious about not compromising on land issues are moving toward the National Union or other rightist parties. And those who are more concerned with religious issues are going to United T orah Judaism and Shas, which have always dealt more effectively with religiously inspired legislation. The NRP has seen its traditional hold on the Ministries of Religious Affairs and Interior eroded by Shas and other parties. Moreover, the NRP does not ha ve a new generation of leaders. Its traditional constituency is having a major crisis of confidence, and the party is doing little to articulate a clear policy preference and/or leadership on their core issue—the settlements. It cannot even decide where to stand on religious issues.

The rise of the Shas Party as a force in Israeli politics has been nothing short of extraordinary. Shas earned four seats in the 1988 election and six in 1992. Then in 1996, when Israelis cast a split ballot for prime minister and the Knesset for the first time, Shas won 10 parliamentary seats. In the 1999 election, it garnered 17 parliamentary seats. If projections are made now for future elections (the next parliamentary election is scheduled for 2003), barring a resurgent Likud Party, Shas could be the single largest voting bloc of any major party. In 2003, Shas could win as many as one-sixth or more of Israel's 120 Knesset seats.

Shas appeals primarily to the underclass and to underprivileged Jews of Oriental or Sephardi origins. [14] Shas provides an array of social services, including day-care centers, pre-school education, cheap summer camps for children, food and clothing for the needy, and a vast socio-educational network. Secular Israelis passionately disdain the manner in which Shas Party functionaries and government civil servants over the last decade have siphoned off millions of shekels into the Shas educational network. Many Shas supporters reflect a sense of disenfranchisement or neglect by the government. Others have a sense of being overtaken in the struggle for economic advancement. Shas voters have reminded elected officials and bureaucrats that the Israeli government does not have the ability, interest, or timing to respond to the daily needs of many in the lower strata of Israeli society. If neither Shas nor Likud are part of a government coalition in the future, they will form a natural alliance to oppose it.

Shas represents more than the Sephardim. Some of its elite are Orthodox but are not in consort with all ultra-Orthodox views, such as holding onto the territories at all costs. Many Sephardim are deeply envious of recent Russian immigrants; two-thirds of those arriving in the past decade hold advanced degrees and have achieved rapid economic successes, but not all are Jewish or are profoundly secular if they are. Shas families, like those belonging to the Ashkenazi *haredim*, have higher birth rates and larger families than most secular Israeli families. Finally, Shas benefits from the fact that most of its supporters serve in the Israeli Defense Forces and thus are more integrated into Israel's economy and society.

Political allegiance to Shas could slip slightly among second- and even third-generation Sephardim who are more affluent, especially if the Likud Party reconstitutes itself in a serious fashion and fields a more secular program. The Shas leadership, though threatening to topple the coalition periodically, probably will be strategic enough over the next decade not to be so demanding that it cannot remain in the ruling government coalition. Regardless of who is prime minister, the Shas Party will need governmental allocations to fund its social and educational network and pay the salaries of thousands of employees in party-related functions.

Many in Israel see Shas as a very dangerous phenomenon. Said one editorial writer in the daily newspaper *Ha'aretz* in 1999:

> Shas is a repulsive political party because it merges ethnicity and ultra-Orthodoxy, which, in effect, is hostile to Israeli democracy, favoring instead a theocracy, like Iran. Together with other ultra-Orthodox parties, Shas turns its back on Western culture and seeks to impose the rules and regulations of a religious ghetto on Israel's secularists.[15]

If any prime minister diverts funds from Shas to resolve the same social problems that the party attempts to address, and the Israeli bureaucracy supplants the Shas network in poor neighborhoods, a slow move away from traditional Shas support will occur. However, this scenario is unlikely. The secular parties that remain perturbed at the amounts of funds that are funneled into Shas operations will continue to be dismayed and to emphasize their secular objectives over those articulated by Shas. The secular Israeli-Shas cleavage will not dissipate in the foreseeable future. While the Shas Party occasionally will be instrumental in supporting the peace process, it will not support measures in the domestic realm that are contrary to its philosophy or party interests.[16]

*Russian Jewish Immigrants.* The Russian community in Israel came in two waves, first in the late 1970s and then after 1989. The first migration was more ideological, the second impelled more by economic motives. A division also exists between Zionist activists and less political settlers.

The 7 percent unemployment rate among immigrants who arrived in the early 1990s was below that of other Israelis. The once-gaping disparity in earnings is closing as Russians steadily move up the economic ladder. Most have bought their own apartments, and half of them own cars. One Israeli commentator, writing in *Ha'aretz*, likened the immigrants' arrival to a $10 billion aid program from the former Soviet states. Economists regard Russian immigration as an infusion of highly trained human capital that Israel itself could never have generated so quickly.

Many Russian immigrants are ignorant of Judaism, and at least a quarter of them are not even regarded as Jewish. Their lack of religious identity has unleashed a firestorm of criticism from more religious groups in Israel, especially the leadership of the Sephardi community.[17] Nevertheless, the Russian immigrants are becoming part of the broad Israeli center in politics, supporting not an ideology but pragmatic group interests. They by no means form a monolithic voting bloc. In 2015, they will vote as they did in 2001, for their economic and social interests.

*Arabs.* The Israeli Arab population was more politically active in 2001 than at any time in Israel's 50-year history. Israeli Arabs constituted 20 percent of the population and approximately 15 percent of the voting public. They held 13 Knesset seats distributed across 3 parties. In 1999, an Arab Justice sat on the Israeli Supreme Court, and the winner of the Miss Israel pageant was an Israeli Arab. The Israeli Arab vote was sufficient in the May 1999 election to tip the balance in Barak's favor. By 2015, as their numbers grow and their representation in the Knesset increases, Israeli Arabs will constitute a significant demographic and civic challenge for Israel's Jewish majority. Their demands for better municipal, educational, and social services will pull at an already squeezed domestic budget.

For many Israelis—Jewish and Arab—the question has become, "Can Israel be a democratic country and Jewish in orientation and favoritism?" On this issue, most Israeli Arabs, religious and secular, are united—they oppose Israel's continued existence as a Jewish state. Most believe that even if the country's Jews make an honest effort to achieve complete equal rights between Arabs and Jews, true equality will not materialize so long as it is the state of the Jewish majority.[18]

## U.S.-Israeli Relations

Washington is not neutral toward Israel or in Arab-Israeli matters. The balance is and will continue to be tilted toward Israel. Washington has no reason to want an unfriendly Israel, and Israel will continue to want strong and deep relations with Washington. Neither another oil embargo nor soaring oil prices is likely to fray the bond in any significant and, most importantly, prolonged manner. The ties that bind are deep, varied, intertwined, incessant, sometimes exasperating, but usually mutually reinforcing. The United States will sustain its innate affinity for the state of Israel. A similar immigrant experience and shared democratic values bind the relationship. But these deep and broad connections have not always meant that Washington has understood Israel or Israelis. American engagement in Arab-Israeli negotiations has deepened Washington's understanding of the complexes and complexity that are uniquely Israeli.

Over the last quarter-century, Washington policymakers have learned the rules of engagement in dealing with Israel on Arab-Israeli negotiating matters. Those rules are now operative. They are:

- Israel prefers that negotiations concerning Arab-Israeli issues or its national security take place under U.S. auspices, preferably with the Congress and the executive branch—where it has influence. Israel does not want the United Nations, the European Union, or any European capital to act as central mediator, facilitator, or guarantor. Israel accepts the participation of others but does not want to transfer to anyone else its special feeling toward Washington nor lose its influence there.
- Israel does not want to be surprised by an unexpected policy initiative, such as the October 1977 U.S.-Soviet Declaration or the September 1982 Reagan Statement. Rather, it insists on consultation, similar to formulating the invitations to the 1991 Madrid Conference and working in concert to evolve the 1997 Hebron Agreement.
- Israeli leaders refuse to be told by outsiders, especially by Washington, and particularly in public, how to behave in their national interests.
- Israeli leaders will not allow any outside party to determine what security needs or concessions should be offered in present or future negotiations. The corollary to this is that Israelis do not function well when they perceive outside pressure.
- Israel will insist on its own timing on national security issues and in resolving domestic issues. Most Arab parties and sometimes Washington would prefer a neutral timeframe that considers the interests of all concerned.

When American administrations see Israeli leaders moving forward in Arab-Israeli negotiations, there is less overt prodding of Israel to move to the ne xt stage in talks. Ho wever, Israelis ha ve accepted the reality that Washington will criticize—either quietly or publicly , depending on the diplomatic moment—any Israeli policy that aims to change the spatial, demographic, or settlement content of the W est Bank.

In 2015, neither the President nor the U.S. Congress will have diminished support for Israeli security or reduced W ashington's involvement and participation in seeking, making, and keeping peace. There is no reason to belie ve that Israel's friends in the United States will be an y less supportive of Israeli security. Not even a recrudescence of the "Who is a Jew?" issue, with all of the anger it stirs in the American Jewish community, can diminish American Je wish support for Israel or its security needs. In monitoring the Arab-Israeli negotiating process, the United States is lik ely to become more in volved diplomatically, physically, and monetarily, just as it did when nurturing the Egyptian-Israeli treaty. American military or ci vilian personnel can be e xpected to participate in a monitoring and implementation function that will arise in a reopened Syrian/Lebanese-Israeli track. If negotiations unfold with Syria and reach critical turning points, Israel will seek closer defense ties with the United States. Israelis will not mind creating additional strategic links between the prime minister' s office and the Ov al Office, between military intelligence agencies, and between the Israeli Defense Ministry and the Pentagon. By 2015, these links could evolve into a defense pact either on the North Atlantic T reaty Organization model or in the form of the U.S.–U.K. special relationship.

## Notes

[1] For discussion of the dangers inherent in the proliferation of weapons of mass destruction, see chapter 10 of this book, "Arms Control: In the Region's Future?"

[2] The Gallup Institute for *Ma'ariv*, May 1, 1998, as quoted in *Mideast Mirror*, May 1, 1998. See also Asher Arian, *Israeli Public Opinion on National Security 1999*, memorandum no. 53 (Tel Aviv: Jaffe Center for Strategic Studies, August 1999).

[3] *Ma'ariv*, November 19, 1999.

[4] Ibid.

[5] The "never again" refers to the promise made by Israelis, in particular Prime Minister Begin, never to allow a holocaust-type action for Jews.

[6] *Ma'ariv*, October 20, 1999.

[7] Economic News, Information Division, Israel Foreign Ministry, Jerusalem, October 24, 1999, accessed at <http://wwwmfa.gov.il>.

[8] *Yediot Aharonot*, October 21, 1999.

[9] John Benaquen, "Israel, The Economic Engine of the New Middle East," *Mideast Mirror*, September 14, 1999.

[10] *Ma'ariv*, November 17, 1999.

[11] Ibid.

[12] Nearly all the ministers in Netanyahu's cabinet (1996–1999) were born outside of Israel.

[13] Ran Kislev, "The Rabbis Changed, Not the IDF," *Ha'aretz*, February 23, 1999.

[14] Sephardic Jews came to Israel over the centuries from countries in the Middle East and Southern Europe; Ashkenazi Jews originated in northern and western Europe and Russia.

[15] *Ha'aretz*, May 25, 1999.

[16] For an assessment of the Shas Party and its leader Eli Yishai, see Leslie Susser, "The Second Most Important Man in Israel," *The Jerusalem Report*, December 6, 1999, 14–18.

[17] *International Herald Tribune*, April 27, 1998.

[18] See Yisrael Harel, "Zionism is Racism," *Ha'aretz*, October 7, 1999; see also Eric Rozenman, "Israeli Arabs," *Middle East Quarterly* 6, no. 3 (September 1999), 15–24.

---

*This chapter is based on a paper that was presented at a conference on* The Middle East in Transition: The Mashreq , *which was held at the Institute for National Strategic Studies, National Defense University, Washington, DC, on November 29, 1999. The chapter was updated to reflect the breakdown in Israeli-Palestinian and Israeli-Syrian talks, which occurred in September 2000.*

Chapter 6
# Palestine: Moving toward a Democratic State?

*Muhammad Muslih*

This chapter has two goals. The first is to identify economic and political trends and issues that could shape Palestinian politics in the next 5 years and beyond. The second is to assess the implications of these trends and issues for questions of succession, the peace process between Israelis and P alestinians, and political stability.

What are the key political and economic changes that are emerging and that are likely to occur in Palestinian society and politics in the medium and long term? What are the changes that are likely to take place as a result of the second *intifada,* and how will they affect the future direction of Palestinian politics? What will be the distinguishing characteristics of the Palestinian political scene in the absence of Palestinian Authority leader Y asir Arafat? How will the P alestinians revise their negotiating strategy in light of the *intifada* and their experience with the Oslo process? In what respects will the current *intifada*

---

*Muhammad Muslih is associate professor of political science and Middle Eastern studies and director of the international relations program at C.W. Post College, Long Island University. He was a visiting scholar at the Middle East Institute of Columbia University and served as political adviser to the Permanent Mission of the United Arab Emirates to the United Nations. His publications include* The Origins of Palestinian Nationalism *(1989),* The Origins of Arab Nationalism *(1993), and* Toward Co-Existence: The Political Program of the P alestine National Council *(1990).*

affect the distribution of power among different Palestinian groups? How should the U.S. Government view these trends and changes, and what kind of role should it play on the Israeli-Palestinian front?

# The West Bank and Gaza

## Geography and Socioeconomic Trends

The West Bank and Gaza Strip fell under Israeli occupation in June 1967. The two territories have a combined land area of about 2,300 square miles, slightly larger than the state of Delaware; among Middle Eastern countries, the only one with a smaller area is Bahrain. Approximately 36 percent of the West Bank is cultivable, 32 percent is grazing land, 27 percent is desert or rocky areas, and 5 percent is natural forest.

East Jerusalem is of particular significance for the Palestinian people of the West Bank and Palestinians in general. Israel annexed this Arab side of the city, which was under Jordanian control from 1948, in June 1967, following its capture in the 6-Day War. Although Palestinians living in East Jerusalem were free from some of the constraints imposed on the West Bank and Gaza by the Israeli military government, they were deprived of many of the rights enjoyed by Israeli Jews. In addition, Israel surrounded East Jerusalem with a ring of Jewish settlements. The West Bank at East Jerusalem resembles the middle of a reversed letter B, and without the city the Mount Nablus area to the north and the Mount Hebron area to the south would have only a narrow corridor connecting them. The potential of West Bank tourism is linked to a physical connection with the religious sites of East Jerusalem. Also, the city houses the financial, trade, and cultural infrastructure of the West Bank, including the power systems serving the areas from Ramallah in the north to Bethlehem in the south.

In an Arab Islamic context, no Arab or Muslim leader would be worth his soul if he were to acquiesce to Israel's retention of East Jerusalem. The city is as central to Islam and Christianity as it is to Judaism. Thus, we cannot realistically envision a durable peace without the settlement of the question of East Jerusalem. This question has as much to do with the viability of a Palestinian entity as it has to do with Israel's legitimacy in a region whose peoples, for the most part, share a culture and world view that is predominantly Arab-Muslim.

The estimated population of the West Bank is 2 million. Projections for the year 2010 put the population at 2.3 million people, making the West Bank (and Gaza) among the fastest growing areas in the world. Fifty percent of the people of the West Bank and 60 percent of Gazans are under age 15. Nearly two-thirds of the total population are male.

The essence of social organization is a network of *hamulas* (extended families) and smaller families, as well as village, neighborhood, and religious solidarities. Palestinian society has a mainly rural character, and even urban centers are closer to the model of small towns than to that of large cities. In the West Bank, 65 percent of Palestinians live in about 400 villages, while only 35 percent live in small towns. Even in Gaza, where close to 85 percent of the inhabitants reside in Gaza City, the culture is predominantly rural.

In the post-Oslo period, the West Bank and Gaza (or Palestine) witnessed both positive and negative socio-economic changes. On the positive side, total Palestinian economic output increased by about 4 percent per year, job increases occurred as reflected in the decline of unemployment (to 12.6 percent during the second quarter of 1999), construction jobs rose to constitute one-fourth of West Bank jobs, the banking sector expanded, and Palestinian economic ministries and institutions were established. On the negative side, Israel's policies of closures, economic strangulation, and collective punishment, especially after beginning of the new *intifada* in September 2000, have had a depressive effect on all socio-economic indicators.[1]

For the next decade, Israeli policies will have decisive influence on Palestinian socio-economic indicators because the latter's economy is largely dependent on the Israeli economy and good will. For example, as was the case in the 8 years since Oslo, border closures by Israel will continue to create a substantial decline both in the level of Palestinian employment in Israel and in the Palestinian-Israeli flow of labor and goods. Production and income in the Palestinian economy will decline by percentages as high as 24 percent, while per capita gross national product will fall by at least 40 percent. Also, the poverty rate, measured at an annual $650 per capita, will increase. Before the new *intifada*, the poverty rate in Gaza was about 36 percent, as compared with 10 percent in the West Bank.[2] This means that over the next decade Gaza will not bridge the gap between its economy and that of the West Bank.[3]

Another economic indicator that seems to be immune to change in the next decade is the willingness and ability of the Palestinian Authority (PA) to shrink the gro wth of its public-sector payroll. Palestinian public expenditures have risen progressively since the first Oslo agreement as the Authority began to take over the public sector functions of the Israeli civil administration in the Palestinian areas that came under the administration of the P alestinian Authority. Wages paid by the PA are estimated between 12 and 14 percent of the P alestinian gross domestic product (GDP), or about 29 P A employees per 1,000 people. In the next 5 to 10 years, the Palestinian Authority will continue to find itself forced to provide jobs to Palestinians rendered jobless as a result of Israeli measures of economic strangulation and to pay money to some Palestinians whose places of residence have been demolished by Israeli military authorities. Man y PA jobs are provided either to reward political loyalists or to keep the rate of unemployment relatively low for political reasons.

A third economic indicator that will prevail over the next 5 to 10 years is the wide gap between the per capita GDP for Palestinians and that for Israelis. Before the second *intifada*, the per capita GDP for Palestinians living in the W est Bank and Gaza w as less than half for what it was for Israelis in 1972 (that is, less than $1,600). This will make Israel an object of en vy and fear to P alestinians and to neighboring Arab countries. It is like having a Somalia (Palestine) next to Switzerland (Israel). A situation like this does not augur well for stability and security .

Other socioeconomic indicators that will continue to exist over the next decade can be briefly mentioned:
- high vulnerability of the Palestinian economy to political fluctuations
- increased Palestinian dependence on the donor community
- economic growth or decline rates that will vary by sector and by region
- disparate living standards in the W est Bank and Gaza
- unstable labor mobility
- expenditure growth that will remain greater than revenue growth
- private investment that will remain a hostage of political developments
- institutional reform and capacity building (that is, infrastructure networks) that will be introduced only if the W orld Bank and donor community focus on initiating such reforms

- balancing existing legislation, building an independent judiciary, and creating a modern market economy that will be a long-term, on-and-off process that will be largely dependent on donors and their policies.

## The Political Environment

The landslide victory of Israeli Prime Minister Ehud Barak in June 1999 raised hopes about the revitalization of a moribund peace process. During the first 6 months of Barak's term in office, the Palestinian Authority and the Israeli government agreed to start negotiations on final status matters (East Jerusalem, water, borders, settlements, refugee right of return, and nature of the Palestinian state) in the hope of reaching a permanent peace settlement. Barak's failure to implement previous agreements—most notably the 1998 Wye Agreement negotiated by his predecessor Benjamin Netanyahu and his policy of building new settlements and expanding existing ones in the West Bank—created resentment and skepticism on the Palestinian side. After a 4-year hiatus, Israel and Syria resumed negotiations under American auspices. Barak himself led the Israeli negotiating team, while the Syrian Foreign Minister, Faruq al-Shar'a, led the Syrian team. In January 2000, Israel and Syria seemed to be within reach of a final agreement. But hope for an Israeli-Syrian deal was dashed with the failure of the prematurely-held Geneva summit meeting between then-U.S. President William Clinton and late Syrian President Hafiz al-Asad in March 2000. For domestic as well as geopolitical reasons, Barak was not willing to accept Asad's demand, which was a full Israeli withdrawal to the lines of June 4, 1967.

The failure on the Syrian front was not only a serious setback for the Clinton administration, which had acted as middleman between Damascus and Tel Aviv, but also made Barak and Clinton focus their attention on the Israeli-Palestinian track. In the spring of 2000, a new Israeli-Palestinian momentum was building. Barak claimed that he wanted to end all aspects of the Israeli-Palestinian conflict. He at least seemingly believed that there was a seasoned Arab leader, PA President Yasir Arafat, with whom he could negotiate a deal. Barak also believed that Arafat's successor would lack the power and prestige to make the difficult decisions required for peace. Arafat, who believed that the Oslo "interim" process had run its course, was skeptical about Barak's willingness or ability to reach a formula acceptable to the Palestinians with respect to all final status issues, as well as an effective mechanism for implementing such a formula.

Despite his skepticism, Arafat accepted the tough choice of going to the U.S.-sponsored Camp David summit in July 2000, mindful that insufficient preparation was made for the summit. As he explained in Ramallah and Nablus a few days before the summit, Arafat thought that if he failed to attend the summit, the Americans and Israelis would blame him for squandering an historic opportunity. "Yet, if I attend," he stated, "and the summit fails, I also will be blamed for its failure. Given this reality, I am determined to muster the political will to go and negotiate in good faith because I don't want to embarrass my friend Clinton or weaken Barak domestically."[4]

In the end, Arafat was proven to be not far from the mark. At the summit, the Israelis and Palestinians failed to reach substantial agreement on final status issues, even though they broke deeply entrenched taboos (for example, the issues of Jerusalem and Palestinian refugees). Both sides also discovered the limits of their positions. For the first time, they presented their true attitudes toward the core issues, thus transcending the "what if" sessions of the past. Also for the first time, President Clinton heard the Palestinian narrative directly from the Palestinians, and not through the filter of Dennis Ross, the Middle East peace coordinator. The summit, however, was not successful. Issues that led to failure include:

- *Israel handled the talks with an occupier mentality* . The Israeli delegation rejected the Palestinian demand for an independent, sovereign, and viable Palestinian state and instead proposed the division of the Palestinian areas into four zones: a zone in the northern West Bank, a zone in the center , a zone in the southern part of the W est Bank, and a fourth zone in the Gaza Strip. A Palestinian who wanted to travel or transport goods from zone to zone had to pass through an Israeli-controlled area. All four zones would be disconnected from each other and under Israel's control. The P alestinians would have neither sovereignty over their airspace nor control over their borders or water resources. The Israelis also proposed the expansion of Jewish settlements in the north, center , and south of the W est Bank, connecting them to pre-1967 Israel through the acquisition of large areas of Palestinian land.

- *Israel proposed a strong military presence in the West Bank to defend against "the danger from the East."* This military presence would be in the form of Israeli bases, patrols, and early-warning stations in the Jordan V alley, along the border with Jordan. The Palestinians believed that the so-called danger from the East w as conjured up to justify Israel' s wish to control Palestinian areas and to impose strict restrictions on the ability of Palestinians to move inside their own state.
- *On the question of East J erusalem, the Israeli delegation insisted on sovereignty over al-Haram al-Sharif.* Washington offered suggestions based on Israel' s demands: dividing the Old City between Palestinian sovereignty over the Muslim and Christian quarters (as defined by Israel) and Israeli sovereignty over the Armenian and Je wish quarters and the W estern Wall; a form of "self-rule" for Arab neighborhoods near the Old City (for example, Sheikh Jarrah, Wadi al-Jawz, al-Suwwana, Shu'fat, and Beit Hanina); and a "sovereign compound" for Arafat and his administration near al-Haram al-Sharif. These areas would be disconnected from each other, and a mosaic of dif ferent rules would apply to each quarter. They also would be disconnected from the rest of the P alestinian "state."
- *The issue of Palestinian refugees was of paramount importance for Arafat and the Palestinians.* "If the Israelis don' t accept the principle of Right of Return, and if no equitable solution is found for the refugee problem, " Arafat stated before the Camp David summit, "then what shall I tell the refugees in Lebanon who supported me and constituted the core of my constituency during my years in Lebanon?" [5] To understand this point, we must recall that Arafat and the Palestine Liberation Organization (PLO), which he has led since 1968, represented a national movement whose adherents lived primarily in exile, particularly in Lebanon. The Diaspora Palestinians (a large portion of the Palestinian people as a whole) had their homes and roots in the three-quarters of Palestine that was captured by Jewish forces in 1948. For nearly 25 years, Arafat and the PLO represented the wishes of Diaspora Palestinians who felt that they had little to gain from anything less than a total return to Palestine, or pre-1967 Israel.

The explosion of the first *intifada* in December 1987 catapulted the priorities of the West Bank and Gaza Palestinians to the top of the PLO agenda. Thus pressed by the *intifada*, the PLO launched a peace strategy consistent in aims and methods with the preferences of West Bank and Gaza Palestinians. The main principles of this strategy include:
- PLO acceptance of United Nations Security Council Resolutions 242 and 338 as the basis for a negotiated settlement with Israel
- the explicit acceptance of Israel as a legitimate state
- an end to Israeli occupation of the West Bank and Gaza and the creation of a sovereign, independent Palestinian state in these territories, with East Jerusalem as its capital
- the rejection and renunciation of violence in all its forms and the adoption of diplomacy as the instrument of political action.

Despite this strategic shift in official Palestinian thinking, Arafat remained committed to the principle of the "Right to Return," which is enshrined in paragraph 11 of General Assembly Resolution 194 (III), adopted on December 11, 1948. The relevant paragraph resolved "that the refugees wishing to return to their homes and live at peace with their neighbors should be permitted to do so at the earliest practicable date, and that compensation should be paid for the property of those not choosing to return and for loss of or damage to the property which, under principles of international law or in equity should be made good by the governments or authorities responsible."[6] Although much of the international community, including President Harry Truman, insisted in 1948 and 1949 that the repatriation of the Palestinian refugees was essential if the Arab-Israeli conflict was to be resolved, Israel refused to accept the principle of return for the Palestinians.[7]

Israel has never showed any flexibility on this issue. This was evident at the Camp David summit, where Israel even refused, as a goodwill gesture, to accept any moral or legal responsibility for what befell the Palestinians as a result of the creation of the Jewish state. All that Israel proposed at Camp David was to allow several thousand Palestinian refugees to return over a 10-year period as part of a "family reunification" plan. A look at the historical record shows that Israeli thinking on the question has not moved an inch forward since 1949 in spite of the peace process and Palestinian recognition of Israel. For example, when Israel came under international pressure to implement Resolution 194 (III), certain doves in the Israeli Foreign Ministry placed a small upper limit on the number of refugees that would be allowed to return and insisted on two conditions that were totally irrelevant to the UN resolution. The conditions were: refugees (not exceeding 100,000 in number) would not return to their original homes but instead would settle in locations determined by Israel; and other Palestinian refugees (about 650,000) would be resettled in the Arab world, and Arabs would agree to sign a peace agreement with Israel. There was a strong domestic opposition to this proposal, and the top Israeli leadership, particularly David Ben-Gurion, endorsed a policy of continuous harassment against the refugees with the aim of pushing them away from the border and deep into neighboring Arab states. [8]

At Camp David, Israel also proposed a compensation plan with funds from the international community, and part of the money would be used to compensate Jews whom Israel encouraged to emigrate from Arab states. The Palestinians could not accept the Israeli proposals. Arafat and the refugee committee knew that the Palestinian refugees had an extremely emotional and deep-seated desire to be given the option to return to their homeland or at least be fairly compensated. Contrary to the prevailing view before the summit, the Camp David talks showed that the issue of refugees is much more complex and difficult than the question of East Jerusalem. [9] The Clinton administration seems to have underestimated the PA commitment to the principle of the Right to Return. Thus no practical mechanism was put in place to reconcile the Palestinian insistence on the Right to Return with Israel's refusal to accept that right. As one senior U.S. official explained, the Clinton administration operated on the principle that pre-1967 Israel "would be the country of all the Jews, [while] the West Bank and Gaza [would be] the country of all the Palestinians."[10] By adopting this position, the Clinton administration ignored one of the root causes of the Arab-Israeli conflict. Moreover, it transformed the refugee problem into an irreversible fact. The position of the Clinton administration contrasts sharply with the U.S. position in 1949. Then, and for years afterward, Washington threatened to reconsider its positive attitude toward the newly established Jewish state if the Israeli government failed to allow the repatriation of the Palestinian refugees, or at least to display flexibility toward this matter.[11]

## Good Governance and Political Order

*Political order* is best defined presently as a goal sought by the Palestinians yet not a reality. There is no Palestinian state or entity capable of developing efficient political institutions and assimilating Palestinian social forces into politics. As we have seen, the Oslo process has produced noncontiguous Palestinian areas divided by Jewish settlements and Israeli "security zones." The Israeli government has used Oslo to divest itself of responsibility for having populated Palestinian towns; in a clever and shrewd way, Israel dumped that responsibility on an underfunded, poorly structured Palestinian Authority, while retaining control over the life of the Palestinians and their natural resources.

Although the PA does not have complete control over its "self-rule" areas, the entry and departure of its own citizens, or trade and limited natural resources, it has managed to make some important achievements since its establishment in 1994. A president (Yasir Arafat) and a legislative assembly (the Palestinian Legislative Council) were elected in 1996. With the help of the international community (World Bank, International Monetary Fund, the United Nations, the European Union, and the donor community), administrative bodies are being established; public services have begun to operate; pluralism has started to emerge; and the Palestinian economy has shown signs of progress in some areas despite the disruptive conditions of Israeli occupation.

Yet the Palestinian Authority, assuming that it will not be crushed by Sharon's right-wing government, has a long way to go in terms of good governance. First, a highly institutionalized political system must be established. This means the development of political structures and processes that are not simply expressions of the interests of particular political or social groups, but rather are expressions of the interests of all Palestinian social forces. Second, a judiciary must be set up that adheres to distinctly judicial norms and that has perspectives and behavior independent of political forces and social groupings. Other steps must be taken to ensure good governance, including:
- a participatory political system
- a vibrant civil society
- institutionalized procedures
- the prevalence of loyalty to the broader institutions of public authority over loyalty to primordial social and economic groupings
- accountability in public office

- sustainable development, and a political systems that is adaptable, coherent, predictable, and diversified in terms of functions and types of organization.

## Two Scenarios for Change

Given the vulnerability of the Palestinian Authority to outside forces and the political culture of *mahsubiyyat* (patronage system) that characterizes the leadership of the P A, it is highly unlik ely that the P A will make extensive changes in the area of good governance over the next 5 to 10 years. Any diagnostic analysis of this question must take into consideration two scenarios.

*Scenario 1: Palestine under Arafat.* This scenario assumes that Arafat will be ali ve and in control 5 years from no w. In this case, we can assume with a reasonable degree of certainty that the Palestinian polity will move slowly and with interruptions toward good governance. A constitutional government that is based on the will of the majority and that is checked and counterbalanced by an effective legislative body and an independent judiciary will be a far-fetched goal. Arafat is not accustomed to thinking of governmental institutions as having representative functions. He will not be inclined to accept an effective system of checks and balances on the executive branch. Furthermore, the Israeli and American insistence on security as *the* overriding goal will make it difficult for Palestinian legislators or judges to limit the powers of the executive; as long as security is the number one priority, Arafat will use the Israeli and American preferences as an excuse for not moving into a new and decisive phase of reform and democratization. In all likelihood, Arafat will continue to use his traditional instruments of political action, including the cooptation of critics, the creation of cabinets that are loyal to him, the exclusion of the Islamist and secular opposition, and the resort to heavy-handed measures against those who oppose his style of leadership.

A good e xample of Arafat's innate inclinations is his restructuring of the Palestinian cabinet on August 4, 1998, in the face of public criticism leveled against his administration for its corruption and incompetence. The following can be observed about the restructured cabinet:

- Arafat introduced 10 new ministers, including 3 who were responsible for the new ministries of prisoners affairs, Jewish settlements, and Parliamentarian affairs.
- With the exception of Yusef Abu Safiyyah, the new cabinet was composed of political appointees rather than technocrats. Twenty-four ministers were members of the Palestinian Legislative Council (PLC), and two ministers who opposed the cabinet changes had their resignations readily accepted by Arafat.
- Ministers accused of corruption remained intact (Nabil Sha'th, Ali Kawasmi, and Jamil Tarifi).
- No individuals opposed to or critical of Oslo, either religious or secular, were represented in the new cabinet.

Arafat avoided appointing critics who hailed from large patrician families, such as Amro, Natsheh, Masri, and Bumedien. In contrast, he was heavy-handed with critics who came from small families such as Hanan Ashrawi, who was transferred from the post of Higher Education to Tourism, as well as Abd al-Jawad Saleh, who ended up with no portfolio. Motives behind Arafat's moves against cabinet members can be summarized as follows:

- Cooptation of PLC members demonstrated Arafat's desire to secure firm support for his position within the PLC. These members, who had spearheaded the campaign against the corruption and incompetence of the previous cabinet, included Salah Ta'mari, Sa'di al-Krunz, and Yusef Abu-Safiyyah.
- Innovation at the Ministry of Parliamentarian Affairs demonstrated Arafat's determination to assume more control over the work of the PLC. This ministry was intended to limit the role of the PLC Speaker and the role of proactive committees that were critical of the Executive.
- Exclusion of the opposition indicated that Arafat was determined to have a cabinet that would endorse his position (in other words, a rubber-stamp cabinet). The appointment of pro-Jordanian ministers, such as Mundher Salah, signaled to Jordan, Israel, and the United States that he was not creating a cabinet of confrontation.
- Composition of the cabinet illustrated Arafat's determination to strengthen his position by introducing key Fatah leaders, such as Hisham Abd al-Raziq and Rafiq al-Natsheh. This

move was meant to pacify the Fatah mainstream whose senior members were lobbying for more positions in the Arafat administration.

The above shows that Arafat did not seem interested in addressing domestic Palestinian concerns, most important of which was political reform. This was clearly expressed by Freih Bumedien, who said that the reason for creating a new cabinet was "the need to work with the situation so it relates to Israel more than the need to deal with the internal Palestinian situation."[12]

In short, Arafat was trying to establish two principles. On one hand, he wanted to relay to Israel and America that he was determined to proceed with the peace process by not introducing political figures opposed to Oslo. On the other hand, by introducing the Ministries of Settlements and Prisoners Affairs, Arafat was trying to switch the attention of active Palestinians from the question of reform to peace process issues.

*Scenario 2: Palestine after Arafat.* The premise of the preceding analysis assumes that Arafat will survive and remain in power over the next 5 to 10 years. But there is a second possibility, or even probability, which rests on the assumption that Arafat will pass away or will no longer be on the Palestinian political scene for health or other reasons. Under this scenario, prediction is extremely difficult.

In this scenario, two questions must be addressed. The first question revolves around the nature of the transfer of power after Arafat's departure from the political scene. There are two views on this subject. First, there is the theory that Arafat's departure will lead to chaos, instability, and violent power struggles among the Palestinian security agencies, as well as criss-crossing struggles within Fatah, which is the backbone of the PA and the PLO. The second theory assumes that the transfer of power in Palestine will be constitutional, orderly, and peaceful. Three factors give credence to this theory. The first is the Palestinian experience itself. Diaspora-based Palestinians, as well as Palestinians living in Gaza and the West Bank, have experience with holding elections, building trade unions, establishing women's organizations, creating parties, and participating in other political activities. Second, Palestinians have an abiding desire for a working democracy and a keen interest in maintaining a united front in the face of Israeli occupation. Palestinians living in the West Bank and Gaza publicly acknowledge an admiration for the workings of Israeli democracy, even though they resent being on the receiving end of Israel's occupation policies. In addition, the smooth process of succession in Jordan, Morocco, and Syria over the past 2 years invalidates the argument of those who assert that Arab leaders are selected through the barrel of a gun.

The second question is multiple: Where will Arafat's successor come from? Will he be favorably predisposed toward introducing the political and administrative reforms that are necessary for strengthening Palestinian institutions and building a viable Palestinian state? In all likelihood, Arafat's successor will emerge from within Fatah. The Fatah focus on Palestinian independence and its adoption of armed struggle for advancing national goals provided the political impulse and organizational dynamic in the evolution of Palestinian national identity. The parastatal institutions that it has built among Palestinian students, women, teachers, and other professionals, together with its bureaucratic elite, formed the nucleus of a quasi-government. By driving mass politics, establishing a national political agenda, gaining recognition and legitimacy, asserting its leadership, fighting for independence, opting for a diplomatic settlement with Israel, and leading the current *intifada*, Fatah demarcated the Palestinians as an autonomous actor in regional and international politics. After more than one generation of struggle and accumulated diplomatic experience, who better understands the meaning and ways of political survival and consensus-building than a Fatah veteran?

At the same time, the new leader will have to consolidate his position of power and make himself acceptable to various Palestinian political forces. This is one of the dilemmas that a new leader will confront: Should he focus on the consolidation of his position at the expense of the peace process (assuming that there will be a peace process), or should he move forward with the peace process and neglect the requirements of consolidating his power? The answer to this question depends on how strong the new leader will be—strong in the sense that he has the ability to impose his will and to withstand countervailing internal and external pressures. There will be forces (Israel and the United States) that may push the new leader to move forward with the peace process and security arrangements with Israel. Simultaneously, there may be forces, both local and foreign, that may pressure him to prove his nationalist credentials and to adopt a maximalist position vis-à-vis Israel and the United States.

The new leader also may have to deal with problems that Arafat could afford to put on hold. For example, Arafat's successor may find himself forced to define the relationship between the institutions of the Palestinian Authority inside the West Bank and Gaza and the institutions of the Diaspora-based Palestine Liberation Organization. Unlike Arafat, he may not be in a position to ignore Palestinian calls for political reform, democratization, accountability, and an end to corruption. In addition, the new leader may be forced to accommodate the Islamic movement Hamas, in contrast to Arafat who clipped the wings of the organization and kept it under the watchful eye of his security services, at least until the emergence of the second *intifada* in September 2000.

Without question, the new Palestinian leader will bring a new mentality and approach. Arafat has not been touched yet by the information revolution. His computer is his memory or a small notebook in his pocket. When he wants to support his point of view or jot down an important piece of information, he pulls out the notebook and searches for a pen, which is readily handed over to him by an aide. This is a typical Ottoman way of managing the daily political affairs of a presidential office. In all probability, the new leader will introduce a new style of administration.

The answers to these two questions are not necessarily definitive or conclusive for three reasons. The first reason is simply *chronological*. The PA is very young. This explains, at least partly, its relatively low level of institutionalization, which cannot be created overnight. Political development, in this sense, is a gradual process, particularly when considered in the context of the post-liberation stage. During this stage, the disruptive legacy of the occupier is still at play and incumbent elites have not yet substituted their experience of building national struggle institutions for the experience of creating state institutions. The younger an organization is, the more difficult it is to predict what will happen once the individual at the top dies.

The second reason has to do with the *autonomy* of a political organization. Although the PA has made some significant achievements in the area of creating public institutions (including institutions responsible for social services, education, and security), its degree of autonomy has been limited because it has been highly vulnerable to Israeli influences. In the words of an independent Task Force report, the "Palestinian Authority has had to establish and operate effective public institutions in a short time span within a framework of limited territorial jurisdiction; geographical fragmentation; nonsovereign control over land, population, and natural resources; and stringent security obligations toward Israel."[13]

Where an organization lacks autonomy, its political dynamic will be greatly impacted by outside influences. This either slows down the movement toward reform or diminishes the ability and willingness of its top leadership to assimilate new social forces without sacrificing organizational integrity. The interests, preferences, and agenda of external forces—in this case Israel and its sponsors in Washington—take precedence over the legitimacy and coherence (that is, ability to prevent the intrusion of disruptive external forces) of the organization.

The third reason is the *gap in our knowledge*. The voice of an important part of the Palestinian people in the West Bank and Gaza is scarcely heard in the West, or heard only in a muted, indirect, and even distorted form. It is the voice of the newly emerging political elites in Palestine. For example, from all the vast coverage, in both English and Arabic source materials, we know in detail and with a reasonable degree of precision about the top leadership of the PLO and the PA. We know a great deal about their politics, backgrounds, attitudes toward critical issues, and style of governance. But we have scarcely a record of the identity and attitudes of a younger generation of political activists who started to emerge after the 1993 Oslo accord and who have been asserting themselves since the *al-Aqsa intifada*. Filling this gap in our knowledge is crucial to the diagnostic, prescriptive, and predictive functions of both researchers and policymakers.

## Identifying New Trends in the Second *Intifada*

For several years, American diplomats in Jerusalem and Tel Aviv have warned Washington that a moribund peace process is fuelling anger, resentment, and despair in the Palestinian street. The explosion of another *intifada* was a matter of time, they argued. Also, Arafat was well aware that the Palestinian street would explode if the Camp David summit failed. In fact, he *pleaded* with Clinton not to hold a summit prematurely. The Palestinian president understood the dangers that would result from failure. But Barak wanted the summit, and Clinton fulfilled the Israeli leader's wishes. Clinton also wanted to crown his second term as president with a historic achievement. He saw in the Israeli-Palestinian front an opportunity that would enable him to go down into history as the American President who helped resolve one of the most comple x problems of the 20 th century. Thus, Arafat's pleas to make more preparations for the summit fell on deaf ears. Araf at's concerns were captured in a remark he made a few days before the summit: "And what if the summit fails and our people e xplode?" Arafat went on to say, "The summit will f ail because Israel was not yet ready to pay the price of peace with us. " He concluded, "I kno w what Barak has in mind and I am neither willing nor able to accept his proposals. The gap between us is too wide and much more work is needed to narrow the gap before the summit. "[14]

Thus, in September 2000, everything unraveled. The provocative visit of Likud Knesset member Ariel Sharon to al-Haram al-Sharif on September 28, 2000, triggered the current *intifada*. Sharon took this step with the authorization of then- Israeli Prime Minister Ehud Barak and Shlomo Ben Ami (who was the Israeli Foreign Minister and Internal Security Minister) under heavy escort and police helicopter guard to assert Israeli sovereignty over al-Haram. Of course, there are other reasons for the explosion of the *intifada*: Israeli control over Palestinian life, including borders, transportation routes, and natural resources; the expansion and building of new settlements in the W est Bank; self-rule areas that are a mosaic of noncontiguous Palestinian communities, divided by Jewish settlements, bypass roads leading to these settlements, and "security zones" under Israeli control; and serious governance problems in the P A-controlled areas, including corruption, a system of patronage, and human rights violations.

Several key turning points, hardly noted in the Arab and W estern media, have manifested themselves during the current *intifada*. The first turning point is lack of cohesion in the 1987–1993 *intifada* and the present one. Civil society organs that emerged in the form of active cooperatives, mass organizations, political shops, and Islamist groups during the 1987–1993 *intifada* have maintained a low profile in the current *intifada*. The once-active unions, student groups, women's societies, charitable and human rights organizations, and a host of other voluntary social formations have confined their activities to demonstrations and funeral processions in towns and cities. Unlike the 1987–1993 period, they do not lead the struggle against Israeli occupation. To be more precise, the y have not launched a ci vilian rebellion. They seem to have resigned themselves to the new reality in relation to the current situation.

The main active forces of the *intifada* are the Fatah *tanzim*, elements of the PA security services, Hamas, Islamic Jihad, and remnants of the Palestinian left. The strategy of these groups is based on armed action, especially against Jewish settlers in the occupied Palestinian territories. In some respects, the military activities of these groups tend to be interdependent in the sense that each one supplies to the military struggle its cadres and particular types of military action. The *tanzim*, which has the largest number of street cadres, carries out the national struggle in Zone C (Palestinian areas that are under Israeli civil and security control) and to a lesser extent in Zone B (full civil Palestinian control and joint Israeli/Palestinian control and joint Israeli/Palestinian security control). The *tanzim* is the unofficial and undeclared arm of the Palestinian Authority. Hamas, by contrast, has launched suicide bombings inside the Green Line. The PA has condemned such bombings, even though it has done little to stop them from happening because, from the perspective of the PA leadership, the Sharon government wants to undo the peace process and to destroy the PA. Thus, Arafat sees no reason why he should help Sharon stay in power.

The second turning point is the process of mass mobilization. The PLO, which was caught by surprise when the first *intifada* emerged, rode the tide and assigned to its number-two man, Khalil al-Wazir, the task of directing it. In this case, the PLO acted as a state surrogate, visibly leading the *intifada* and sending directives to local activists in the field. In the current *intifada*, Arafat and the senior members of his administration are staying behind the scenes. They issue no directives; they do not participate in demonstrations or candlelight marches; and they take no responsibility for any military action. Why? The answer lies in the Israeli and American understanding of the PA as playing primarily a security role. Because the PA has to fulfill stringent security obligations toward Israel, Arafat implemented these obligations when he felt that he had a peace partner. But Sharon is far from being a peace partner. Thus, Arafat is not taking any risks. Some Palestinians close to him maintain that he neither leads the *intifada* nor even plays a role in it.

Arafat does not want to alienate the U.S. administration and the remnants of the peace camp in Israel. He also does not want to give Sharon an excuse to launch a large-scale military assault against the PA and the areas that are theoretically under its control. At the same time, Arafat does not want to jeopardize his standing as a leader of the

Palestinian struggle for independence. This is why he has advocated a wait-and-see attitude. He does not stoke the flames of the *intifada*. Nor does he try to stop it because he knows that the Palestinian street will not let him do that. However, if Arafat gets political concessions from Israel (for example, the lifting of closures, a freeze on settlements, the development of an international or multinational monitoring force) or if he gets some attention from the White House, he may be positively inclined toward curtailing the growth of the *intifada* through his security services and the leverage he can exercise over the *tanzim*, which is the largest and most effective force in the street.

A third turning point manifests itself in new trends that are crystallizing and that might strike roots in Palestinian politics over the next 5 years and beyond. These include:

- Palestinian determination to make the occupation costly for Israel in terms of human life and material losses, regardless of the punishment that Israel inflicts on the Palestinians. Palestinians will continue to follow what can be called *siyasat al-nafas al-tawil* (the policy of patience and endurance). There will be no turning back, even if Israel unleashes the full force of its military power.
- Fatah's role will continue to expand, and the movement—by virtue of its armed struggle and its ability to mobilize the Palestinian street—will remain the dominant political force over the next decade. Thus, Fatah will remain the main pillar of any Palestinian state or entity that may emerge in the next 5 to 10 years.
- Hamas will continue to lag behind Fatah, unless Israel destroys the Palestinian Authority and Fatah. If this happens, Hamas will become the only viable organized group that is able and willing to take initiative and play a central role in the national struggle.
- Palestinians will continue to target Jewish settlers in the West Bank and Gaza, to isolate them and instill fear through a sustained war of attrition.
- Palestinians will raise the ceiling of their national demands in any future negotiations with Israel. It is highly unlikely that they will return to the status quo ante (that is, the incrementalism or the "peace by pieces" approach of the Oslo process).

- Palestinians will continue to resent unlimited American support for Israel and Washington's inability or unwillingness to play the role of an active and semi-objective middleman between Palestinians and Israelis.[15]

## The U.S. Role

The American Government should understand that emerging trends in Palestine will continue to develop their own momentum regardless of Israel's overwhelming military power. The Palestinians will no longer live with the status quo or with the incrementalism of the Oslo process. The Madrid/Oslo era is over. The Palestinians have fallen back on armed struggle because they were deeply disappointed with the outcome of Oslo and the American embrace of the Israeli position at the July 2000 Camp David II summit. The Palestinians and their leadership believe that President Clinton was hesitant and timid at Camp David and that he allowed Israel to dictate the agenda without taking into consideration U.S. strategic interest in the region. Also, from the Palestinian perspective, Clinton did not make sufficient preparations for the Camp David summit. The two parties went to a hastily arranged summit with their positions on final status issues too far apart. With the failure of Camp David and the unwillingness or inability of the United States to change Israel's position on final status issues, the only viable option was to look for another approach or model. This, for many Palestinians, was the model of Hizballah.

Indeed, the Palestinians were aware of the differences between the situation in Palestine and the situation in South Lebanon when they launched the second *intifada*. They knew that Hizballah had the active support of two major regional powers, Syria and Iran. They also knew that they would be alone in their confrontation with Israel. Yet they resorted to armed resistance, believing that it was imposed on them by Israel's continuous occupation and control over their life. They believe that they gave diplomacy more than one chance. They also believe that they made the necessary concessions for peace.

Despite their frustrations, Palestinians still see a pro-active U.S. role as the only hope to counterbalance a power equation that greatly favors Israel. America is the only power that the Palestinians recognize must play a key role in the peacemaking process. America has the essential power and leadership to promote, sustain, and reinforce peace.

A timid U.S. approach has serious implications for its interests in the region. It puts America's Arab allies on the defensive vis-à-vis their publics. It also hampers American efforts to promote and defend its interests in the Gulf.

It is dangerous for the U.S. Government to turn back and squander the legacy of previous administrations. To maintain regional peace and stability, the United States must involve itself by using not only friendly persuasion but also a package of carrots and sticks. This is needed if the peace process is to be saved. Richard Nixon and Henry Kissinger, Jimmy Carter and Cyrus Vance, and George Bush and James Baker used this approach and pressed reluctant Arabs and Israelis to move forward. This approach led to several breakthroughs, including peace agreements between Egypt and Israel as well as Jordan and Israel. American perseverance also has buttressed the Oslo process and produced some important achievements, especially in the area of security. Washington must understand that the peace process can act as a safety net for its regional strategy. If this process collapses, the safety net will collapse, too. The Arab masses are no longer timid, and the quiet that prevails in the Arab street may well be the calm before the storm.

## Notes

[1] The World Bank Group, *West Bank and Gaza Update*, West Bank and Gaza Resident Mission, Third Quarter 1999, 9–11.

[2] Radwan Shaban, "Socio-economic indicators and border closures", *New Visions for the Economic and Social Development of the West Bank and Gaza: A summary of an international conference sponsored by the Economic Development Institute of the World Bank and The French Institute for International Relations*, accessed at <www.palecon.org/papersdir/visions.html>.

[3] On the Gaza economy, see Sara Roy, *The Gaza Strip: The Political Economy of De-Development*, 2nd ed. (Washington, DC: Institute for Palestine Studies, 2001).

[4] Personal communication between Arafat and author, June 2000.

[5] Ibid.

[6] See text of resolution in *Official Records of the General Assembly, Third Session, Part I, 21 September to 22 December 1948*, Resolutions, 21–25.

[7] Mark Tessler, *A History of the Israeli-Palestinian Conflict* (Bloomington: Indiana University Press, 1994), 311.

[8] Ibid., 313–314; Benny Morris, *The Birth of the Palestinian Refugee Problem, 1947–1949* (Cambridge: Cambridge University Press, 1987), 280–282.

[9] The Camp David material in this chapter is based on private discussions with Israelis, Palestinians, and Americans who wish to remain anonymous, and on a discussion with Arafat in August 2000; Akram Haniyeh, "The Camp David Papers," *Journal of Palestine*

*Studies* 30, no. 118 (Winter 2001), 75–98; the report of Mahmud Abbas (Abu Mazin) of September 9, 2000, on the P A negotiation affairs, accessed at <www.nad.gov.ps>; and a summary of a report of the Palestinian negotiating team in *al-Quds al-Arabi* (London), July 25, 2001, 9.

[10] Private communication with author on December 27, 2000.

[11] Morris, 256 ff; Itamar Rabinovich, *The Road Not Taken: Early Arab-Israeli Negotiations* (New York: Oxford University Press, 1991), 27.

[12] *Jerusalem Post*, August 6, 1998, 3.

[13] "Strengthening Palestinian Public Institutions," Executive Summary: Report of an Independent Task Force sponsored by the Council on Foreign Relations (New York: Council on Foreign Relations, 1999), 7.

[14] Personal discussion between Arafat and author, June 2000.

---

*This chapter is based on a paper that was presented at a conference on* The Middle East in Transition: The Mashreq, *which was held at the Institute for National Strategic Studies, National Defense University, Washington, DC, on November 29, 1999. The chapter was revised to reflect the* al-Aqsa intifada, *which began in September 2000.*

Chapter 7
# Iran: Can the Islamic Republic Survive?

*Mark J. Gasiorowski*

For several years, Iran has been locked in a fierce power struggle that has pitted conservatives, who want to preserve the strict Islamic regime established after the 1979 revolution, against reformers, who want to liberalize the Islamic regime in various ways. Although both factions have worked earnestly to increase power and influence, the struggle remains deadlocked, despite the landslide victories of reformist Mohammad Khatami in both the May 1997 and June 2001 presidential elections. Certain long-term trends are now unfolding that should slowly shift the balance of power in favor of the reformists during the ne xt 10 to 15 years. Ho wever, in the more immediate future, various events could lead to a break in the deadlock and to victory in the struggle by either the reformists or conservatives. As a consequence, it is impossible to say with any certainty what will transpire in Iran during the next 15 years.

---

*Mark J. Gasiorowski is professor of political science at Louisiana State University. He specializes in Third World politics, Middle East politics, and comparative and international political economy. Dr. Gasiorowski has been a visiting professor at the faculty of law and political science Tehran University. He is the author of* U.S. Foreign Policy and the Shah: Building a Client State in Iran *(1991) and coeditor (with Nikki Keddie) of* Neither East Nor W est: Iran, the So viet Union, and the United States *(1990).*

This chapter examines the various trends affecting Iranian politics and identifies the scenarios that are most likely to emerge during the next 15 years. More specifically, this chapter reviews a number of important demographic, social, and economic trends that are likely to influence the long-term course of Iranian politics; examines public opinion in Iran and how these trends are likely to affect public opinion in the future; speculates about the political scenarios that are likely to emerge during the next 15 years; and finally considers how these scenarios may affect Iran's foreign policy and the resulting implications for U.S. foreign policy.

## Demographic and Social Trends

One of the most important trends unfolding in Iran is the maturation of a large baby boom generation that was born in the 1970s and early to mid-1980s. Iran's population growth rate rose significantly in the 1970s, as a result of improvements in sanitation and health care and higher income levels associated with the oil boom.[1] Population growth rates rose even further during the first several years after the revolution, as Iran's new Islamist leaders encouraged larger families and implemented a variety of other policies that raised birth rates.[2] Population growth then fell sharply in the late 1980s and 1990s as family planning measures were implemented to reduce the socioeconomic strains engendered by the high growth rates of the early post-revolution era.

These trends produced a large demographic bubble that has been working its way through Iran's population. In 1994, 14.3 percent of Iran's population was between the ages of 10 and 14 (born in the early 1980s) and 20.4 percent was between 15 and 24 (born in the 1970s).[3] These numbers are significantly higher than the corresponding numbers for 1976 (12.8 and 19 percent). The population cohort born in the late 1950s and 1960s (aged 25–39) was relatively large in 1994, while the cohort born in the late 1980s and early 1990s (aged 0–9) was relatively small. Taken together, these numbers indicate that Iran in the year 2000 has a very large cohort of young adults aged 16 to 30 (34.7 percent of the 1994 population), a relatively large cohort of early middle-aged adults aged 31 to 45 (19.8 percent), and a relatively small cohort of older adults aged 46 and above (18.1 percent).

These three age cohorts differ not only in size but also in their connection to the revolution. The oldest cohort was above the age of 24 in 1979, which implies that its members experienced the revolution as adults and have clear memories of the prerevolution era. The middle cohort was aged 10 to 24 in 1979 and therefore viewed the revolution and the period of postrevolutionary ferment as impressionable teenagers and young adults. To a much greater degree than older Iranians, the members of this cohort were involved in the revolution, the post-revolutionary frenzy of political activity, and the politically charged war with Iraq. As a result, they became swept up in the intense political socialization that surrounded these events. This cohort can be described as the *children of the revolution*. The youngest cohort was under the age of 10 at the time of the revolution and younger than 19 when the Iran-Iraq war ended in 1988. Its members did not experience the political socialization of the revolution and postrevolution periods and have no clear memory of the prerevolution era, making them the *grandchildren of the revolution*.

These three cohorts also differ considerably in their levels of education. Primary, secondary, and postsecondary education levels have increased substantially in Iran since 1960.[4] The children of the revolution attended primary school in the 1960s and 1970s and secondary school in the 1970s and early 1980s, making them much better educated than the cohort of older adults. The grandchildren of the revolution attended primary school from the late 1970s through the mid-1990s and secondary school from the mid-1980s through the present, making them even better educated than the children of the revolution. This sharp increase in primary and secondary education raised Iran's overall adult literacy rate dramatically, from 22.8 percent in 1966 to 36.5 percent in 1976, 47.7 percent in 1985, and 72.1 percent in 1995.[5] World Bank statistics also indicate that the grandchildren of the revolution, who began to finish secondary school in the late 1980s, benefited from the sharp increase in postsecondary education that has occurred since the revolution. The statistics reveal that these age-related differences in education are especially dramatic for Iranian women, whose educational opportunities have improved more rapidly than those of men since the revolution.[6] Iran's female adult literacy rate has increased from 24.3 percent in 1976 to 42.7 percent in 1981 to 65.8 percent in 1994.[7]

Finally, another important social trend in Iran has been the rapid increase in urbanization. The proportion of Iran's population living in urban areas has grown from 41 percent in 1970 to 50 percent in 1980 to 60 percent in 1997. [8] Thus, Iranian society now is not only younger and better educated than it was in the past but also more urbanized.

## Economic Trends

The Iranian economy has performed poorly since the revolution, with generally slow or negative growth and moderately high inflation.[9] Two broad factors account for this poor economic performance: First, the revolution and the war with Iraq severely disrupted the economy from 1978 through 1988. Second, since the revolution, economic policymaking has been guided largely by political, rather than economic, considerations. Government officials have maintained tight control over the economy, keeping much of the economy in state hands and relegating the private sector largely to peripheral activities, such as construction and retail trade. Public spending has been oriented toward redistribution and other political objectives, resulting in huge subsidies and other expenses that drain public coffers and distort prices. The government has been unwilling to use monetary policy effectively to curb inflation and, until recently, maintained a multiple fixed exchange-rate system that left Iran's currency seriously over-valued, discouraging exports and encouraging imports. The dominant role of the state and its over-regulation have allowed corruption to flourish in recent years. These problems have been abetted by Iran's high oil revenues, which have enabled the Iranian rentier state to avoid many of the fiscal constraints faced by others. These various problems, together with the U.S. economic sanctions and uncertainty about the future, have discouraged both foreign and domestic private investment, further stifling economic activity. Taken together, these factors have set economic development back two generations in Iran, with real per capita income today remaining roughly 40 percent below its 1977 peak. [10]

Since the late 1980s, Iran's leaders have increasingly realized that substantial economic reform is needed to improve the country's economic performance. They have implemented two 5-year development plans (1989–1994 and 1995–2000) and recently have unveiled a third, each aimed at revitalizing the economy by implementing reforms.

The first plan was hampered by opposition in parliament, which until 1992 was dominated by Islamic leftists who opposed reforms that might adversely affect the poor, such as privatization, subsidy cuts, exchange rate liberalization, and tight monetary policy. The Islamic leftists were decisively defeated in the 1992 elections, raising hopes that the new parliament would be more supportive of economic reform, which had become a major objective of President Ali Akbar Hashemi Rafsanjani's government (1989–1997). However, the conservatives who dominated the new parliament soon moved in a populist direction and blocked key elements of the second plan, largely emasculating it. In addition, despite the existence of various social safety nets, a series of small-scale riots rooted in poor economic conditions occurred throughout the country in the mid-1990s, leading the government to back away from some of the more painful reforms embodied in the second plan. Finally, oil prices remained fairly low during most of the decade, further undermining Iran's economic performance.[11]

President Khatami is a moderate Islamic leftist who initially placed greater emphasis on political rather than economic reform. As a result, economic policy during Khatami's first two years in office was given a low priority and failed to address Iran's major problems.[12] The government shifted its priorities toward economic reform in the summer of 1999, when it began a much-needed effort to unify the exchange rate. In the fall of 1999, Khatami unveiled the third development plan, an ambitious effort to reform the economy that calls for extensive privatization, increased foreign investment, expansion of non-oil exports, cuts in subsidies, and efforts to increase tax collection and reduce bureaucracy. However, after Khatami submitted the plan to parliament, his conservative opponents quickly began to pick it apart, raising rather than lowering subsidies, maintaining price controls, and limiting foreign borrowing. After parliament approved the amended plan, the Council of Guardians ruled that key elements of its privatization initiative were unconstitutional, further weakening the plan. The government protested that the changes imposed by parliament would have a devastating effect on the plan, bringing the economic growth, inflation, and unemployment rates during the period covered by the plan to 4, 18, and 19 percent, respectively, from the targeted rates of 6, 12, and 16 percent.[13] Predictions by reputable independent observers are even more pessimistic.[14]

The fate of the three development plans clearly illustrates the political obstacles to better economic performance in Iran. These obstacles will persist as long as the current power struggle between reformists and conservatives remains deadlocked, with politicians in both camps using economic policymaking to achieve partisan political advantage. While it is difficult to say where Iran is headed during the coming years, it seems likely that this deadlock will persist for some time. Thus, the prospects for meaningful economic reform are not positive. In the absence of meaningful reform, Iran's economic performance will continue to depend heavily on oil prices, which are expected to remain erratic in the coming years.[15] Consequently, Iran's economy is likely to remain stagnant for the foreseeable future.

Continued economic stagnation could have ominous consequences for Iranian politics. The greatest concern is that the cohort of grandchildren of the revolution discussed above has entered the job market in large numbers in recent years, producing two new workers for each new job created. Unless a substantially higher rate of economic growth can be achieved on a sustained basis, the unemployment rate, which is 16 percent,[16] will continue to grow in the coming years, adding to the discontent of Iran's restive youth. Although high youth unemployment and other economic problems have not yet translated into explosive unrest, this could quickly change—especially if the sociocultural and political liberalization that has occurred in recent years ends. The state of the economy will be a key factor affecting Iranian politics.

## Trends in Public Opinion

Several interrelated factors have produced a dramatic shift in public opinion in Iran in recent years, creating strong popular pressure for reform. First, the revolutionary fervor that gripped Iran in the early 1980s has virtually disappeared, as Iranians have realized that many revolutionary ideals were unattainable and as the excesses and hardships caused by the revolution have become increasingly apparent. Second, the large, better-educated grandchildren of the revolution cohort, now aged 16 to 30, has entered the political arena, creating a substantial bloc of relatively sophisticated, pragmatic young people who are generally disenchanted with the Islamic regime and strongly favor reform.[17] Third, the economic difficulties discussed above have created widespread discontent and considerable disillusionment with the Islamic regime, especially among young people whose future prospects in many cases are bleak.

This popular pressure for reform focuses on three main areas. Most importantly, Iranians want economic reforms that will provide more employment, curb inflation, and raise living standards. Unfortunately, few Iranians are sophisticated enough to know what kinds of reforms are needed to achieve these outcomes, and many do not appreciate that effective economic reform requires short-term sacrifice. Moreover, while Iranians complain a great deal about the economy (and while economic conditions have resulted in occasional protests and riots during the past decade), price subsidies and other safety-net programs have helped mute some discontent. As a result, popular pressure for economic reform is unfocused and has not yet become a major factor in the Iranian factional power struggle.

Second, many, though certainly not all, Iranians favor further easing of the strict sociocultural restrictions, especially restrictions on *hejab* (women's dress code), gender relations, and access to Western culture and media. These issues are especially important to women and young people for obvious reasons. Third, many Iranians favor more extensive political liberalization, both to make the state more accountable and to increase the prospects for economic reform and sociocultural liberalization. The advocates of political liberalization are mainly educated people, including not only many of the revolution's grandchildren but also many of its children (now aged 31–45), who have experienced the excesses of the revolution most acutely. President Khatami and his reformist allies have strongly emphasized the need for sociocultural reform and political liberalization, so the pressure for reform in these areas has given the reformists a strong base of popular support, especially among women and young people.

The depth of this desire for reform has become increasingly apparent in the 1990s through election results, intellectual trends, and various forms of popular protest. Its strongest manifestation came in the May 1997 presidential election, which Khatami won with 69 percent of the vote.[18] Eighty-five percent of people under the age of 29 voted for Khatami, as did a large majority of women, making young people and women his two largest constituencies. Khatami won a majority of votes in all but two of Iran's 27 provinces, indicating that the desire for reform is strong not only in the major cities but also in provincial towns and rural areas. Moreover, an astonishing 91 percent of the electorate actually voted, dwarfing the 55 percent turnout rate of the 1993 presidential election. [19] These results were virtually duplicated in the February 1999 nationwide municipal council elections, in which 75 percent of the seats in Iran's 112 largest cities went to reformist candidates and only 12.5 percent went to conservatives.[20] These two elections provided clear proof that a large majority of Iranians favor reform.

Although the desire for reform is widespread and deeply felt, only a small minority of Iranians seem to oppose the Islamic regime, judging from casual conversations, attendance at Friday prayer services, and widespread adherence to conservative styles of dress, which are widely viewed as statements of political preference. Moreover, many Iranians who do oppose the Islamic regime do not favor active steps against it because they recognize that it remains broadly popular and they believe that only slow, evolutionary change is feasible. The clearest indication that only a small minority of Iranians are willing to work actively against the regime is the student-led riots of July 1999. These riots remained fairly limited and did not spread to other sectors of the population. Thus, the movement for reform symbolized by the election of Khatami seeks to liberalize the Islamic regime rather than dismantle it.

This popular pressure for reform undoubtedly will continue to grow during the next 15 years, as the children and grandchildren of the revolution become increasingly important actors and as economic hardship persists, which appears to be inevitable. As long as meaningful reform seems possible, the societal forces that favor meaningful reform almost certainly will continue to work peacefully within the parameters of the Islamic regime to foster it. However, if the prospects for reform fade, the forces favoring it—especially young people—could turn against the regime and resort to violence, as began to occur during the July 1999 riots.

The growing popular pressure for reform notwithstanding, it has not translated into strong pressure for change in several key aspects of Iranian foreign and defense policies. Although many Iranians favor better relations with the United States, most still harbor resentment about past U.S. policy toward Iran and are skeptical about whether the two countries can have an even-handed, mutually beneficial relationship. As a result, the efforts by Khatami and others in recent years to promote rapprochement with the United States have not generated a substantial base of popular support, which would have facilitated these efforts. Iranian rapprochement with Western Europe and pro-Western Arab states has been quite popular, but these initiatives have not depended on popular support. Iranians generally remain sympathetic to the Palestinian cause and skeptical about the Arab-Israeli peace process; thus, any effort to moderate Iran's position on the peace process would face significant, though perhaps not substantial, popular opposition. Similarly, any effort to abandon the Lebanese Hizballah would encounter significant opposition. Finally, there is strong support in Iran for a powerful military apparatus and little opposition to the development of weapons of mass destruction (WMD), so moderation in this area might also encounter significant popular opposition.

## Probable Political Scenarios

Growing popular pressure for reform has led to the emergence of two reformist factions among the Iranian political elite during the past decade. The first, which is generally referred to as the Centrist faction, consists of close relatives of Rafsanjani and technocrats who held high positions in the Rafsanjani government. The Centrists were the architects of the economic and sociocultural reforms carried out during Rafsanjani's tenure. They remain closely associated with Rafsanjani and his moderate views, advocating Western-style structural adjustment measures of the sort that were embodied in the first and second development plans, continued sociocultural liberalization, and political liberalization. Their main organizational vehicle is the Servants of Construction Party.

The second reformist faction is a diverse group of Islamic leftists, many of whom served in the government of Prime Minister Mir Hossein Mousavi (1981–1989). Islamic leftists have moderated considerably since their defeat in the 1992 parliamentary elections. Their main focus now is to promote democracy in Iran, though they also advocate sociocultural liberalization and economic development measures that protect the poor. They also have created a number of political organizations over the years, most of which are now grouped in the Islamic Iran Participation Party. Khatami is a moderate Islamic leftist, and his cabinet includes both Centrists and Islamic leftists. [21]

The Centrists and Islamic leftists are aligned in a tenuous coalition against the conservatives. The conservatives are a diverse group that includes Islamic traditionalists whose main goal is to preserve the Islamic sociocultural restrictions currently in place, hard-line revolutionaries who mainly want to preserve the system of political institutions and power relations established after the revolution, and opportunists whose family or professional connections have led them to align with the traditionalists and hard-liners. The conservatives are united by their opposition to the political and sociocultural reforms advocated by the reformists. Some conservatives have supported the economic reforms embodied in the three development plans, while others have opposed these reforms for opportunistic or tactical reasons. The conservative opposition to political and sociocultural reform has led them to align themselves closely with Ayatollah Ali Khamenei, who, as Leader of the Islamic Republic, is the successor to Ayatollah Ruhollah Khomeini. As such, he symbolizes the political and sociocultural achievements of the revolution. Khamenei, in turn, has drawn close to the conservatives during the past decade, though he does occasionally back the reformists on certain issues. The main political organizations of the conservatives are the Militant Clerics' Association and the Islamic Coalition Organization.

Although the reformists have made some progress in achieving their goals during the past decade, the power struggle between them and the conservatives is deadlocked, with neither faction fully able to control the state apparatus and thus to implement its agenda. Because of their overwhelming popularity, the reformists have triumphed in recent presidential elections, enabling them to control much of the executive branch. However, because the constitution gives the Leader control over the security forces, judicial apparatus, and radio and television media, Khamenei has been able to keep these vital institutions out of reformist hands. The conservatives also wield extensive influence over foreign policy, both through the Leader, who has final say on major foreign policy issues, and through the national security council, which is about equally divided between reformists and conservatives.

Before the February 2000 parliamentary elections, the absence of an effective party system prevented the reformists from bringing their overwhelming popularity to bear on parliamentary elections, enabling the conservatives to control this important body from 1992 until 2000. The reformists worked energetically to change this, however, and the conservatives lost control over parliament in February 2000. Nevertheless, the conservatives control the Council of Guardians, which can veto legislation passed by parliament, and they have considerable influence over the Expediency Council, which mediates disputes between the Council of Guardians and parliament. In sum, the overwhelming popularity of the reformists has been offset by conservative control of key institutions, leaving the power struggle between the two factions essentially deadlocked in recent years.

This deadlock in the factional power struggle is likely to persist in the short term (that is, for the next 2–3 years). Reformist success in wresting control over parliament from the conservatives in February 2000 was an important victory, but the conservatives can still block parliamentary legislation through the Council of Guardians, and they still control several other key institutions. Moreover, disputes between the leftists and Centrists that emerged during the election campaign could weaken the reformist faction. Consequently, reformist success in the parliamentary elections has not ended the deadlock in the power struggle. Their success in the 2001 presidential election will probably not decisively affect the struggle in the near term. Khatami is barred constitutionally from seeking a third term, and his ability or inability to realize any elements of the reformist agenda could impact on their ability to elect another reformist.

In the longer term, three alternative scenarios should be considered: a peaceful evolution toward reformist victory; a conservative crackdown; and a continuation of the current deadlock over power between the reformists and the conservatives.

*Reformist Victory.* Many close observers of Iran believe that the pressures for reform discussed above will make future reformist victories inevitable. Two key trends would play a crucial role in contributing to more reformist victories. First, most conservative leaders are now more than 60 years old, and some are over 70. By contrast, almost all of the key reformist leaders now are under 60, and most are under 50.[22] Consequently, during the next 15 years, almost all present conservative leaders will disappear from the political scene, while most reformist leaders will remain politically active. In particular, Khamenei, who is 61 and reportedly has health problems,[23] is likely to step down as leader within the next 10 to 15 years, raising the possibility that this position might be filled by a more moderate figure. Second, as popular pressure for reform continues to grow, conservative leaders increasingly will see the need to adopt reformist positions, either to win elections or to prevent popular unrest from reaching levels that threaten the existence of the Islamic regime. Indeed, this trend has already begun to unfold, with some conservatives de-emphasizing or abandoning their opposition to political and sociocultural reform and adopting economic reform as an issue with which to attack the reformists. With most established conservative leaders disappearing from the scene and their successors moving toward reformist positions, the reformist cause will inevitably triumph, according to this argument.

Two alternative long-term scenarios seem equally plausible in the face of growing pressure for reform.

*Conservative Crackdown.* In this scenario, the conservatives respond to pressure for reform by using their control over security forces to carry out a crackdown similar to the one at Tienanmen Square in 1989. They outlaw and repress open dissent, arrest reformist leaders, and replace the populist authoritarianism that has prevailed in Iran since the revolution with strictly coercive rule. This approach essentially would entail a decision by conservative leaders to sacrifice the Islamic regime's popular base to safeguard their dominant position. The success of this approach would depend on the loyalty of security forces, which was brought into question when many Revolutionary Guards and military personnel reportedly voted for Khatami in May 1997.[24] However, security forces remained loyal during the July 1999 student-led riots, and a group of Revolutionary Guard commanders even issued an extraordinary warning to Khatami at that time, which some observers interpreted as a coup threat. [25] A crackdown of this sort would create tremendous anger and opposition among the large majority of Iranians who favor reform. Since the conservatives strongly oppose sociocultural reform and could not implement political reform under these circumstances, the viability of this approach might require rapid, large-scale economic reforms that would produce a sustainable wave of prosperity, similar to that which occurred in China after the Tienanmen Square episode. Although it seems unlikely that the conservatives would carry out such economic reforms, this certainly cannot be ruled out. Consequently, a crackdown is a distinct possibility, though its long-term viability is uncertain.

*Persistent Deadlock.* A third scenario that could play out during the next 15 years is a continuation of the deadlock that now exists in the factional power struggle, with sociocultural and political reform continuing at the slow, erratic pace that has prevailed since the late 1980s. There is no compelling reason to think that either the reformists' popular support or the conservatives' institutional powers will change substantially in the near future, so the rough balance of power that has existed between the two is likely to continue at least for several years. While the demographic and social trends discussed above should gradually expand the reformists' base of support in the coming years, they are not likely to have a substantial impact on the factional power balance for perhaps 5 to 10 years. In the meantime, the conservatives may find ways to adapt to these trends. Moreover, most leaders in both camps have been acting cautiously, seeking only incremental progress on their respective agendas, avoiding factional confrontation, and often restraining more militant colleagues. This caution is likely to persist, reducing the possibility of a confrontation that results in victory by one faction or the other.

A number of unforeseeable factors could affect the likelihood of these three scenarios during the next 15 years, making it impossible to predict with any certainty which of them will occur. *Economic conditions* could affect the Iranian political future in two fundamental ways. First, if economic conditions improve during the next few years as a result of economic reform, high oil prices, or some other factor, the popularity of Khatami and the reformist camp is likely to remain high. This would increase the likelihood of a reformist victory and reduce that of a conservative crackdown or continued factional deadlock. Conversely, economic stagnation or deterioration would probably undermine reformist popularity and make a conservative crackdown or factional deadlock more likely. Second, continued economic stagnation could trigger an outburst of rioting at almost any time, perhaps leading to a major confrontation in the streets and a showdown between reformists and conservatives. If the security forces remain loyal and the rioting is contained, conservatives might seize the opportunity to carry out a crackdown. However, if the security forces refuse to back the conservatives or if rioting spirals out of control, reformists might achieve victory through an Iranian "Velvet Revolution." A showdown of this sort thus could lead to either a conservative or reformist victory, with the outcome remaining uncertain until the end.

Other domestic and international political factors could affect the likelihood of these three scenarios. Rioting triggered by political events, such as the imprisonment or murder of a popular figure or the blatant rigging of elections, could produce a factional showdown. A split in either the reformist coalition or the conservative camp would undermine the affected faction and perhaps lead to a break in the deadlock and victory by the opposing faction. The death or retirement of a powerful figure such as Khamenei or Rafsanjani also could alter the factional power balance and lead to a break in the deadlock. Better relations with the United States during the next few years could lead to the dismantling of U.S. economic sanctions, a larger American presence in Iran, and a reduction in Iran's harsh rhetoric toward the United States, strengthening Khatami and the reformists and depriving conservatives of one of their main rhetorical weapons. Another regional war or crisis could also affect the Iranian political future in unpredictable ways.

A third key set of factors involves the *timing* of some of the trends and changes discussed above. Khatami has been in office now for 4 years but has had few concrete achievements. There is a growing danger that he and the reformist camp will be discredited in the public eye if they cannot claim to have solved some of the country's pressing problems soon. Consequently, if Iran does not experience improved economic conditions, a breakthrough in relations with the United States, or some other positive development during the next few years, then public support for the reformists may begin to fall sharply, tipping the power balance in favor of the conservatives. Similarly, since the factional deadlock has hampered economic reform in recent years (as discussed above), an early break in the deadlock might produce a substantial improvement in economic conditions, benefiting whichever faction is in a position to claim credit for it. Moreover, while continued deadlock might prevent significant economic improvement, it would give demographic and social trends more time to play out, further expanding the popular base of the reformist faction and reducing that of conservatives. Thus, if the reformists can maintain popularity and prevent a conservative victory for the next 5 to 10 years, their chances of prevailing in the power struggle should improve considerably.

Finally, in the tense and uncertain environment that prevails in Iran, the political instincts and skills of principal actors will be critically important. In particular, the future of the factional power struggle will depend on how Khatami, Khamenei, and Rafsanjani— the three most important figures in Iran—act during the next few years. Foresight and ingenuity will be at a premium; miscalculation could be fatal for either faction.

## Trends in Iranian F oreign P olicy

Iranian foreign policy has moderated substantially since the 1980s, as revolutionary zeal has dissipated and leaders have come to appreciate the benefits of moderation. Iran has largely abandoned efforts to export Islamic revolution, reducing its ties to most, though not all, radical Islamist groups, and even clashing with or criticizing groups such as the T aliban in Afghanistan and the Islamist guerrillas in Chechnya and Algeria. Similarly , Iran has lar gely abandoned its efforts to destabilize its neighbors, markedly improving its relations with the moderate and conservative Arab states and showing considerable restraint toward Iraq, the Caucasus states, Afghanistan, and Pakistan, despite the instability in these countries and the hostility several have displayed toward it. Iran also has worked hard to improve relations with the European Union (EU) countries, ending the assassination of Iranian dissidents in Europe, negotiating a deal with Britain over the Salman Rushdie af fair, and moderating its rhetoric toward these countries.[26]

Each of these initiatives has proceeded with a fair degree of consensus among Iranian leaders and between the reformist and conservative factions. Also, there has been relatively little criticism of them even from more marginal groups and individuals. A considerable consensus exists on several other key foreign policy principles, including the importance of maintaining an independent foreign polic y, acting as a leader in the Islamic world, projecting an image of solidarity with underdeveloped countries, and maintaining a strong military apparatus.

The consensus on these initiatives and principles suggests that they are likely to remain central cornerstones of Iranian foreign policy for the foreseeable future, regardless of which of the domestic political scenarios discussed above takes place. As a consequence, during the next 15 years, Iran almost certainly will continue to exercise restraint in the region, work toward full normalization of relations with the EU countries and the moderate and conservative Arabs, pursue an independent foreign policy favoring Islamic and underdeveloped countries, and maintain a strong military apparatus. Iranian military planning almost certainly will continue to include the development of at least some WMD capabilities, which are not at all unpopular among most Iranians and are almost universally accepted among the political elite as instruments of deterrence that are vital to Iranian security .[27]

A lack of consensus marks three other important foreign policy issues: rapprochement with the United States, Iran's posture toward the Arab-Israeli peace process, and its support for terrorist groups such as Lebanon's Hizballah, Hamas, and Palestinian Islamic Jihad. Most Iranians know and care little about these issues, though they are generally wary of the merits of rapprochement with the United States, skeptical that the peace process will bring justice for the Palestinians, and unaware of the violent character of these terrorist groups and governmental involvement with them. Thus, public opinion has little impact on these issues. However, opposition to the United States and Israel and support for Lebanese and Palestinian Islamist guerrillas have featured prominently in the mythology of revolutionary Iran, leaving many members of the political elite still strongly committed to these causes and making it difficult for others to back away from them. Most conservatives and some Islamic leftists still strongly support these causes, due partly to their ideological and xenophobic outlook as well as to the emotional appeal and demagogic value these causes hold. Ayatollah Khamenei's hard-line position on these issues has been especially influential. Most reformists and a few prominent conservatives now cautiously favor rapprochement with the United States and a reduction or end to Iran's opposition to the peace process and support for terrorist groups, though it is difficult for them to say so publicly. Still, they have not worked energetically to change Iran's policy on these issues because the domestic political costs would outweigh the potential benefits and because domestic issues are much more important to them.

The factional divisions that underlie these three issues suggest that progress on each of them will depend at least partly on how the factional power struggle plays out in the coming years. If the reformists achieve victory, they will have much more latitude to pursue rapprochement with the United States and reduce the Iranian opposition to the peace process and support for terrorist groups. Because most reformist leaders remain ambivalent about these issues, the extent to which they would do so depends on the inducements that Iran is offered by the United States and other interested parties. If the conservatives achieve victory and manage to consolidate control, they undoubtedly will be much less forthcoming than the reformists on these issues. However, since they almost certainly would want an end to U.S. economic sanctions and perhaps other concessions and since their opposition to these issues is partly opportunistic, they would probably be willing to bargain over these issues, making some progress possible. The least propitious scenario for progress on these issues is a continuation of the current factional deadlock in which the conservatives use almost any mention of these issues as an opportunity to seek partisan advantage. Under these circumstances, reformists will remain unwilling to spend scarce political capital on these issues as long as the costs outweigh the potential benefits. It seems unlikely, therefore, that any substantial progress will be made in resolving the main disputes between the United States and Iran as long as the power struggle remains deadlocked.

In addition to the outcome of the factional power struggle, a number of other factors could have a considerable impact on these three issues and on Iran's broader foreign and defense policies. First, Iran is more likely to be forthcoming on these issues and act moderately in general if its economy continues to stagnate or deteriorates further since it will have more incentive to seek an end to American economic sanctions and other concessions. This will be especially true if economic conditions produce further rioting or other political instability.

Second, the outcome of the Arab-Israeli peace process (whatever it might be) will have a substantial impact. A successful conclusion to the peace process would obviate Iran's opposition to it and thus remove a major obstacle to U.S.-Iranian rapprochement. It might also weaken Hizballah, Hamas, or Palestinian Islamic Jihad or, at least, lead these groups to adopt more moderate postures toward Israel. Of course, these groups might remain hostile and even increase their attacks on Israel if the peace process succeeds, perhaps making Iranian relations with them even more problematic. Alternatively, a collapse of the peace process might lead Iranian hard-liners to increase ties to these groups and persuade some U.S. officials to blame Iran for the collapse, clouding the prospects for rapprochement. As long as the peace process remains inconclusive, Iran's opposition to it and support for these groups will remain serious impediments to U.S.-Iranian rapprochement.

Third, Iran's posture on these three issues and its broader foreign policy will be affected by the posture that America maintains toward Iran (see below). Fourth, the Iranian attitude toward these and other issues will depend partly on the policies of the EU countries and, to a lesser extent, other regional and global actors since these countries can provide many of the economic benefits that Iran wants from the United States. Thus, Iran is more likely to be forthcoming on these issues if America can harmonize its policy toward Iran with the policies of the EU countries and these other actors. Finally, Iran's foreign and defense policy will be affected greatly by any changes that occur in its security environment, such as greater instability in some of the neighboring countries or another regional war. While it is impossible to predict what changes of this sort might occur, it is easy to envision several that could lead Iran to adopt a more hostile foreign policy or to expand its military apparatus further, including WMD capabilities.

## Implications for U.S. Strategic Interests

The foregoing discussion touched on a number of trends now emerging in Iran that could have a substantial impact on U.S. strategic interests during the next 15 years. Some of these trends are fairly certain to play out, while others are much less so.

We can be fairly certain that Iran during the next 15 years will continue to exercise restraint in the region, work toward full normalization of relations with the European Union and Arab countries, pursue an independent foreign policy, and maintain a strong military apparatus. It is also quite likely that the Iranian economy will continue to stagnate. These conclusions suggest, above all, that Iran is not likely to pose a direct military threat to U.S. forces in the region or to American allies such as Israel, Turkey, Saudi Arabia, and the other Gulf Cooperation Council countries. Iran also is not likely to pose a military threat to any of its other neighbors, unless they directly threaten its interests as the Taliban did in the fall of 1998. Iran's WMD development almost certainly will continue, remaining a major strategic concern for the United States. While Iranian leaders may show some flexibility on this issue,[28] it seems unlikely that they will forego WMD development entirely in the absence of a comprehensive ban on weapons of mass destruction in the region (including Israel and probably Pakistan). The likelihood of continued economic stagnation will place additional pressure on Iran's leaders to exercise foreign policy restraint and seek economic concessions from Europe, Japan, and the United States. As a result, economic sanctions will remain the most important bargaining chip that the United States can wield in its relations with Iran in the coming years.

The prospects for U.S.-Iranian rapprochement and an end to Iranian opposition to the peace process and support for terrorist groups during the next 15 years are much less certain. Progress on these issues will depend on how Iran's factional power struggle plays out, with positive movement most likely to occur if the reformists consolidate control and least likely if factional deadlock persists. Also, progress on these issues will be affected by factors such as the state of the Iranian economy.

These conclusions have a number of implications for U.S. policy toward Iran during the next 15 years. First, the United States must continue to exert pressure on Iran and remain vigilant for signs of change in both Iran's domestic politics and its foreign policy. The American military presence in the Persian Gulf, though now aimed primarily at Iraq, helps to ensure that Iran will not act aggressively. There is no compelling reason to reduce the U.S. presence in the Gulf on Iran's account, though this could be a useful bargaining chip in future bilateral negotiations. The United States must continue its various efforts to interdict Iran's acquisition of weapons of mass destruction since Iran almost certainly will continue to seek these weapons, regardless of its commitments under international arms control agreements and the enticements that America and other countries might offer. The United States also must continue to monitor Iran carefully, watching both for signs that the factional power struggle might break in one direction or the other and for changes in the Iranian posture on major foreign policy and defense issues.

Second, the desire of most reformists and some conservatives to achieve rapprochement with the United States suggests that American officials should expand the limited efforts that they have been making recently to foster constructive engagement with Iran. Dialogue between the United States and Iran is not possible now, mainly because the reformists (who favor it) do not see how potential benefits outweigh costs—costs that the conservatives would impose on them for pursuing dialogue. This problem is likely to persist for some time.

The United States now should work toward preparing the groundwork for dialogue when it becomes possible. This involves several things. First, U.S. officials should clear away some of the underbrush that will hinder future dialogue through actions such as speeding up settlement of the "frozen assets" issue, making remorseful statements about past American policy toward Iran, and emphasizing that the United States seeks an even-handed, non-domineering relationship with Iran. These matters are important to Iranians and will hinder rapprochement until they are resolved. Second, U.S. officials should continue to encourage *people-to-people dialogue,* which has had a powerful effect on Iranian views of America. Third, U.S. officials should offer Iran "teasers" that would demonstrate the benefits of rapprochement, using statements that emphasize the mutual interests of the two countries on various issues; back-channel messages soliciting Iran's views on these and other issues; and small, appropriately chosen unilateral concessions.

When some form of dialogue becomes possible, the United States should explore the possibilities of negotiating changes in Iran's behavior on three main issues of concern: WMD development, opposition to the peace process, and support for terrorist groups. The main bargaining chip held by U.S. officials is various American economic sanctions on Iran. These sanctions include not only trade and investment embargoes but also U.S. opposition to pipelines across Iran, oil swaps, and international bank loans.[29] Although they do not say so openly, Iranian leaders are anxious to have these sanctions lifted. Iran also would be interested in a lower U.S. military presence in the Persian Gulf as well as access to spare parts for its U.S.-made military equipment. Negotiations also could focus on cooperation in areas of mutual interest, such as the containment of Iraq and conditions in South Lebanon, the Caucasus, and Afghanistan. Iran's willingness to negotiate would depend on who is in power, domestic political conditions faced by its leaders, the state of the economy, and the relative importance of these various issues at the time.

In addition to eliciting concessions and more moderate behavior from Iran, constructive engagement, if pursued appropriately, could have the added benefit of strengthening the reformists and increasing the likelihood that they will prevail in the factional power struggle. Successfully forging rapprochement would strengthen the reformists by increasing their popularity among Iranians who favor it, giving a boost to the economy for which they could claim credit, and depriving the conservatives of the ability to use the "Great Satan" card against them in the domestic power struggle. Since the reformists are more likely than the conservatives to steer Iran in a moderate, cooperative direction, this benefit from constructive engagement could be as valuable as any concessions Iran might make on the issues mentioned above. Of course, American officials must be careful not to embrace the reformists too closely since the conservatives could use this to attack them and undermine the process of rapprochement.

Third, U.S. officials should try as much as possible to harmonize American policy toward Iran with that of the EU countries, Japan, and the moderate and conservative Arabs. Iran can obtain many, though not all, of the economic benefits that it needs from the EU countries and Japan. Therefore, if the United States falls far behind these countries in forging rapprochement with Iran, its ability to use economic sanctions to elicit concessions will decline. Also, America must work closely with its European and Arab allies to stop Iranian WMD acquisition efforts and to maintain Persian Gulf security.

In seeking rapprochement with Iran and moderation in its foreign policy, U.S. officials must be patient. Iran's relationship with the United States and other major aspects of its foreign policy are deeply caught up in the factional power struggle. They will not change quickly, and the United States can do little to hurry them.

## Notes

[1] World Bank, *World Development Indicators* (Washington, DC: World Bank, 1998).

[2] Jahangir Amuzegar, *Iran's Economy Under the Islamic Republic* (London: Taurus, 1997), 61–62.

[3] United Nations, *Demographic Yearbook, 1996* (New York: United Nations, 1998), 198–199; United Nations, *Demographic Yearbook, 1982* (New York: United Nations, 1984), 194–195.

[4] World Bank, *World Development Indicators*.

[5] Ibid.

[6] Ibid.

[7] United Nations, *Statistical Yearbook* (New York: United Nations, various years).

[8] World Bank, *World Tables, 1991* (Washington, DC: World Bank, 1991), 322–323.

[9] International Monetary Fund, *International Financial Statistics Yearbook* (Washington, DC: International Monetary Fund, various years).

[10] Ibid. For good overviews of Iran's economy since the revolution, see Amuzegar, *Iran's Economy Under the Islamic Republic*; Kaveh Ehsani, "Iran's Development and Reconstruction Dilemma," *Middle East Report* (November-December 1994), 16–21; and Hamid Zanganeh, "The Post-Revolutionary Iranian Economy: A Policy Appraisal," *Middle East Policy* 6, no. 2 (October 1998), 113–129.

[11] On the problems that plagued the first two development plans, see Hooshang Amirahmadi, "Iran's Development: Evaluation and Challenges," *Third World Quarterly* 17, no. 1 (1996), 123–147; and Amuzegar, *Iran's Economy Under the Islamic Republic*, 338–359.

[12] Jahangir Amuzegar, "Khatami and Iranian Economic Policy at Mid-Term," *Middle East Journal,* 53, no. 4 (Autumn 1999), 534–552.

[13] Jahangir Amuzegar, "Iran's New Economic Plan: A Preliminary Review," *Middle East Economic Survey* 42, no. 41 (October 1999); Mehrdad Balali, "Iranian Officials Doubt Quick Economic Recovery," *Iran Focus* (November 30, 1999); "Guardian Council Opposes Khatami's Privatization," *Iran Weekly Press Digest* (December 11, 1999).

[14] *The Economist Intelligence Unit, Country Report: Iran*, 4th Quarter 1999 (London, 1999), 5, predicts economic growth rates of 2.3 and 3.2 percent in 2000 and 2001 and inflation rates of 27 and 35 percent.

[15] *The New York Times*, December 20, 1999, C–32.

[16] "Iran Eyes Move to Market Economy," Reuters, October 14, 1999.

[17] For a good overview of the attitudes of this cohort, see "The Post-Khomeini Generation," *The New York Times Magazine*, November 1, 1998.

[18] In the 2001 election, Khatami garnered 77 percent of the vote, although fewer Iranians voted than did in the 1997 election.

[19] "Young Iranians Help Elect Moderate," Associated Press, October 23, 1997; "A Moderate in Tehran," *The Washington Post*, May 26, 1997; "Vote Breakdown Contradicts Pre-Election Predictions," *Iran Times* (Tehran), June 2, 1997.

[20] "IRAN: Khatami Council Victory," *Oxford Analytica*, March 9, 1999.

[21] For a more extensive discussion of these factions and the issues discussed in the next few paragraphs, see Mark Gasiorowski, "The Power Struggle in Iran," *Middle East Policy* 7, no. 4 (October 2000), 22–40.

[22] Of the conservative leaders, Khamenei was 61 in 2000, Mohammad Yazdi 69, Ahmad Jannati 74, Ali Akbar Nateq-Nouri 57, Mohammad Reza Mahdavi-Kani 69, Ali Akbar Meshkini 75, and Habibollah Asgharowladi 58. Rafsanjani was 66. Of the reformists, Khatami was 57 in 2000, Abdollah Nouri 51, Gholam Hossein Karbaschi 46, Ataollah Mohajerani 46, Said Hajjarian 47, and Mehdi Karrubi 63.

[23] See, for example, "Ailing Iranian Leader Cuts Short Speech at Khomeini Mausoleum," Agence France Presse, June 4, 1998.

[24] Many close observers of Iranian politics, both in Tehran and abroad, claim that electoral districts with large numbers of Revolutionary Guard or armed forces personnel voted strongly for Khatami. However, the author has not seen any concrete analyses of this issue.

[25] "Iran's Revolutionary Guards Denounce Khatami, Students Claim Coup Bid," Agence France Presse, July 20, 1999.

[26] For a good overview of Iranian foreign policy, see Mahmood Monshipouri, "Iran's Search for the New Pragmatism," *Middle East Policy* 6, no. 2 (October 1998), 95–112.

[27] Iranians across the political spectrum are comfortable with the development of nuclear weapons and medium- and long-range missiles. Although few Iranians have a sophisticated understanding of the implications of these types of weapons, they implicitly see them as instruments for deterring both nuclear and conventional attack by Israel, the United States, Iraq, and perhaps Pakistan. Iranians are more ambivalent about biological and chemical weapons because of the gruesome toll that these weapons took during the Iran-Iraq war.

[28] Iran is probably least likely to give up its development of intermediate-range missiles since they are essential to its presumed goal of achieving minimal deterrence against Israel and other regional threats. Long-range missiles and nuclear warheads are expensive and technologically difficult to develop, so Iran might be willing to forego development of these weapons if offered suitable enticements. It might also be willing to forego them under certain circumstances because Iranians feel more ambivalent about biological and chemical weapons and the international opprobrium associated with them.

[29] For an overview of these sanctions, see Kenneth Katzman, *U.S.-Iranian Relations: An Analytic Compendium of U.S. Policies, Laws and Regulations* (Washington, DC: The Atlantic Council of the United States, 1999).

---

*This chapter is based on a paper that was prepared for a conference on* The Middle East In Transition: The Persian Gulf, *which was held at the National Defense University, Washington, DC, on January 21, 2000.*

Chapter 8

# Iraq: Another Saddam on the Horizon?

*Adeed Dawisha and Judith S. Yaphe*

This chapter will describe the political, economic, and social realities that shape present-day Iraq, outline those historical and cultural characteristics that have affected its past and could determine its future, and speculate on trends and possible scenarios for change in Iraq. Our discussion will be grounded in facts that reflect current trends and speculative in considering possible futures. W e may not, however, be optimistic.

## Current Trends and Realities

Many scholars and policymakers imagine that politics in Iraq is the brainchild of one evil man who is responsible for creating and inflicting on Iraqis the conditions that define a uniquely authoritarian and repressive system of political and social controls. While Saddam Husayn undoubtedly has refined the methods of oppression —physical, psychological, and intellectual—we should remember that oppression

---

*Adeed Dawisha is pr ofessor of political science at Miami University , Ohio. In addition to over 60 book chapters and journal articles, Dr. Dawisha is the author or editor of eight books and one monograph. His latest book is* Arab Nationalism in the Twentieth Century: From Triumph to Despair *to be published by Princeton University Press in early 2003.*

and violence are part of Iraq's ancient and contemporary history. They were tools of statecraft long before Saddam came to po wer, and the y probably will remain such after he leaves the scene.

## *Guarding the State: Trends in Political Repression*

If the present is any guide to the future, Iraq in 2015 could resemble Iraq in 2000—a society in which nearly 50 percent of the population is under the age of 16, in which an entire second generation has grown up and another become middle-aged not knowing any rule but that of Saddam Husayn, his family, clan, and party, and not having any direct knowledge or experience of the outside world—two generations born since 1980 that will have known only wars, sanctions, and repression. It could be an Iraq in which Kurd mistrusts Arab, Sunni mistrusts Shia, Shia mistrusts everyone, and Iraqis are linked more by the fear of the outside than of the terror within the state. Conversely, it could be an Iraq free of sanctions and of the republic of fear that has kept Saddam and the Ba'th Party in power since 1968.

Iraq in theory is a republic with an "elected" national assembly headed by a Shia, a Kurdish vice president, and a president who in 1996 won 99.6 percent of the popular v ote. In theory, the R evolutionary Command Council approves all laws and official decisions.

The reality is far different. The present system of political control in Iraq resembles a series of concentric circles. At the center are Saddam and his immediate family—his sons Uday and Qusay, his cousin Ali Hassan al-Majid, and his half-brothers Barzan, W atban, and Sabawi.[1] At various times, family members have held all the powerful posts—for example, as defense, intelligence, or interior minister—but mostly they serve as heads of the various and redundant security and intelligence organizations that protect Saddam.[2] The second circle consists of loyalists primarily from Saddam's home re gion, the city of T ikrit, and his tribe and clan of the Bayjat and the Alb u Nasir. Included in this circle are the predominantly Sunni Arab tribal confederations of northwestern Iraq—especially the Dulaymi, Jabburi, and Duri tribes. These tribes are most closely associated with Saddam and his own tribe, the Bayjat, which is a branch of the Dulaymi confederation. Their members serve mostly in the Republican Guard; the Special Republican Guard, which acts as a bodyguard force for Saddam himself and to protect special weapons of mass destruction (WMD) sites and materials; and the other security and intelligence organizations in the military.

The third circle includes non-clan, non-tribal Iraqis who have been with Saddam from the early years of the Ba'th Party, when it was a clandestine organization focused primarily on assassinating Iraq's leaders.[3] The few loyalists who have survived decades of purges include Deputy Prime Minister Tariq Aziz, a Chaldean Christian; Vice President Izzat Ibrahim al-Duri, reputedly a devout Muslim; and Taha Yasin Ramadhan, a Mosuli, once head of the Ba'th Party paramilitary group. They owe their survivability to their lack of ambition, their lack of a power base in the party or the government, and their apparent lack of independent popularity among Iraqis. The outermost circle, the most marginal and tangential one, includes the Ba'th Party and its members. Over the past 30 years, Saddam has purged the party leadership, in particular its intelligentsia and anyone with the potential to become a rival or the ability to attract a popular base.[4] For many Iraqis, such as Professor Dawisha, discussion of eliminating the party as a viable institution would have been blasphemous 20 years ago, but today it seems a given.[5]

The scheme of concentric circles conceptualizes Saddam Husayn as the grand patriarch, the source of all power, influence, and status. It depicts the flow of power from the center—Saddam—through his sons to his cousins, and then to the outer circles. The system is based on control, fear, repression, and the cult of personality. Much has been written on this system, and the physical and intellectual oppression that has marked Saddam's rule does not need to be rehashed here.[6]

## *Political Dualism*

In the late 1970s, many Iraqis believed there was a chance to move away from this oppressive style of rule. Saddam had established a relatively popular base in Iraq. The methods of oppression were in place but, at the same time, while Iraqis feared Saddam, they also respected him. In this contradictory dualism, Saddam appeared to be a successful and ambitious young leader. He had initiated popular socioeconomic programs, including nationalization of the Iraqi Oil Company, and resolved, albeit temporarily, the war with the Kurds and the Shah of Iran. He had encouraged all Iraqis—Sunni and Shia, Arab and Kurd—to participate in the Ba'th Party and governance of the state, and he projected a theory of Iraqi nationalism that transcended ethnic and sectarian differences. Some Iraqis saw in these new themes and programs the possibility that if his popularity continued, Saddam would not need to continue policies of oppression. Some even speculated about the chance of some political liberalization.

These feelings became even stronger after the Iraq-Iran War (1980–1988), when Iraq emerged "victorious" and Saddam himself conceded the sacrifices of the Iraqi people. There was talk among his inner circle about liberalization, about opening the system, and about getting a few political parties to compete. Saddam encouraged these hopes by announcing plans for a constitution. In those days, some Iraqis believed it was possible that, somehow, the Grand Patriarch had realized that it was time for a change and that he knew that if a change came, given the kind of political conditions that pertained at that time, he might very well emerge as the popular leader. Saddam repeated this pattern after the Gulf War in 1991 when he reminded Iraqis—and the West, the real target—of his promised constitution and briefly named Assembly head Sadun Hammadi prime minister.

Hopes for peace and political liberalization disappeared immediately after the Iraq-Iran War and again within several months after the end of the Gulf War, when it became obvious that Saddam had no intention of changing his style of rule and that the absence of war would not lead to any such "foolish ideas."[7] Iraqis were left with a system where the power of the state was based almost entirely on institutionalized physical and intellectual oppression. In the view of the authors, few countries have had a similar plethora of competing and redundant intelligence and security services—all inter-connecting, crisscrossing each other, and meeting at the apex of the pyramid based in the presidential palace. These organizations, control of which has increasingly been placed in the hands of Saddam's younger son Qusay, include the special security organization, the *Amn al-Khass*; the general intelligence organization, the *Amn al-Am*; and the military intelligence organization, *al-Istikhbarat al-Askariyah*. All are part of what makes Iraq a *mukhabarat* (police) state. These are umbrella organizations, and there may well be hundreds of these in the services filtering down through the local levels throughout the state. They have done their job well thus far. They certainly have kept Saddam in power in the decade since the occupation of Kuwait, the imposition of sanctions, the end of the Gulf War, and the failure of the rebellions, all interspersed with several abortive coups. Moreover, they have displayed an impressive ability to penetrate most of the opposition groups inside Iraq and abroad.[8]

## *Is Terror Enough?*

People in the Arab world today—not illiterate poor peasants but intellectuals, academics, journalists, the people of the professions in Cairo, Amman, and even Washington—believe Saddam survives in power not just because of his awesome secret services or heroic self-view. Four out of five Arabs believe that Saddam Husayn remains in power because the United States wants him to be there. Why is this so? "Arabs uniformly believe that there is no way that Saddam Husayn could have survived a decade of the almost draconian sanctions on Iraq, had the United States not wanted him to be there."[9]

Most analysts acknowledge the force of conspiracy theories in this region and say that they are more sophisticated and easier to accept than is reality. And reality indicates that Saddam owes his survival to the kind of security arrangements that he has perfected in more than 30 years of rule. While the United States is spending $100 million on the opposition, Saddam has spent at least five times as much every year for the past 30 years to perfect his kind of rule. We have a long way to go if we are to think of undermining him.

Having said that, we are convinced that the stability of Saddam's regime today does not compare to its stability 20 years ago, before the war with Iran began. His rule undoubtedly has been undermined, and he is weaker today than at any time in the past. But this is relative, not absolute, weakness. Whether his strength is tenuous enough that his removal can be confidently predicted is not clear and may never be. Saddam will continue to rule in the only way he knows how—through physical, intellectual, and psychological oppression and social controls; by means of torture, imprisonment, and executions; and with his special military and security services.

No independent recourse is available inside Iraq. Saddam's older son, Uday, now an "elected" member of the National Assembly, is increasingly in charge of the intellectual oppression that all the media now come under.[10] He uses his control of the media to accuse other ministries of poor performance or to attack ministers for incompetence.[11] When there is a clash of interests between Uday and anyone, Uday always comes out on top. Only Saddam can restrain his accusations and ruminations in print.

In some respects, one could argue, this amount of control should become more difficult in these days of satellite dishes and the Internet. (Baghdad announced in early 2000 the opening of its first cyber café.) This sense of "freedom by Internet" is deceptive. Iraqis will not have even the limited amount of cyber freedom allowed Iranians under Mohammed Khatami or Syrians under Bashar al-Asad. Iraq is probably the last bastion in the Middle East against this kind of intrusion of the information revolution. Conditions for intellectual thought and social freedoms will only become more difficult than they were before the wars. But, we must also note that the Iraqis have been probably some of the most successful perpetrators of keeping information within Iraq. Given the extent of internal paranoia and eavesdropping, with foreign visitors monitored by their government-appointed "minder," Iraqis are very cautious in discussing internal politics with anyone, Iraqi or non-Iraqi.

## Institutions in the Last Circle of Power

Other institutions historically have shared a degree of political power, especially in the years of the monarchy (1920–1958) and after the 1958 revolution.[12] Few would argue that the National Assembly is relevant or useful, so what other institutions are relevant? Since seizing the presidency in 1979, Saddam has reinvented Iraq and its institutions in several images.

The Ba'th Party was the premier institution when Ahmad Hassan al-Bakr and Saddam Husayn took power in 1968. In the 1970s, the party had more than one million members, with party members dominating both senior policy and decisionmaking bodies—the Cabinet and the Revolutionary Command Council.[13] Membership in the party gave legitimacy to Iraq's leaders and opened the path to advancement for its members. There was no alternative institution or political party allowed in Iraq. In particular, the military had to be Ba'thized—that is, made idologically pure with ideological monitors—if it were to serve Saddam loyally.

Saddam began to replace the party with the cult of personality in 1979, when he removed his cousin Bakr from the presidency and assumed the office himself, and he orchestrated and held a party conference that featured ritual denunciations, self-criticisms, confessions, and instant executions. The party, in effect, was marginalized, its role reduced to that of mobilizer rather than bestower of legitimacy and credibility. Party members were replaced first by members of Saddam's family circle and later by the tribes after a dramatic post-Operation *Desert Storm* makeover. In all the reinventions and makeovers, one principal has remained paramount—Iraq is ruled through the institution of the Grand Patriarch and Leader Saddam Husayn, his cult of personality, and his circles of po wer.

The transformation of the party from a key defining political institution to an irrelevant body accelerated in the early 1970s. By 1973, 6 years before Saddam moved Bakr aside and assumed leadership openly, the outlines of the personality cult and the emer gence of the duality within the Ba'th Party were discernible. Over the next 6 years, the Ba'th Party became a secondary institution to the presidenc y. Within a year of his ascension to the presidenc y, Saddam himself began openly to denigrate the party and adv ance the cult of personality , saying, for example, there is no need for anyone to become a member of the party. Rather, any true patriotic Iraqi, meaning a patriotic Iraqi who accepts Saddam Husayn as his president, is a Ba'thist. This implied there was no need for anyone to be institutionally connected to the party. If you were a true patriot, if you were a true Iraqi, then you were a Ba'thist.

By the be ginning of the Iraq-Iran W ar, the party had lost all claims to a preeminent role and authority . Saddam had reduced the importance of the slogan "unity , Arabism, and socialism" inherent in Ba'thist ideology, denigrated party membership, and treated party leaders with scorn. Michel Aflaq, a Syrian Christian and an original founder of the Ba'thist movement, was kept in seclusion in Baghdad and was posthumously converted to Islam by Saddam. After Operation *Desert Storm*, the process of marginalization gathered momentum. Saddam blamed the party, which w as in total disarray , for allo wing the rebellions in northern and southern Iraq to occur . Its members became tar - gets of the opposition and regime security forces. [14] Saddam began to believe that his regime's survival depended not so much on the middle classes, which throughout the 1970s and 1980s had been the bulwark of his support through the Ba' th Party, but on the tribes. The incentives once doled out to loyal party members now went to tribal leaders in exchange for their loyalty , support, and assistance in maintaining local security.[15]

## Factors Affecting Iraq's Once and Future P olitics

It is unclear what institutions will survive to 2015 in Iraq. By their nature, certain institutions—for example, the military and the intelligence and security services—would seem sure to survive, given any regime's reliance on them for protection and a po wer base. Less certain, however, is the fate of the family, in this case Saddam' s family, and the Ba' th Party. The cult of personality , continual purges of the military and the b ureaucracy, and the changed necessities of a sanctioned Iraq together ha ve virtually eliminated an y party, political, or military institution that in other regional societies and at other times in Iraq pro vided leadership, stability, and some de gree of protection for civil society. Today, no central or single institution still commands the respect of the people, with the possible exception of the military, which historically has played a major role in Iraqi politics. Furthermore, Saddam's one-party state has destroyed or absorbed almost all aspects of civil society—unions, professional organizations, the press, chambers of commerce, and any other independent forms of association. It has tried to weaken, displace, or co-opt traditional patterns of community leadership—the *sayyids* (learned men) and the *shaykhs* (tribal notables). Religious institutions—the Sunni and the established Shia ones—are controlled by the state as well.

Other, more elusive sets of factors will help shape Iraq's future. The first are demographic and economic. Beginning in the early 1980s, war and sanctions weakened the economy and severely reduced the ability of the state to provide for or shelter many of those who depended on its safety net. Deteriorating economic conditions and Saddam's inability to pro vide for his inner circle of supporters almost certainly impelled him in 1996 to accept United Nations (UN) Security Resolution 986—the first oil-for-food resolution—and a return of high oil prices in 1999 probably saved him from harder times. The second factor is more a historical one—tribalism. In many ways, it continues to shape events and loyalties in Iraq as it does in some other Middle Eastern societies. In all cases, regardless of the political future of Iraq, deteriorating economic and social conditions could doom any current and future regime that was less draconian than that of Saddam Husayn.

## *Demographic Trends*

Iraq's population continues to gro w, despite the impact of sanctions. The country no w has more than 22 million people by Baghdad' s estimate, with more than half of the population under 16 years of age. This half of the population essentially has grown up since 1980, with an estimated 40 percent born since 1989. Most Iraqis have known no ruler but Saddam and have no experience but wars, economic deprivation, and sanctions. Most are growing up poor, ill-educated, and with no vision of the future. These Iraqis are not part of the elite around Saddam, many of whom have enriched themselves on sanctions and control of lucrative monopolies. They face a bleak future and see little to encourage them.

Iraq is a socially polarized country, perhaps more now than at any time in its history. Ethnic and religious divisions between Shias and Sunnis, Arabs and Kurds, have sharpened especially since the second Gulf War and the two major uprisings in the south and the north in 1991. The statistics are confusing: ethnically, Arabs are 75 percent of the total population, Kurds are approximately 20 percent, and 5 percent are neither Arab nor Kurd. Religiously, the Shia—Arab and Iranian-origin Shia living primarily in the south and the shrine cities of An-Najaf, Karbala, and Baghdad—comprise 65 percent of the total population of Iraq; Arab Sunnis—Saddam's kind of Iraqi—are less than 20 percent of the population. The Kurds are primarily Sunni, but there are Shia Kurds (*fayli*) and there were Jewish Kurdish tribes as well. Most Kurds live north of the 36th parallel in the area known since 1991 as the security zone in which Iraq's military is forbidden to drive or fly. Iraq's Shia live in central and southern Iraq. No neat division exists between the Sunni and Shia. Shia tribes predominate in large areas of southern Iraq, but many Iraqi tribes, including Saddam's, have Sunni and Shia branches.

## *An Eroding Economy*

The economic situation for Iraqis under war and more than a decade of sanctions has been grim. Before the second Gulf War, Iraq had a gross domestic product (GDP) of $80 billion. Baghdad "borrowed" approximately $80 billion from its oil-rich Gulf neighbors—Kuwait, Saudi Arabia, Qatar, and the United Arab Emirates—to fight the war with Iran. Since the end of the war, the GDP has dropped by an annual average rate of about 6.8 percent. From 1989 to 1996, the gross national product shrank by more than 80 percent, while the population increased by approximately 60 percent. The amount of money Saddam's regime was able to hide away in foreign accounts has not been assessed, although some economists have estimated that the regime siphoned off 15 percent of oil revenues into secret accounts that were used to fund purchases of illicit goods, including acquisition of

WMD technology. The U.S. Government estimates that Baghdad gave up approximately $120 billion in oil revenues in the 1990s rather than comply with UN sanctions and weapons inspections.

What is the social impact of all this on Iraq? The greatest toll, of course, is among the poorer classes. If Iraqi government projections can be believed, thousands of children are dying every year because of sanctions. Numerous international organizations and nongovernmental humanitarian agencies have confirmed these figures, but they receive their data from the Iraqi government. They are not independent collectors, although some have been observers. Although the actual statistics are unknown, the costs of war and sanctions have been and remain high, especially for those not in favor with the regime, for those in the south suspected of rebellious sympathies, and for the apolitical middle and poorer classes. Their suffering is great, and the impact on their negative view of their fate, their future, and their seeming abandonment by the outside world could be long lasting. The middle classes have been literally decimated. One cannot talk about a middle class in Iraq today in the same sense that one did 20 years ago. Many members of the middle classes today have been reduced to conditions of abject poverty. A small section of that class associated with Saddam has grown wealthy from sanctions. But generally, the vast majority of the middle class not associated with the regime has suffered badly.

Deteriorating economic conditions have had a devastating impact on personal and professional loyalties. Once-loyal party members who spent their time and energy promoting and policing the party no longer have the time or energy for these activities. This became very apparent in the 1990s, when because of the economic conditions, a streak of criminal activities pervaded Iraq—carjacking, highway robbery, burglary, beggary, and prostitution. This situation is in stark contrast to Iraq in the 1970s and 1980s when the rule of law, albeit Saddam's law, reigned. One could walk in cities at any hour of the night and feel safe from molestation, attack, and harassment. The state provided security from personal crime, if not from state crime. After 1992–1993, that sense of personal security had completely disappeared because of low wages, lack of jobs, and the high cost of food and other necessities—brought on by sanctions and the regime's control of purchasing and distribution.

Saddam called on the party, which had always seen itself as another arm of security, to protect the streets as it had in 1972, when a psychopath was killing people with an ax—a rare event in contemporary Baghdad. In 6 months, he had killed so many people that the Iraqi government put the army into the street. Alongside the army were members of the Ba'th Party, who routinely patrolled the streets of Baghdad when called upon by Saddam.

This time, Saddam's call prompted little response. Few members of the Ba'th Party went into the streets. Devotees who had once spent much of their time in party activities now needed to hold several jobs to make ends meet. This left little time for revolutionary thoughts and revolutionary activities, even for committed Ba'thists who still believed in party ideals. They could not have stopped the kind of criminality rampant after 1992. Saddam appeared on television twice saying, "Where are the faithful members of the Ba'th Party?" Nothing happened. That lack of response was indicative of the loss of Ba'thist commitment. Party members expected to respond to the Leader's call were actually moonlighting, driving cabs, and working in shops and restaurants to support their families.

The Iraqi government today will claim that the security situation is under control and that the criminals are ethnic and sectarian opponents of the regime who are merely traitors who were picked by Iran. This is very difficult to confirm, since no one can go there and ask about conditions. The few journalists who are allowed into Iraq are taken around by the regime in the south and allowed to visit the north to photograph happy Kurds and Bedouin and starving women and children. They cannot see actual conditions or gauge personal sentiments. They cannot see that the roots of resentment against state and society are very deep in the south and north and that Iraqis can do little in terms of power relationships at this moment. A population that is growing at a rate higher than that of most countries in the region, that is young, impoverished, internally polarized, and externally isolated from the rest of the world, plays into the current and future problems of Iraq.

One factor that is particularly damning for Iraq's future is the abrupt and tremendous decline in educational standards. Most schools in Iraq now operate in three 3-hour shifts a day because buildings are run down and educational materials are not available. Teachers are in short supply because they are paid about $2 a month. University professors are paid the equivalent of $12 a month. Creating one of the most advanced educational systems in the Middle East and setting high standards of education for all Iraqis were significant accomplishments of Saddam Husayn's rule that made Iraq one of the most envied countries in the region. This strong educational base helped to produce the scientists and technicians who developed Iraq's advanced WMD programs. What can the future hold for these Iraqis?

## *The Reinvention Trend: The Party Versus Tribalism*

Tribalism as a theory and a reality shaped Iraqi politics before Iraq was a state, during the years of monarchy and republic, and under Saddam. Large confederations and extended families dominated the political landscape, with loyalties to family, clan, and tribe in many instances superceding those created by 20th-century movements including Ba'thism and the new Iraqi nationalism fostered by Saddam. Tribal ties, in fact, brought Saddam to power—he was a cousin of President Ahmad Hassan al-Bakr as well as the chief enforcer of the Ba'th Party's security force. For Saddam, tribal values and loyalties as well as Ba'thist ideology and Arab nationalism were intended to enforce pride in his and the country's uniqueness. More importantly, they gave the Iraqi leader tools to reinforce his own power and control. Many Iraqi military officers and intelligence and security service officials are recruited from prominent tribes because of their links to President Saddam Husayn's family, clan, and tribe. Their selection also presumes their adherence to traditional values of loyalty, honor, and courage—historic characteristics of the "tribe" that Saddam values highly.[16]

In the 1960s, the party represented, in theory, the new Iraq. It was supposed to appeal to all Iraqis—Sunni, Shia, and Christian, Arab and Kurd. The party was to provide all with special and equal status—meaning membership brought privileges not available to non-party members and accorded Arab and Kurd, Sunni, Christian, and Shia party members the same access to position, education, and other status determinants in the new society. In the early years, party functionaries held high positions in the government and security services.

In contrast, most tribal units claim to trace their roots to a common ancestor or family. In modern, post-revolutionary Iraq, their personal ties were not supposed to promote their status or advancement. However, tribal lineage, symbols, and culture were integrated into the state culture to enhance the status, legitimacy, and power of the ruling elite. This focus has been first and foremost on prehistoric myths and on the Arab Sunni clans and tribes related to Saddam. In 1976, the government ordered Iraqis to drop their tribal/family names to mask how many Tikritis, Dulaymis, and others close to Saddam's clan were in key positions. For the next decade, they would not be identified as at-Tikriti, al-Mosuli, or ad-Duri. The change was temporary.

Saddam used the institution of the Ba'th Party to rise to power, but he reinstated kinship networks to rule Iraq. In the months following Iraq's invasion and occupation of Kuwait, Saddam portrayed himself as an Islamist and a seeker of justice for the Palestinians and the downtrodden of the Arab world. These reinventions had no effect on the internal political dynamic. After the loss of the Gulf War and the abortive rebellions that discredited the party, Saddam revived a tribal policy intended to help him maintain a degree of law and order. He used qualities identified as "tribal" to build loyalty to himself as the Republican Shaykh, the father of his people, the essential Iraqi, and to enable him to rule as tribal godfather, the dispenser of wisdom, justice, wealth, and punishment. He mobilized clan and family networks into the military and security services, giving them control of institutions of coercion, violence, and terror. He rewarded the loyalty of tribal leaders by allowing tribal law to prevail in many areas and bestowing on them guns, cars, and privileges. In return, they acknowledged his leadership. Reports of coup plotting after the war, however, reveal to outsiders the extent to which certain powerful tribal federations and extended families—in particular, the Jabburi, the Dulaymi, and the Ubaydi— had been recruited into the security and intelligence services as well as key military units in the Republican Guard and the Special Republican Guard. These networks extend the narrow base of the ruling elite, provide manpower to help it control the state and society, and bring a semblance of stability to the power structure. Tribal solidarity and values are a source of cohesion, loyalty, and discipline. Most importantly, they provide Saddam with a sense of trust in a normally conspiratorial environment where power struggles are the norm.

## Looking to the Future

If Saddam understands the factors and influence that constitute power in Iraq, so too will a successor. In the decade between the 1958 revolution, which ended the monarchy, and the July 1968 coups, which brought the Ba'th Party directly to power, Iraq experienced four successful coups and several abortive ones. To Saddam and others in the

Ba'thist regime of 1968, the lessons of the previous 10 years taught that power based solely on military officers, party bureaucrats, or government civil servants would not succeed. And subsequent lessons have shown as well that an ideology based solely on Arabism, unity, or economic justice does not bind Iraqis together.

The future would seem bright economically, especially with the discovery of more than 200 billion barrels in new oil reserves. If so, Iraq's current reserve of 112 billion barrels plus the new discovery far exceed those of the current oil power, Saudi Arabia. However, even this kind of potential oil production—even if the Iraqi projection of producing 6-8 million barrels a day by 2010 comes true—may do little to alleviate the economic blows that Iraq has sustained since 1980. If we are looking toward 2015, Iraq will need more than a decade to return to its 1980 level.

Of the following three scenarios for political change in Iraq, one of the first two is more likely to occur than the third.

## *Saddam or Son Continues in Power*

This is the most likely scenario. Saddam has survived more than 30 years in power, including in the last 20 years two major and devastating wars, 10 years of UN-imposed sanctions, the loss of more than $120 billion in oil revenue, and several abortive coups. In 2015, he will be 78 years old. He is, by all accounts, healthy and intent on maintaining power.[17] If he lives, he rules. Iraq has no retirement plan and no tradition of transferring power by other than violent means. If Saddam still rules in 2015, Iraq will remain as it is now, perhaps with the usual concessions to necessary ethnic or tribal blocs, certainly with the collusion of his military and security services. A variant on this scenario is the accession to power of Qusay. Having watched the succession of Bashar al-Asad in Syria and hoping to avoid a family feud between his two sons, Saddam may be preparing the way for Qusay by promoting him to the Ba'th Party Regional Command and placing loyalists from his generation in positions of power in the government and the party bureaucracy. Speculation in 2001 centered on Saddam's relinquishing power to Qusay as a way to end sanctions, but this prospect is highly unlikely. In any event, Qusay would continue the customs and practices of Saddam to consolidate and retain power. He could do no less and feel secure in Baghdad.

## *The Military Takes Over*

While this possibility is less lik ely than the f irst, Iraq's military has played a direct role in state politics since it was created by King Faysal I in 1932. Military of ficers, including Saddam's uncle Khayrallah Talfah,[18] took part in an aborti ve anti-British coup in 1941, and military officers were prominent among the ranks of early Ba'th Party leaders, including General Ahmad Hassan al-Bakr . Despite political indoctrination, countless and continual purges, and forced retirements due to popularity, Iraq's military—its Regular Army and its elite Republican Guard— have remained loyal to Saddam and Iraq. Y et of the coup attempts that have been reported or acknowledged in the last 10 years (there have been at least four), all occurred within the ranks of the Republican Guard, and perhaps even from within the ranks of the Special Republican Guard, although there is no w ay to confirm this. Conventional wisdom holds that the Republican Guard is the b ulwark of Saddam's regime. Its officers and corps come from T ikrit, from tribes that ha ve long been prominent in Iraqi political society and having strong links to Saddam. These coups have not been instigated from or by "outsiders, " as Baghdad usually proclaims, not from Shia units of the Regular Army or by disaffected Ba'thists in Syria.

Before being heartened by this indicator of dissent within Saddam's support base, remember that these were *abortive* coups, made perhaps not for political reasons but for less ideological and more personal ones. There is no sign that any conspirators were unhappy with authoritarian rule, just with Saddam' s authoritarian rule. There are no indications that the dissent in volved hopes for democrac y, civil justice, or political freedom. And none of the abortive coup attempts appears to have come close to succeeding. Even the assassination attempt on Uday in December 1996 may have been more of a personal vendetta than a political statement, opposition claims not withstanding. Conspirators in any of the plots may have been more concerned with loss of economic privileges, monopoly concessions, property, or even women. Some of the conspiracies seem to have been efforts at blood revenge for the murder of a senior military officer and family member who was a member of the Dulaymi or Jabburi tribes. More significantly, the plots had been infiltrated, apparently in their early stages, by the intelligence services. Continuing efforts to remove the regime— regardless of the motivations and the fact that the Republican Guard is the locus of unrest—do not constitute proof of instability or political weakness. Saddam remains in control, and in 2015, we could still be talking about Saddam Husayn, his aging sons, and how they are ruling and ruining the country.

Two traditions are at work in this respect: Iraqi military participation in every coup since 1936, and authoritarian rule, even in the more enlightened days of monarchs and "elected" prime ministers. These traditions are part of Iraq's political culture. Contrary to the popular view, Saddam Husayn is not the inventor or instigator of oppression and authoritarianism in Iraq. Iraq since the 1930s—certainly since the 1936 coup attempt—has been ruled by an authoritarian system that routinely oppressed political opponents, parties, and ethnic groups. During the monarchical period in the 1940s and 1950s—when Iraq had political parties, parliamentary debates, and elections—elections were rigged, people were imprisoned for their political beliefs (especially Communist Party membership), and many were persecuted.

The coup attempts noted above involved prominent military officers as well as important tribal and social figures. If a military coup occurs, the chance of a successor regime that is authoritarian is very high. None of the generals probably have much regard for democratic values or politically liberal practices. They have been schooled in the ways of the Saddam regime and have had their hands bloodied in all his repressive operations against the Iraqi people over the last 30 years. A military coup would be difficult to accomplish and has only a slim chance of succeeding. However, the tradition of attempted intervention by the military is likely to continue.

## *A Democratic Overthrow*

In the third and least likely scenario, peaceful change occurs, instituted or instigated perhaps by opposition groups inside or outside Iraq and helped by the United States and the West. The assumption is that the Iraqi "opposition," in all its diverse elements, will bring democratic institutions, elections, political transparency, and liberal political rule to Iraq. The political programs of most of the groups—the secular, London-based Iraqi National Congress; the Shia-led, Iran-based Supreme Council for the Islamic Republic of Iraq; and the Kurdish groups—all emphasize their adherence to Western-style democracy and the rule of law.[19]

We do not share these assumptions. First, any opposition based outside the country and having little recognition or support within the country would have great difficulty making a revolution, even with support from a superpower or neighbors. Saddam may succumb to a military coup, but Iraq will not collapse because of external forces. Even if a coup were to succeed in Iraq, it is very unlikely that the exiles sitting in London or P aris or Amman would be in vited to take over the government, and even if they were, that they would institute democratic rule. It is interesting to note how authoritarian the opposition groups are, including the self-proclaimed democrats and liberals. The leaders of these groups tolerate no opposition from the others, and personal animosities dominate relations among the groups.

## Ramifications for U.S. Aspirations and Activities

It seems axiomatic that U.S. interests in 2015 would be better served by anyone but Saddam and that Iraqis would be better off under any other leader. Iraq's neighbors, Europe, e ven the UN, will mo ve quickly to recognize a successor to Saddam and hope that quick recognition will ensure political and economic stability . By 2015, this may be moot. Sanctions almost certainly will have been lifted or ignored for years.

Oil and economics, tribes and tribalism will still be important factors in Iraq. A successor regime will probably have to make concessions to prominent economic interests and tribal leaders in order to gain powerful allies, consolidate its rule, and stabilize large parts of Iraq. The successor to Saddam will have to accommodate the anachronistic demands and visions of powersharing of the prominent tribal chiefs with the needs of a modern and potentially wealthy state. He will have to ensure the tribes do not challenge the growth of civil society and associational politics for those Iraqis who do not depend on these extralegal groupings for their well being and survival.

Tribal loyalties will remain difficult to sort out, especially for those unread in tribal history or politics. Many families, including Saddam's, have Sunni and Shia branches in their e xtended family tree. To successfully challenge Saddam in 2005 or 2015, an Iraqi would need to have popular recognition, supporters in military or party bureaucracy, and a netw ork of family and tribal supporters. Saddam has let few Iraqis with these qualifications survive. If the challenger were to succeed, few outside or inside Iraq would question his legitimacy. If the ne w leader had promises or had recei ved outside assistance beforehand, then he would assume continued support. If not, Iraq's neighbors, as well as most European and Asian governments, will not hesitate to recognize the new leader.

The United States will not have much time to consider its options. Swift recognition may help assure regime stability and limit post-regime blood feuds. It will also accord corresponding influence to those governments quick to respond favorably and willing to live with the consequences of their decision. The United States and Iraq's neighbors could be committed to ensuring Iraq's survival and territorial integrity against internal forces determined to weaken central authority or dismantle central government. The issue of Kurdish self-rule almost certainly will remain on the Iraqi political agenda, as will past U.S. and European support and sympathy.

The second Gulf War personalized the relationship between Saddam and the United States into a virtual vendetta on both sides. Will this have changed by 2015? Or, with or without Saddam, will Americans and Iraqis still mistrust each other, and will Iraqis still believe Saddam's accusations that the United States was intent on keeping Iraq weak if not destroying it? It is difficult to see how the perceptions of the generation coming of age under Saddam and sanctions will change radically. Whoever comes to power after Saddam will need legitimacy, whether he is authoritarian or democratic. The only way to gain legitimacy and acceptance is by providing economic improvement and stability to the Iraqis. In this, the United States will be pivotal. Just as Iraqis and many Arabs think that the Americans are strong and powerful enough to keep Saddam in power, they also think that the United States is the greatest economic power and that its economic wishes will be fulfilled. There is probably truth to that belief. If the United States becomes instrumental in Iraq's economic turnaround, then we might have some influence on the kind of political direction the new leadership takes. If we provide the economic and technological assistance Iraq needs to rebuild, open up trade, and even initiate security discussions, then we probably would have some influence in shaping political direction. In any event, the United States should care about what happens in Iraq, because even if Saddam is replaced by another authoritarian regime, the United States probably will have far greater influence on the successor than it has now or will ever have with Saddam.

It is difficult for many observers to see Iraq changing literally overnight into a democratic, liberal society—some Iraqis believe democracy impossible in a country so deeply divided by sectarian and ethnic tensions; others ardently espouse the creation of democratic institutions under the aegis of a coalition government that would see Iraq through the transition to an open society and politics (similar perhaps to the provisional government headed by Afghan leader Hamed Karzai). Change may be coming in the countries neighboring Iraq—for example, Iran, Kuwait, and Syria. We are not sure, however, that the same changes will come to Iraq. The country has been an unforgiving police state for more than 30 years and over the last decade has been in virtual isolation from the rest of the world. Popular attitudes have been shaped by brutality, xenophobia, and mistrust—hardly the kind of environment in which liberal ideas and proclivities can grow. Is there a possibility of change? Yes, but we are not sanguine about it happening by 2015.

## Notes

[1] Saddam's cousin and brother-in-law, Adnan Khayrallah Talfah, and his sons-in-law, Hussein and Saddam Kamil, were once part of this inner circle. All are dead, probably at the order of Saddam. Adnan Khayrallah, then a popular defense minister, was killed in a helicopter crash, and the sons-in-law died in a shoot-out at the family farm. They had defected to Jordan in August 1995 and were lured back to Iraq one year later under an alled amnesty. Saddam claimed their murder was the result of family/tribal justice and not his decree.

[2] Saddam's half-brother Barzan was intelligence minister and chief security thug for several years after the revolution, a position later held by his other half-brothers, Sabawi and Watban; cousins Adnan Khayrallah Talfah and Ali Hassan al-Majid both served as defense minister. Saddam's second son, Qusay, now controls the intelligence and security forces, including the Special Republican Guard.

[3] In 1958, the 21-year-old Saddam attempted to assassinate Iraqi leader Qassim. This heroic exploit is enshrined in Iraqi memory and a museum is dedicated to preserving the bloody shirts, car, and weapons Saddam used as he shot at Qassim and then fled, wounded, across the border to Syrian exile.

[4] In 1979, when Saddam finally assumed open control of Iraq as President, he ordered the execution of many party leaders and long-time associates as well as its leading theoretician, Abd al-Khaliq al-Samarrai, who had been in prison for years.

[5] Israeli scholar Amatzia Baram argues that the party remains an effective institution in Iraqi politics. See "The Ruling Political Elite in Ba'thi Iraq, 1968–1986," *International Journal of Middle East Studies* 21, no. 4 (November 1989), 447–493.

[6] See, instead, Kanan Makiya, *The Republic of Fear* (University of California, 1998) and *Cruelty and Silence* (University of California, 1993).

[7] Author Dawisha admits he "entertained such foolish ideas."

[8] This judgment derives from comments by dissidents fleeing Iraq in September 1996 after Iraqi troops entered Irbil and arrested many regime opponents seeking safe haven among the Kurds and above the 36$^{th}$ parallel, which marked the no-fly, no-drive zone for the three predominantly Kurdish provinces of northern Iraq. Baghdad had been invited to attack by Kurdish Democratic Party chief Masoud Barzani, who wanted Saddam to contain his Kurdish rival Jalal Talabani, head of the Patriotic Union of Kurdistan.

[9] Adeed Dawisha, comments at conference on *The Middle East in Transition: the Persian Gulf*, held at the National Defense University, Washington, DC, on January 21, 2000.

[10] In "elections" in April 2000, Uday received 99 percent of the vote cast for members of the Assembly but failed in his bid to become Speaker. His ambition was foiled by Saddam, who apparently felt it was more important for former prime minister Sadun Hammadi, a Shia and a prominent Ba'thist, to remain Speaker of the National Assembly. Uday did not attend a session of the Assembly until December 2000.

[11] Both Uday's uncle Watban and cousin Hussein Kamil had been criticized in *Babil*, Uday's newspaper, criticism Kamil took as a warning to leave Iraq in 1995.

[12] The Hashimite Kingdom of Iraq lasted from its invention by the British in 1920 through the assassination of King Faysal II in 1958. Prime ministers, regents, and generals usually wielded more power than the monarchs, their cabinets, or parliaments. Nuri al-Said, prime minister in the 1940s and 1950s, despised the National Assembly, which he saw as too democratic, and he tried to manipulate its members and authority. He was murdered in the 1958 revolution while trying to flee Baghdad dressed as a woman. See Phebe A. Marr, *The Modern History of Iraq* (Boulder: Westview Press, 1990) for the most accurate accounting of Iraq's turbulent political history.

[13] See Adeed Dawisha, "Identity and Political Survival in Saddam's Iraq," *Middle East* 53, no. 4 (Autumn 1999), 553–567; and Marr, *The Modern History of Iraq*, 226–227.

[14] Dawisha, "Identity and Political Survival in Saddam's Iraq."

[15] For additional discussion on the tribal factor in Iraqi politics, see Amatzia Baram, "Neo-Tribalism in Iraq: Saddam Hussein's Tribal Policies, 1991–1996," *International Journal of Middle East Studies* 29 (February 1997), 1–31; and Judith S. Yaphe, "Tribalism in Iraq, the Old and the New," *Middle East Policy* 7, no. 3 (June 2000), 51–58.

[16] Ibid.

[17] Opposition reports in summer 2000 claimed that Saddam had cancer and was undergoing treatment by European doctors who arrived by French or Russian planes allegedly defying the embargo and making humanitarian flights into Baghdad.

[18] Talfah was a staunch anti-British Arab nationalist whose singular contributions to Iraq's history, besides the 1941 coup attempt, were a book entitled *Three Things God Should Not Have Made: Persians, Flies, and Jews*, and a reputation for venality so excessive that Saddam had to remove him as mayor of Baghdad.

[19] See, for example, the political agenda of the Iraqi National Congress at <www.Iraqinationalcongress.com or www.iraqfoundation.com>.

---

*This chapter is based on a paper that was presented at a conference on* The Middle East in Transition: The Persian Gulf, *which was held at the Institute for National Strategic Studies, National Defense University, Washington, DC, on January 21, 2000.*

Chapter 9

# The Arab Gulf: Will Autocracy Define the Social Contract in 2015?

## F. Gregory Gause III and Jill Crystal

This chapter examines the nature, processes, and pace of change that are likely to occur in the countries comprising the Gulf Cooperation Council (GCC): Saudi Arabia, Kuwait, Bahrain, Qatar, the United Arab Emirates, and Oman. It also considers the factors and traditions that will probably continue to shape decisionmaking well into the 21st century. The first part of this chapter focuses on identifying key indicators that analysts can use to judge the direction of Saudi political life. It concludes by considering how these processes of change might affect U.S.-Saudi relations over the next 15 years. The second part concentrates on the five smaller GCC states.

*F. Gregory Gause III is associate professor of political science at the University of Vermont and director of the University's Middle East Studies Program. Dr. Gause is the author of* Oil Monarchies: Domestic and Security Challenges in the Arab Gulf States *(1994) and* Saudi-Yemeni Relations: Domestic Structures and Foreign Influence *(1990).*

*Jill Crystal is associate pr ofessor of political science at A uburn University. Her publications include* Oil and Politics in the Gulf *(1995) and* Kuwait: The Transformation of an Oil State *(1992) and "Civil Society in the Arab Gulf States," in* Civil Society in the Middle East *(1995).*

## Identifying Change in Saudi Arabia

The analyst of Saudi Arabia is presented with an interesting paradox when thinking about the prospects for "change" in the Kingdom. On one level, Saudi Arabia seems to have changed little over the past 30 years. The same people, literally, are making the decisions now as made them in 1970. Caution and incrementalism characterize daily decisionmaking. The Saudi leadership's emphasis on their country's adherence to tradition and strict interpretation of the Hanbali school of law underscores the conservative nature of Saudi society.

Yet, on another level, no country in the Middle East has changed more in the past few decades than Saudi Arabia. It has gone from being very poor to very rich to somewhat rich. It has gone from having a predominantly rural population to an overwhelmingly urban one. It has gone from distressingly low levels of literacy to a substantially educated population. While Saudi Arabia's leaders have remained essentially the same, the Saudi population has witnessed enormous change.

Therefore, when talking about change in Saudi Arabia, we have to be careful in defining just what we mean. Some analysts focus exclusively on the extreme scenario of regime change via social revolution or military coup. Of course, a regime change in Saudi Arabia would be extremely important, but it is not likely in the near to medium term. Focusing primarily on regime change obscures less dramatic but important change on other levels of Saudi politics and society. Transformations in state-society relations, economic trends, shifts within the Saudi regime, and changes in Saudi foreign policy all stand to exert a significant impact on Saudi Arabia's long-term direction.

This chapter assesses the processes of change that are likely to occur in Saudi Arabia over the next decade. It identifies key indicators that analysts can use to judge the direction of Saudi political life. It concludes by considering how these processes of change might affect U.S.-Saudi relations over the next 15 years.

### *Processes of Change: Incremental Change*

Two different processes of change are important to understand when assessing Saudi political, social, and economic life. The first is continuous incremental change that is extrapolated from existing trends. These changes are relatively easy for analysts to discern, though their potential consequences are unclear. The second is discontinuous, sharp, and sudden change. These kinds of changes are, by their nature, extremely difficult to anticipate. Five areas are likely to undergo continuous incremental change that will have a substantial cumulative impact on political, social, and economic realities in Saudi Arabia are demographics, education, political opposition, the private sector, and the ruling family .

*Demographic Change.* Population growth rates in Saudi Arabia are among the highest in the world—3.04 percent per year as of 2000. Even if we assume that overall population figures are somewhat exaggerated by the Saudis for domestic and regional political reasons, we can anticipate that the Saudi population will be considerably larger in 15 years' time. At current rates of increase, it is expected to double in 23 years. In 2000, 42 percent of the total Saudi population w as 15 years of age or younger .[1] As a result, an enormous demographic bulge in the younger age categories will continue to work its way through the school system and into the workforce over the next decade. The immediate consequences of this demographic change are clear: greater demands on the aging Saudi infrastructure (for example, schools, roads, electricity, water, health care), and thus greater demands on the Saudi state. Indeed, population growth is a major factor driving the cautious economic reform efforts in the Kingdom. While the demographic boom could stimulate the Saudi economy by providing a larger market for domestic industry , the Saudi state will also need to provide more services and create more jobs with fewer per capita resources than in the past.

Financing these services is a major challenge. W e already are seeing efforts by the Saudis to increase user fees for goods and services, including electric rates, gasoline prices, and health care for expatriates. Privatizing state-owned service industries will mean increased prices and, perhaps, increased ef ficiencies. New infrastructure investments will require large amounts of private capital, because the Saudi state no longer has the resources to upgrade the power and water sectors. Corporate taxes reportedly have been considered, although this option is still in the conceptual stage and far from implementation. In any event, demographic realities assure that these issues will not go away any time soon.

Is "Saudization" of the workforce a desirable goal? The number and role of foreign workers in the Kingdom is a key issue that will be affected by the demographic boom. Saudi officials have been calling for increased hiring of Saudi nationals in private sector jobs. Approximately 75 percent of the estimated 8 million workers in Saudi Arabia are foreign, many of whom work for low pay and have no job security. Saudi employers are reluctant to hire Saudi w orkers because they demand higher salaries and are harder to control than foreign workers; the government will have to provide the private sector significant incentives to encourage hire of Saudi workers. Over the next 15 years, the number of foreign workers will surely decrease, at least at the middle management level, as some of these jobs go to Saudis. Foreign workers have always been marginal in the Saudi political equation. The ease with which the government expelled hundreds of thousands of Y emenis in 1990 testif ies to their political irrelevance.

But the increasing role of Saudis in the workforce, particularly the private sector workforce, could have two important consequences by 2015. First, the integration of Saudis into the workforce will require some kind of negotiation of the social compact with the Saudi private sector that increases that sector' s economic and political po wer. This could lead, in turn, to greater influence for a burgeoning Saudi nonroyal middle class and a lessening of influence for the peripheral members of the Al Sa'ud f amily. Second, o ver the longer term, more Saudis in the private sector workforce could lead to a shift in the organizational focus of Saudi political life. Saudis mobilize politically around "cultural" political issues, such as the role of Islam in the state. Saudis working in the private sector might reorient their demands around economic issues, as Saudi labor in the oil sector did in the 1950s. However, such a shift w ould be predicated on a substantial change in employment patterns. Demographic forces are pushing that wa y, but other factors could work against this kind of change.

*Education.* Changes in education parallel the demographic boom. As the population grows, so will the number of literate citizens who have had at least some formal education in schools. They certainly will not share a single political viewpoint—not all will be strict Islamists nor will the y be "Western-style liberals" (that is, adv ocates of Western political institutions or practices). Man y Saudis will ha ve graduated from the Islamic university system with degrees in Islamic law, sciences, or religious studies. As literate and educated citizens, they should have the tools to engage in a more active and organized political life. They can more easily access sources of information and authority outside the control of the state, whether low-tech sources such as books, pamphlets, and petitions, or high-tech sources such as the Internet. The expansion of literacy is occurring contemporaneously with the expansion through technology of the sources of information available to readers and viewers. Over the next 15 years, the Saudi population likely will become more politically discerning and critical in its evaluation of the government.

Graduates of the Saudi school system have been taught to take a national, rather than a regional or tribal, view of their political loyalties. They have been exposed, at least at the university level, to contacts that cut across the old ascriptive ties. Not only will the Saudi educational system produce more literate citizens, but it will also encourage them to eschew narrowly based client-patron ties and form attachments that cut across older social divisions. [2]

These ideas do not necessarily mean that Saudi Arabia will see a blossoming of political activism over the next 15 years. Translating political interest into mass-based activity is difficult. It requires organizational networks over which the Saudi state continues to exercise substantial control. Yet it does mean that the pool of Saudis who are potentially mobilizable for political activism will grow, and the Saudi regime will face an increasingly sophisticated and potentially critical public.

*The Opposition.* To the extent that organized, mass-based movements affect the Saudi political scene over the next decade, they will remain centered in the Islamic establishment. While demographic, educational, and economic changes might open the door down the road to new forms of political organization, for now the Islamic establishment is the only place where there are the organizational resources and the social space required for bottom-up political organizing. Islamic activism is a force that could draw the Saudi leadership away from the United States on many foreign policy issues, particularly on public displays of alliance with America, and on sensitive political issues, such as the Arab-Israeli peace process, that are marginal to immediate Saudi security concerns. The extent to which such movements appear will depend on numerous factors, including the success of government monitoring and coercion, the state of the economy, and unpredictable regional factors. But if such movements do appear over the next 15 years, they will likely be "Islamist" in orientation.

*The Private Sector.* The private sector will inevitably grow in political and economic importance over the next 15 years. The private sector will have to employ more Saudis, generate more wealth, purchase state industries, and invest in the Saudi infrastructure. To entice it to do those things, the regime will have to pay more attention to the private sector and give it a greater role in the decisionmaking process. The private sector is already exerting greater influence in some economic areas, such as in the preparations for Saudi Arabia to join the World Trade Organization.

The private sector possesses the organizational capacity to act as an interest group through the system of regional chambers of commerce and the national-level council of chambers, but it does not behave as a force for regime opposition. On the contrary, the business community relies on the state and wants to work with it. Tensions will emerge on a range of issues as the role of the private sector in the economy grows—for example, employment of Saudis, taxation, the judiciary (particularly the role of shari'ah courts in contract law), and the role of the ruling family in the business world. These tensions likely will be resolved within the existing consultative framework between the political leadership and the business community. The private sector will continue for the next 15 years to be a force pushing the Saudis toward greater economic openness and reform. A shift in the attitude of the business community toward the regime—in which private business either gives up on the regime or begins to see itself in opposition to the regime—will be a signal of serious problems ahead.

*The Ruling Family.* If the general Saudi population grows substantially over the next 15 years, proportionately the Al Sa'ud themselves will grow at an even faster rate. This "boom" within the Al Sa'ud will necessitate a redefinition of family membership, including a reassessment of the role of marginal members of the family. These changes will be particularly critical in the business realm. Will marginal members of the ruling family be able to claim exemptions from judicial rulings in contract disputes? Will they have an unfair advantage in competing for state contracts against "commoner" businessmen? Dissent within the family over such a redefinition could create political problems for the Saudi leadership and could contribute to factionalization of that leadership.

These incremental, practically irreversible trends will change the environment of Saudi politics over the next 15 years, but not in ways that will present immediate threats to the stability of the regime. Because these trends are well known in the Kingdom, they will not surprise the top decisionmakers. What these trends will do is define the agenda of Saudi politics—with economic and employment issues playing a much larger role and with the role of the Al Sa'ud in the private sector broadly understood as requiring increased attention. These trends will also change the context in which political decisions are made, because Saudi decisionmakers will be facing an increasingly literate and informed public that has the resources to organize politically. These trends do not pose an y major challenges to the U.S.–Saudi bilateral relationship. The y do, however, hold out the prospect that Saudi leaders (looking to burnish their nationalist, Arabist, and Islamist credentials with that increasingly literate and informed public) might want to distance themselves from controversial U.S. policies in the Middle East more generally—on the Arab-Israeli front and on Iraq most immediately .

## *Processes of Change: Discontinuous Change*

The second kind of change that can occur in Saudi Arabia is discontinuous change—that is, e vents that will happen suddenly , without warning, and will alter the political landscape within the Kingdom.

*The Price of Oil.* The world oil market experienced drastic price fluctuations during the 1990s, most dramatically at the end of the decade. Oil prices, after falling by more than one-third from 1997 through 1998, nearly quadrupled in 2000. These price fluctuations have had an enormous impact on the Saudi fiscal situation. During the 1980s and early 1990s, the Saudis had fiscal cushions to ride out oil price fluctuations. They drew down the substantial financial reserves that they had built up in the 10 years after the 1973 price increases. They borrowed domestically from wealthy Saudi banks. Even as oil prices fell in the 1980s, the Saudis maintained high levels of government spending and contributed substantial amounts to the Iraqi war effort against Iran. Operation *Desert Storm* wiped out most of their financial reserves, and continued deficit spending in the 1990s drove their internal debt level to more than 100 percent of the gross domestic product (GDP), well above the guidelines for fiscal stability recommended by international financial agencies. In effect, by the end of the 1990s, the Saudis were more dependent upon their yearly oil revenues to finance government spending than at any time in the previous 25 years.

With oil prices declining and the ability of the state to f inance its deficits severely reduced, 1998 was a particularly bad year for the Saudi treasury. Hedge fund managers be gan to speculate against the Saudi *riyal*, betting that the balance of payments deficit would force a devaluation. The Saudi government had to use the borrowing power of Saudi Aramco, the state oil compan y, to tap the international capital markets for loans. Also, in December 1998, the government worked a currency swap with the United Arab Emirates to bolster its hard currency holdings. This "stealth" fiscal crisis drove the Saudis to take the lead among the Organization of Petroleum Exporting Countries (OPEC) and non-OPEC oil producers in arranging the production cut agreement of March 1999 that led to significant price increases (in conjunction with an earlier than expected recovery in East Asian oil demand).

A continuation of the current high prices could reduce the impetus for economic reform within the Kingdom. More importantly , price decreases could have serious political consequences, as the Saudis no longer have the resources to ride them out. Price decreases could lead to tensions with the United States if the Saudis work to push prices up when Washington might not fa vor that course. Price decreases also could lead to conflicts within the elite about the direction to take to meet the subsequent fiscal crisis, whether to cut government spending and impose immediate costs on the population or to take the financial risks that deficit spending entails. Lower oil prices do not immediately translate into popular discontent or upheaval, but they certainly contribute to public grumbling.

*Succession.* It is entirely possible that the next 15 years will pass without any serious succession issues in the leadership of the Kingdom. There are plausible candidates for kingship from the generation of Abd al-Aziz' s sons who are no w in their early- to mid-60s, and thus the succession might continue to work its way through that generation. But it is also possible that the next 15 years will see the switch in the succession line to the generation of Abd al-Aziz' s grandsons. No blueprint exists for how that shift will be accomplished. T ransferring the succession to the next generation will be a momentous decision within the Al Sa'ud family because it will affect the prospects of many ambitious and powerful people for the remainder of their lives. While the family has long displayed a talent for sticking together and preventing their differences from becoming public, the earlier history of the Al Sa'ud contains numerous precedents of serious intrafamily political fights, the most recent being the struggle between King Sa'ud and Crown Prince Faysal in the late 1950s and early 1960s that ended in 1964 with Sa'ud's deposition by a family council and Faysal's assumption of the kingship.[3]

*External Environment.* The Saudis enjoy a more benign regional environment now than at any time in the previous century. Saddam Husayn remains a problem, but his ability to pose a significant military threat to the Saudis is much reduced. Tehran has greatly reduced its efforts to spread its revolutionary version of Islam into the Arabian Peninsula and is now seeking improved state-to-state relations with Riyadh. Despite periodic bumps in the road, the Arab-Israeli peace process could move once again in a direction that reduces the chances of regional upheaval and helps the Saudis maintain their close ties to the United States. The breakdown in Israeli-Palestinian negotiations and renewal of the *intifada* in September 2000 for the first time clearly linked that crisis to U.S. policies in the Gulf in the minds of the Saudis. While the Saudis, like all the Arab governments, supported the Palestinians and condemned Israel at a special meeting of the Arab League in Cairo in October, 2000, they clearly were not enthusiastic for declaring *jihad*, as Saddam Husayn urged. The Saudis supported the Clinton administration's proposal for peace in 2000, probably because it called on Israel to cede control of the Haram al-Sharif and other predominantly Arab and Muslim sections of the Old City of Jerusalem to the Palestinian Authority. Crown Prince Abdullah's proposal made to the Arab League summit in Beirut in March 2002 included similar terms—normalization of relations for Israel in exchange for withdrawal to its positions on June 4, 1967 (that is, withdrawal from the Old City, Gaza, and the West Bank).

One can imagine scenarios where external regional events could have an impact on Saudi domestic politics and foreign policy (for example, an Islamist revolution in Egypt or a renewal of Arab-Israeli war), but they do not seem to be likely at this time. A more likely regional crisis is a civil war in a post-Saddam Iraq that leads to a wider regional conflict. The Saudis would inevitably be dragged into such a conflict, if not militarily, then certainly politically. But it is unlikely that such an Iraqi scenario would have a significant spillover effect into Saudi domestic politics.

No one of these discontinuous changes could shake the basic regime stability in Saudi Arabia. In combination, ho wever, they might present a serious threat to the regime. If a serious fiscal crisis were to occur contemporaneously with a regional crisis that had spillover effects into Saudi domestic politics, and if there were divisions over succession within the Al Sa'ud, then the elements for significant regime instability would be in place. Similar circumstances prevailed during the Sa'ud-Faysal crisis, and the Kingdom was fortunate to emerge from that episode. Any one of these discontinuous changes could lead to a rocky period in U.S.-Saudi relations. Fiscal crisis might lead to Saudi efforts to manipulate oil pricing and production in ways that Washington might find unacceptable. Saudi polic y toward the United States would inevitably become tied up with any serious internal splits within the ruling elite, e ven if Washington took great pains to remain aloof from Saudi factional struggles. A regional Middle Eastern crisis could lead the Saudis, as has happened before, to appease regional actors and trends that the United States opposes.

## *Indicators of Change*

Four key indicators provide hints about the direction of Saudi domestic policies and politics.

*The Women's Issue.* The role of w omen is a k ey symbolic issue in the debate o ver the direction of Saudi society . It has become the marker for a whole range of issues stemming from the ability of the Kingdom to adjust to domestic change as well as changes in its relationship with the rest of the world. Important groups, including some within the ruling family, have made the greater inte gration of Saudi women into society and t he economy a centerpiece of their more general reform efforts. Others, most notably the religious establishment and members of the ruling family , have staked out this issue as the place to resist what they see as the secularization and W esternization of Saudi Arabia.

It would be wrong to focus on the *cause célèbre* of the Gulf War—that is, w omen's driving—as the core of this issue. Those demanding greater rights for women will leave that emotion-laden topic aside and concentrate on less inflammatory elements, such as workplace access and the role of w omen in the economy more generally . The 1999 decision to allow women to obtain their own citizen identity cards, albeit without photos, is an interesting first step in this direction. If the driving issue is raised, it will be in a piecemeal fashion—women being able to drive with family members, during working hours, in certain areas of the Kingdom, with permission from their families. More telling, although women comprise more than 50 percent of the student population, especially at the university level, less than 5 percent are in the Saudi workforce.

The framing of this debate is key. If the reformers are going to win, they have to frame the issue as one of economics. Women represent a critical, untapped potential that could make an important contribution if they are integrated into the Saudi workforce. Integrating them into the economy would reduce dependence on foreign labor and reduce the Saudi balance of payments deficit (fewer foreign workers means fewer remittances). If the conservatives are going to win, they have to frame the issue as one of morality. The side that can define the debate on this question will be able to define the debate on a whole range of other social and economic issues. It bears close scrutiny as an indicator of the direction of Saudi society.

*The Fiscal Situation.* The status of the government budget is a key indicator of whether the Saudi government can alter the current, unsustainable relationship between increasing demands for government spending and an almost exclusive reliance on oil for government revenue. If the government cannot control spending, a fiscal crisis of serious consequences, such as devaluation of the *riyal* or inflationary spurts, looms.

In 1998, the year of the "stealth" fiscal crisis, the government budget deficit was approximately 45 billion Saudi *riyal* (SR) ($12 billion), about 25 percent of the total budget and about 9 percent of GDP. Despite announced plans in the middle of 1998 to cut spending in light of the decline in oil prices, actual 1998 spending was almost exactly what was budgeted. In 1999, with oil prices improving markedly, there was plenty of money to go around in Saudi government circles. Still, the government budget recorded a 34 billion SR deficit ($9.1 billion), about 19 percent of the total budget and about 6.5 percent of GDP. With the revenue bonanza, the government overspent its targets by 16 billion SR, about 10 percent of the original planned expenditures. Moreover, the government's revenue estimates were based on a price of oil lower than the yearly average. With only sketchy, preliminary figures released by the Saudi government, it is difficult to determine how the extra money was spent.

These two budget years, one with low oil prices and one with rising oil prices, point to a number of problems in the Saudi fiscal situation. The obvious problem is overreliance on oil revenues to fund government expenditure. The inability of the Saudi government to manage expenditures—to cut spending when it says it is going to cut spending—and the large fluctuations between estimated revenue and actual revenue in times of oil market instability are equally troubling. Realistic budgets with more transparent accounting procedures are a necessary part of the economic transformation of the Kingdom. International financial and economic institutions will demand it. Domestic and foreign investors will demand it. Citizens will demand it. Can the Kingdom's political leaders learn to live with such a radical change in the way the government keeps its books and writes its checks?

*Private Saudi Money.* Can wealthy Saudis be persuaded to invest in the domestic economy to a greater extent than they do now? The money is there, and the need for domestic investment in the Saudi economy, particularly infrastructure projects, is clear. The level of domestic private investment will be an excellent indicator of economic confidence for those who know the country best. Indications that Saudi investors are repatriating capital, as domestic investment opportunities grow, would be an excellent sign of confidence. Conversely, Saudi failure to attract the capital of domestic investors would be a disturbing sign.

*Splits in the Ruling Family.* Open conflicts among senior members of the Al Sa'ud on succession issues or important public policy issues would constitute an important warning sign that serious regime instability could be in the offing. This indicator must not be confused with the constant rumors of palace intrigue that are the stuff of any closed, monarchical system. This indicator refers to conflicts within the family that become too public to deny, on the model of the Sa'ud-Faysal struggle. If the ruling family divides into factions publicly, those factions will look to mobilize support throughout society, opening up the political field to social movements that, once mobilized, might not be controllable from the top. Worst-case scenarios of serious political instability in Saudi Arabia begin with irreconcilable splits among the ruling elite.

## Patterns of Change and the Future of U.S.-Saudi Relations

The incremental changes sketched out above will not have an immediate effect on U.S.-Saudi relations. None change the fundamental mutual interests that tie the two governments together. The Saudis need to accommodate economic change in the face of demographic growth. Oil market uncertainties underscore the importance of Riyadh's ties to the United States, the world's leading economic power. The social changes resulting from these incremental trends could drive the Saudi leadership to seek some public distance from U.S. policies in the region to prove its independence to the increasingly politically aware Saudi population. Already we see a less intense and less public level of coordination between Washington and Riyadh than was true 10 years ago. Unlike their smaller GCC neighbors, the Saudis continue to worry about an American military presence on their soil. When changing circumstances reduce the need for Operation *Southern Watch*, we can expect an almost immediate Saudi request to redeploy those American forces outside the Kingdom (though the Saudis are now more willing than before 1990 to see American forces permanently stationed in the Gulf itself, just not in Saudi Arabia). Particularly on issues that the Saudis do not see as central to their own security, such as the Arab-Israeli peace process (and particularly Jerusalem), we can expect to see Riyadh take positions that are at variance from those of the United States. But this scenario is in many ways a return to the pre-1990 situation, not a drastic change in U.S.-Saudi relations.

The most serious disruption in the relationship, of course, would come from a sudden change of regime in Saudi Arabia. If there were revolutionary regime change, the new regime would inevitably distance itself from the United States. It would still sell oil to American companies because any Saudi government will need oil revenues to survive, but it would delink itself from the United States on the political and military levels. It is unlikely that any one of the discontinuous changes described above could lead to such a revolutionary regime change. Contemporaneous crises in the fiscal, family, and foreign policy areas could lead to a regime-threatening scenario, but the chances of such a coincidence of crises must be considered low. The worst-case scenario is also the *least* likely scenario.

Within the context of regime continuity, the most likely scenario for a crisis in U.S.-Saudi relations revolves around Saudi oil policy. If the Saudi government is unable to alter the fiscal pattern of the last three decades—almost exclusive reliance on oil for government revenue and ever-increasing demands on state spending driven by the demographic surge—then Riyadh will have to rely on higher oil prices to fund its day-to-day expenses. It cannot draw down financial reserves as it did in the 1980s. It is reaching its limits in terms of domestic borrowing. Tensions are just beginning to emerge in the United States over Saudi oil policy in the price run-up of 1999. Should a similar set of circumstances occur at a time when the U.S. economy is not as robust as it is now, the pressures within the United States for a more confrontational policy toward Saudi Arabia on oil issues will be even greater.

## Identifying Change in the Smaller Arab Gulf States

Trends that will affect Saudi Arabia will also affect Kuwait, Bahrain, Qatar, the United Arab Emirates (UAE), and Oman, members with Saudi Arabia of the GCC. In particular, social trends revolving around demographic, economic, and political issues could affect the internal balance of power in these societies (among tribes, sects, classes, and other groups) or bring new actors (for example, women and a new generation) to the forefront of politics.

### Economic Trends

Two related but distinct economic issues shape politics in the Gulf today and will continue to do so in the coming decade: globalization and economic restructuring. Globalization is probably the less significant of the two issues. In the Gulf, globalization is not new; oil globalized these economies decades ago. Nonetheless, states will have to think about globalization as they attempt to diversify and develop markets abroad. Their modest efforts to export products or services other than oil have already alerted them to the vulnerability that globalization creates (that is, the Asian financial crisis and Russian economic problems).

*Economic restructuring* is the larger problem. It involves cutting costs and raising revenues. Absent much higher oil prices, we will see through 2015 the continuation of the austerity measures of the past decade as states introduce new policies: limiting the provision of public services by cutting public subsidies, restricting access to public services, allowing public services to deteriorate, and curbing state employment. These policies will fall disproportionately upon some groups, in particular public sector employees, women, the poor and middle class. But where they fall is, to a degree, a matter of state policy and thus within the government's control.

*Raising revenues* is the second issue. The coming years will see discussion about diversification to create new engines of growth but little actual movement. The region's economies will continue to be dominated by oil, even if (as in Bahrain or Oman) that means dominated by the oil of other oil-producing states. States will find it hard to change the dominant sector owing to limitations of resources, potential, and state capacity. The local private sector is too weak and tied to the state to do it itself. Foreign capital has little to attract it outside the oil sector, and its ventures into other areas elsewhere in the region (for example, sports tourism in Bahrain) have not been overwhelmingly successful. Weak though the local business community is, it will use its efforts to try to limit foreign capital.

Consequently, what we are likely to see are efforts to raise *government* revenues in the form of more taxes. This may take the form of income taxes, but since these have created opposition in the past, we will more likely see an increase in user fees. The key question here will be who gets taxed. There has been some effort in each state to tax foreigners (for example, in health services, or a tax on hiring expatriates), but the limits to such taxes are quickly reached and in any event are at cross-purposes with efforts to attract foreign investment. User fees tend to hit the middle class hardest, and taxing ordinary people will draw attention back to money spent on civil list and other ruling family subsidies.

A related issue is dealing with the concomitant international pressure to move in the direction of the market economy and to shift tasks from the public to the private sector. Here, the trend will likely be for governments carefully to allow more foreign capital into the oil sector, to turn some noncrucial tasks over to the private sector in an effort to save money, and to embrace some degree of a market ideology in an effort to legitimize austerity measures (that is, telling citizens, in effect, that the economic problems they face are the result of the market, not state policy, thus absolving the state of some of the blame for economic bad times). Nonetheless, there will be no significant enduring moves toward the private sector, because regimes have relatively little to gain and much to lose in terms of the political control that flows from control of the economy, because sooner or later these privatized firms will get into trouble and, because, since their owners are well placed, the government will bail them out by buying into the businesses, as has historically occurred in Kuwait. It is important to remember that moves to market are not irreversible.

This expansion of the market, however tempered and self-serving, nevertheless creates two kinds of tension. First, it af fects people's interests: there are winners and losers, and it is useful to identify the losers to determine whether they are likely to organize and form coalitions and whether the government is likely to identify and co-opt them. Some of the big losers include specific groups in the bureaucracy who either have done relatively well by state employment compared to their prospects in the private sector or are likely to get cut first. In the Gulf, this includes women, minorities, Shias, some tribes, the elderly, and state employees generally. One consequence may be an emer ging tendency for opposition to organize around sectors perhaps through clientele networks, in turn possibly precipitating a corporatist response from the government.

Of course, there are also winners in the privatization process. These include some members of the b usiness community, but here there is much variation from state to state. In some states (for example, Kuwait and perhaps Dubai) where the indigenous business community is relatively strong, elements of the business community may push for more economic liberalization, albeit a liberalization that includes partnership with the government. Divisions could emerge between those merchants situated in one sector (whose interests lie primarily in rent seeking) who will lobby the state, and those with diverse interests and more capital who may be in a position to shape broad policy and possibly would be more interested in economic liberalization.

In other states, where the private sector is weak and co-opted, the ruling family is best placed to move in should economic liberalization occur. Their presence will undercut real mo ves toward liberalization. This is quite likely to occur in Qatar, for example. Moreover, where the b usiness community is weak, it will be less able to prevent policies aimed at limiting the number of expatriate workers by hiring nationals, a prohibitively expensive restraint on emerging private sector even with help. The point, again, is that people's interests will be af fected by these changes, and we can expect that those whose interests are hurt will attempt to organize to protect those interests.

The move toward the market also precipitates a debate over values: whether economic growth at all costs should be the primary goal or whether other values (such as job security, the environment, sustainable communities, and community values) also should be goals. This debate about values is a central if often less visible element of the globalization process today. During the Cold War, the two ideological choices were clear, as were the policy prescriptions. If people are attracted to communism, a little attention to social justice (for example, land reform outside the Gulf) might be a good thing. But today it is unclear what the alternative to the market is. The market appears hegemonic now largely because the opposition to it is disorganized, but this should not be confused with an all-encompassing embrace of the market.

In the Gulf there is no particular ideological commitment to the market and no consensus on its values. There is certainly no interest in letting the market set the price of oil. To the extent that the move toward the market deepens, it will be accompanied by a debate over the values implicit in the market. In focusing on interests, on the losers in the globalization process, we should not ignore this battle over values. The Islamists have staked a claim to this issue already, condemning materialism and linking it to corruption and royal excess. If economic restructuring actually occurs, one result may be a heightened ideological dimension to politics as a debate over values emerges. We should not confuse the real efforts at economic restructuring with acceptance of the market, and if ideologues can organize those whose interests as well as values are affected, this could be an important element of political debate. If states become more open politically, this is likely to appear as a debate over whether decisions related to growth should be made by the market rather than the state or perhaps even through a democratic process. We see a hint of this in Kuwait in recent debates over investment legislation.

Oil prices of course affect the severity of these trends. Lower prices will heighten pressures to introduce austerity measures and to privatize; higher prices will simply delay this. But prices themselves are largely out of the hands of the GCC states, turning instead on what the Saudis are willing to do and more broadly on market forces—especially changes in the U.S. economy—and the likelihood of current growth rates continuing into the future.

## Social Trends

To understand the impact of these changes, we need to think about which social groups are important. Two kinds of groups are worth examining: identity groups and interest groups. Interest groups (that is, groups based on economic interests) form along lines of class and sector. In terms of class, business and labor are worth thinking about in the Gulf. In most Gulf states (except perhaps Kuwait and the UAE), the old business community (the pre-oil merchant elite) was replaced in the postwar period by a new business elite, economically dependent on and subordinate to the state. Whatever its origins, the first interest of this class is its economic well-being. It assures that interest by lobbying the state (thus shaping policy formulation) and by colonizing the state bureaucracy (shaping policy implementation). As a result, it has mixed feelings about the market. If economic liberalization continues apace, this class might well divide. On one side would be those with more capital and diverse business interests (generally, the older established business families), who stand to benefit from and thus favor economic liberalization. On the other side would be those with interests lodged primarily in one sector who might prefer to stick with rent seeking and would lobby the state to limit economic liberalization, perhaps by working with state employees of the same clan or tribe (as the Najdis have prevented economic reforms in Saudi Arabia).

It is a popular misconception that this class is pro-democratic; it is not. Even in Kuwait, this class has for the most part been uninterested in electoral politics. Elsewhere, it is so tied up with antiroyalist sentiments (Qatar) or antiregime sentiments (Bahrain) that it is hard to gauge the depth of democratic sentiment. Generally, because the strategy of working with and through the state bureaucracy has been largely successful in persuading rulers to protect core merchant interests, merchants continue to support the rulers. This support, however, is conditional and passive. As a class, the merchants might well support *any* regime that would distribute wealth its way and guarantee the requisite investment stability.

*Expatriate Labor.* Labor, overall, constitutes a less important social group, as it is generally clearly divided between expatriates and nationals. Today's working class is overwhelmingly foreign (98 percent of private sector employees in Kuwait, for example, are expatriates). This dependence on foreign labor is not a problem politically. Highly transient and internally divided by nationality, employment conditions, residential patterns, and social networks, expatriate labor lacks the incenti ve and ability to act cohesi vely. Although labor has grievances, it has a strong incentive to cooperate. Its interests are economic; its politics are at home.

There is no reason to think that these trends will not continue; the governments have learned a good deal about controlling foreign labor over the years. Nonetheless, it is worth remembering that foreign labor was not always completely outside politics. Strange as it seems from the perspective of the 1990s, in the 1950s and 1960s expatriates and nationals were engaged in political con versation in Kuwait. In Qatar, mass naturalization forged a working-class Qatari identity . The point here is that foreign labor' s quiescence is not natural b ut is the result of government policy. Just as good polic y has contained foreign labor , bad policy might repoliticize it, especially if foreign labor were to join with some kind of local ally—perhaps a dissident prince moving into an expanding private sector and using his workers to stir up trouble, or well-placed families joining with expatriates to develop a growing market niche in the drug trade. The point here is that, while unlik ely, it is conceivable that expatriates could be used politically again.

Two formal mechanisms are used to control foreigners. The first, and less important, mechanism for controlling expatriate labor is labor law, which bans collecti ve action generally and constrains e xpatriate labor particularly. Second, and more importantly , the state in effect has privatized the policing of expatriates. The most important legal structure shaping e xpatriate labor is a Residence La w, the application of which is left largely to the private sponsorship system and the sponsor. Actively policing the lar ge expatriate community is beyond the bureaucratic capacity of the government, and there is sufficient harmony of interest between the state and sponsoring nationals that daily control can rest within the pri vate sector. Behind pri vate control lies a public threat of deportation, a threat so effective it need rarely be used.

Nationals could become a problem only if real economic liberalization occurs, serious austerity measures are implemented, or the state institutes a genuine policy of forcing the private sector to hire nationals. It is useful to remember that labor was once quite important politically in the Gulf. In Qatar , the labor mo vement allied with ruling family dissidents to reshape policy in the 1950s and 1960s. In Bahrain, it once succeeded in building bridges across sects. But the policies of control devised for expatriates (residence laws and deportation) would not work on nationals. Nationals thus far have been contained primarily because they have few grievances, but if this changed, the government would be poorly equipped to handle or ganized labor.

Is labor likely to become a political force? Perhaps, but not as it was in the past. One likely and potentially stable scenario for containing labor is a corporatist one, where the government orchestrates a compact between labor and business and labor agrees to give up some tactics (for example, strikes) in exchange for institutionalized input and some guaranteed floor of concessions. Such a policy would be consistent with the historically close business-government relationship but requires political skill.

*Public sector employees* are another important group and one that is wary of moves toward the market. The growth of the state in the last several decades has created a large group of people with a vested interest in sabotaging privatization. Not everyone who works for the state will oppose liberalization. Those more likely to favor it are those who can most easily mo ve into the pri vate sector, namely the young, men, and members of the more socially dominant groups well established in the pri vate sector (largely, the older Sunni f amilies). Those who have done better in the public sector than they would likely do in the private sector and would probably suffer disproportionately from cutbacks in state employment include women (in education and health care), Shias, bedouins (in the military and police), and groups of more marginal political significance (for example, the old nearing retirement). These groups have problems with the private sector as currently structured and have put a good deal of effort into colonizing the state and may be more reluctant to change. But these also include some more powerful groups: members of the ruling family controlling ministerial fiefs, business interests lodged in key ministries (for example, commerce and finance in Kuwait), and Islamists with holds on *awqaf* and education. These groups may be more reluctant to see their fiefs dismantled.

If the right coalition of these groups were to object to privatization, the government might well be responsive. The rulers, after all, have an independent interest in preserving a large public sector. It not only pro vides patronage channels b ut also gives the government the ability to monitor and sanction and, for that matter , tax those who work for it. The government will try to minimize firing public sector employees by first replacing expatriates with nationals, with predicable consequences: a reduction in the quality of services provided, which will only delay the problem. In some Gulf states (for example, Kuwait), that process is already well under w ay.

*Identity Issues.* In addition to groups organized around interests, groups organized around identity—tribe, sect, gender , or generation—are important. T ribal identification is common throughout the Gulf, although most important in Kuwait. There, tribes were naturalized later and thus were unable to move into the private sector when it was first established. Consequently, they depend more on public-sector jobs. The state has always had mixed feelings about tribes because of their uncertain loyalty and ties across borders. But tribes also are an asset, because their social cohesion actually f acilitates loyalty. What happened in Kuwait tells a story of broader importance.

In Kuwait, some 15 tribes constitute about 65 percent of the population and hold the majority of assembly seats, but this was not always so. T ribes were brought into the political process in the 1950s and 1960s through government policies that settled bedouins and gave them police and military jobs in exchange for electoral support. A key goal was to use the bedouins to counterbalance the power of the merchants. At first, the tribes were lo yal to the ruler , but, as with other allies, they began to develop their own agendas. Since these agendas were initially economic (delivering services to the typically poorer tribal constituencies), they could be easily addressed (at least as long as oil revenues held up) through existing clientele networks. Thus, tribal representatives ran as service candidates, continuing the original arrangement with the government of votes for services. But bedouins faced continuing discrimination from the urban merchant population and in state employment. As oil revenues fell, even those motivated primarily by economic concerns began to look for other avenues of political expression. Meanwhile, the assembly itself became a power base for tribal representatives, who now looked within that structure for allies. Some bedouins in the 1980s turned toward the liberals. But this was an uneasy alliance, in part because of the different underlying constituencies; the liberals were wealthy , the tribes poor . An Islamist alliance seemed more promising. After 1992, the two main Islamist groups gained footholds in bedouin areas. The *amir* was forced to respond. In the 1999 elections, he moved to curb tribes, banning tribal primaries and detaining and fining some tribal candidates, including former representatives, for ignoring the ban. The tribes in turn refused to support him on the issue of women's suffrage.

In addition to tribal divisions, the *sectarian* divide is an especially important one in Kuwait and Bahrain, although its importance has waxed and waned over the decades and may continue to do so. In most states, the marginality of the Shia population and the hostility of the dominant Sunni opposition, whether liberal or Islamist, means that as long as the government is not overtly hostile, the Shia may well prefer the existing regime to any likely Sunni opposition, especially Islamist. But existing alliance patterns are not given. In Kuwait, Islamists have struck some tentative working alliances across the sectarian divide. In the past in Bahrain, Shias and Sunnis worked together in opposition to the government. As is the case with tribes, Shia loyalty can shift (so long as Iran stays quiet).

*Gender* is another important line of social stratification, although historically not politically important. Recent extension of suffrage in Oman and Qatar and efforts to do the same in Kuwait, if successful, could lead to the eventual emergence of women as an interest group in politics. Turning women into another special interest group might not have been the intention when suffrage was extended, but it might be an unintended long-term consequence. Women have a debt to the ruling family for putting suffrage on the agenda, but they may get over that; others have. There are certainly no insurmountable stumbling blocks to their participation in politics. Also, there is nothing new about a public role for women. Before oil, most men spent much of the year away at sea, forcing women to take public roles; in any event, seclusion was something only the rich could afford.

One development that could politicize women would be cutbacks in state employment, the effects of which would fall disproportionately on women who have benefited from professional employment in the state. Women working in the state sector have enjoyed conditions more sensitive to the needs of working parents (generous maternity leave, hours that match the schools) than those in the private sector. If the economy worsens, the participation rates of women in the labor force will continue to climb. If enfranchised, women conceivably could develop a corporate agenda and pressure other blocs to include women's issues on their platforms. The liberals and Islamists might then develop a women's platform, probably focusing on social issues; if the economy weakens, on employment. Liberals and Islamists both could take on this issue, and both could go either way. Liberals could either support women, especially merchant-class women, or hang them out to dry—both of which they have done before. Islamists could espouse a traditional family ideology, calling for a retreat from the workforce to protect jobs for men, or Islamists could define and support an agenda based on an "appropriate" working environment for women. It must be kept in mind that their core constituency is poor or middle-class households, where women's employment income is less discretionary. The point here is that gender could be a line of stratification that could be incorporated into the political systems rather easily.

*New Agers.* Another emerging social group is the new generation. Age, as gender, is a universally important stratification. People form different interests at different ages. Young people are concerned with access to higher education and jobs; adults are concerned with their children's education, and still older adults with retirement. Schools create annual cohorts of graduates. Links established in youth and perhaps crystallized by a shared political experience endure a lifetime, making age and generational change critical to politics. This is especially true in the Gulf, where age is such a culturally defining trait that seniority, even by a few months, confers authority. Rapid improvements in public health and education in the region have produced an unusually large and experientially different baby-boom oil generation. In the Gulf, the generations are defined by the economy (oil boom and post-boom) and by political events (wars and successions). Soon, the key division will be between those who remember the Gulf War and those who do not.

The large, diverse, younger generation is a demographic reality. What is less clear is what this generational divide means. Certainly, some consequences are obvious—more demands on the state for schools, jobs, and services. It also is less clear that this generation will form a distinct political pressure group. They are more educated, but higher education neither confers similar beliefs nor pushes people in a particular political direction (giving them, for example, a more Western or liberal orientation). In the 1960s, students returned from Western educations to become Arab socialists; in the 1980s, they returned to become Islamists.

The important difference may be a new style of politics that is national in scope and inclusive in rhetoric. College graduates have learned to develop personal networks that cut across family, tribal, and other lines and can draw, to a degree, on those networks to mobilize people on political issues. The shared experience of this generation has created a national arena for politics. This is not to suggest that members of a new generation will not identify along lines of sect or class or clan but rather that they will have a greater ability to build bridges and alliances across these lines, perhaps using the ideology and organization of generation as a fulcrum. The extent to which this generation will form a distinct pressure group turns on two factors: whether they are attacked along generational lines (for example, if governments cut state expenditures by dramatically cutting new hires) and whether people so affected turn to institutions in which young people predominate (such as sports clubs or university organizations) rather than established institutions, such as those of the extended family.

*Family Ties.* Families are another important group. Businesses are family-based. Government is family-based (the ruling family is shorthand for political power). Families are also important because they temper disputes and provide the informal links that keep otherwise conflicting interest groups working together. Family ties prevent sharp polarization along ideological lines and explain why politicians who argue heatedly at a political forum (where this is allowed) chat amicably afterward. Even in closed states, the family patriarch mediates the family's relationship with the state, agreeing, for example, to discipline a dissident son, should the ruler release him. When all goes well, rulers can delegate a significant degree of policing of this sort to the family.

The most important family is the ruling family. Many political observers have correctly attributed regime survival to ruling family solidarity and control of key state institutions, especially the sovereign ministries. As a whole, this system of family rule works, although the success of the system ranges from high (in Kuwait) to poor (in Qatar). But might the ruling family crack? Possibly, but the likelihood would depend on its size (more likely where it is especially large, as in Qatar and Saudi Arabia) and also perhaps on how moves to the market are greeted by the ruling family. Those with fiefs in the public sector may resist efforts to move toward the market. But in those states where the private sector is especially weak and co-opted, the ruling family is best placed to move in should economic liberalization occur. Shaykhs can be expected to move into an expanding private sector, either directly or as silent partners with other families (including perhaps, as decades ago, behind Shia families). Those of the younger generation, less bound by deals of the past and facing fewer public opportunities, might be especially inclined in this direction. Such movement will cause tension because of the nonmarket advantages the shaykhs enjoy and the consequent tendency toward moral hazard. Should business ventures fail, their partners cannot trust them to honor their agreements, nor take them to court to enforce those agreements. If insufficiently checked, the shaykhs entering business can effectively sabotage any moves toward the market. In turn, this might provoke the ruler to constrain the family by threatening cutbacks in perks and allowances or paring the civil list, acts that could bring internal dissent to the surface.

If a succession crisis were to emerge while all of this is going on, then family disputes could become public, with two predictable consequences. First, the process w ould be nasty, as it was in the 1950s when official lines to the ruling families originally were established in most of these states. Second, ruling family factions would seek alliances as they have in the past with whatever groups are powerful. In the 1950s and 1960s, those were Arab nationalists and labor; today , it would be the Islamists. Islamists may not be fans of the ruling family generally, but they have their factions, too, and such an alliance is not unthinkable. Regimes can survive these contested moments, but at a cost. Coups (as in Qatar), even though they eventually stabilize, throw off the entire political dynamic for a while because they force everyone to re-rack clientele networks.

All these identity groups, from family to tribe, will remain important in the coming years because membership in identity groups (although not the alliances between them) is relatively fixed; people are born into them. This rigidity is both a strength and weakness. The strength lies in the fact that associational life is natural and difficult for the state to pre vent. People of the same sect w orship together, the same age study together, the same clan dine together , the same gender socialize together. This is a particular strength in politically closed states but a drawback in more open states. If states liberalize politically, these groups will ha ve to modify their strate gies. To win electorally, any identity-based group must e xpand beyond this narrow base and find a way to cast itself more broadly without losing its core concerns in the process.

## Political Trends: The Opposition

The major opposition players in the GCC states are the Islamists and the liberals. As elsewhere in the region, liberalism has shifted away from its broad commitment to Arab nationalism toward political liberalization. Governments, increasingly concerned with religious opposition, began shifting support to the liberals after the Iranian revolution. The Gulf War hastened this shift, especially in K uwait, as liberals were forced to disconnect from their historical association with now-discredited Arab nationalism. The result was that liberals reconstituted themselves under this unifying but vague appeal for more political openness.

In the coming years, a key issue for liberals will be to decide where they want to build their core base, especially if economic liberalization occurs. Will it be on a se gment of the emer ging business community, as it is in K uwait, or on an increasingly less af fluent middle class? Liberals, already weak, may split over this issue, which would further degrade them.

Islamists face the same dilemma. They need to attach their emphasis on moral values to interests. In the Gulf, where the constituency of the dispossessed is weak er, Islamists ha ve emphasized broad, nonmaterial issues by entering the moral void left by the decline of socialist ideologies and the rise of rampant materialism. They have sought a base in the middle class, but some Islamists have also acquired money and institutions (for example, Islamic banks). They may decide to reach out to a rising business community composed of new merchants, Shias, minor Sunni families, or bedouin, all eager to break into a historically closed b usiness community.

Interests thus will be an important part of political decisionmaking in the coming years. The interaction between Islamists and liberals will reveal the strength of each. The stronger the Islamists are, the more the liberals will turn to the government for support and backing. The weaker the Islamists are, the freer the liberals will feel to criticize the government. Nonetheless, while ideological frameworks do not determine behavior, they shape it. Ideas sometimes de velop a momentum of their own. Having for whatever reason, even the most cynical, bought into a particular set of ideas, one is sometimes stuck with the package. Liberal ideas drew them to support w omen's suffrage, which some may come to regret (as in Kuwait). Islamists are more likely to gravitate toward certain issues, such as reform of the criminal justice system, which may not be terribly popular.

Both liberals and Islamists have tried various tactics. Each state has seen something of a prodemocratic movement and some realization of their aims (for e xample, elections of v arious sorts in Qatar, Kuwait, and Oman). These trends are likely to continue. States lacking consultative councils are likely to see the opposition push for them; states possessing them will see pressure to expand both participation and contestation. Economic liberalization also may exert prodemocratic pressure, not because the business community is prodemocratic, but because economic liberalization may lead to reform of the legal system. Investors demand a stable le gal environment and a predictable system for settling disputes. But once legal reform is on the table, if only because the business community needs to know the rules and that the courts will enforce them, then liberals can link it to their longstanding demand for an independent judiciary, and Islamists can link it to judicial reforms related to *shari'ah*. An unintended consequence of economic restructuring may thus be a more thoroughgoing legal reform. Legal reform is a potentially important issue because only a legal structure, a judiciary, has the po wer and patience to check tendencies toward excessive force. Parliaments and press can do little but draw attention to isolated incidents. Both lack the tenacity necessary for the thoroughgoing reform that elicits continued responsible beha vior. Only courts can provide this. At some level, both Islamists and liberals understand this and so place legal reform on their agenda. They share an important, although often unacknowledged, common ground—they both oppose an element at the core of authoritarianism, arbitrariness. Both would like to see arbitrary government, even if benign, replaced by the rule of la w, God's or man's.

Several groups have adopted a primarily nondemocratic approach to the state. For groups holding especially controversial ideas in closed systems, it is a useful tactic to present their ideas as apolitical, voicing dissent in nonideological terms while simultaneously trying to expand a support base and organizational structure. They criticize the government, as Islamist groups do, not for what it does (that would be political) but for not doing it well. This is a good strategy: who can object in principle to good government? Even if the rulers could find allies with the bureaucracy (where surely many would object to good government), it w ould be a hard position to criticize publicly. Finally, some groups have, at least historically, adopted antidemocratic or violent tactics. This has typically occurred (as in Bahrain) where the government closes prodemocratic avenues.

## *The Rulers*

All Gulf rulers have relied on a combination of three strategies to contain the opposition: representation, regulation, and repression. While Gulf rulers have tried to manipulate and balance opposition groups, for example by co-opting and fragmenting supporters or opening and closing ci vil society, the strategies at the extremes are most interesting.

Political liberalization is al ways a top-down affair, a calculated reaction by the ruler to secure support. That it occurs in the presence of pressure from below should not obscure this fact. Liberalization has generally taken the form of appointed consultative bodies and will likely continue to do so. But the movement toward elected, albeit still largely consultative, bodies pioneered by Kuwait has been followed in more modest measure in Oman and Qatar. This trend may continue lar gely because elections serve several useful goals. First, elections are a pressure valve, relieving a public demand for increased participation. Campaigns allow people to vent. Electoral politics also tame the opposition and marginalize the violent groups. It is no coincidence that Kuwaiti Islamists and Shias participate politely, compared to their Saudi or Bahraini counterparts. Moreover, should elections f ail to tame the opposition, they allow the ruler to gauge opposition strength and identify leaders to be targeted for repression or co-optation, should representation lead in unfortunate directions. Elected institutions can be made to tax and share in the resultant unpleasantness. In Qatar, municipality elections were held just after municipality funds were slashed (leading to the resignation of the minister, although he had other problems). Elections reinforce the *amir*'s legitimacy abroad (meeting international, including occasionally American, pressure for liberalization) but more importantly at home. Elections are popular; by permitting them, the *amir* shares in their legitimacy. In Kuwait, for example, the *amir* has convened and reconvened the assembly when that le gitimacy was most threatened (for example, in 1963, when Iraq threatened Kuwait; in 1981, after Khomeini came to power; and in 1992, after K uwait's liberation). But elections reinforce the ruler's legitimacy in more subtle w ays. By standing abo ve the chaos of partisan politics, he appears to represent a shared national interest neglected by petty elected politicians. Finally, rulers can use elected bodies to pressure for better international agreements, arguing that they cannot sign on to some agreements because of the opposition they would face at home. The Kuwaiti *amirs* have used this argument (the potential opposition agreements would prompt in the assembly) since the 1960s—then with the oil companies, today with arms purchases and reopening relations with Jordan.

The transformation of the National Assembly in Kuwait indicates the success that rulers can have in manipulating these bodies if they persevere. In Kuwait, the *amir* achieved a body that he could work with in part by manipulating the electoral rules, a skill he has honed over time. In the 1967 election, for instance, this manipulation was untutored: ballot stuffing and other irregularities occurred that were so crude they prompted representatives to resign and the public to call for new elections. A more subtle 1981 redistricting, by contrast, created the small constituencies (most candidates win with around 3,000 votes) that make arguments over petty local agendas (enhancing the *amir*'s visible ability to stand abov e them) more lik ely. In the 1970s and 1980s, the *amir* simply closed the assembly. In 1990, he attempted a partially appointed assembly; by 1999, he had learned to close it, push through legislation, then hold new elections, allowing him to both benefit from the legitimacy elections conferred and also present himself as a leader above partisan factions. The *amir* also supports and manipulates particular factions, thus promoting di vision. In this way, the amir both recalibrates the body to achieve a composition more to his liking and also stands above seemingly petty squabbling. This may be a trend. In the future, the *amir* may well continue to play with electoral rules and procedures. He could close the assembly and reschedule elections, manipulate suffrage, perhaps even redistrict. His ability to exert this kind of tempered control over the assembly renders it a more palatable model to the other Gulf states.

The problem with the politically liberal strate gy, however, is that once concessions, such as allo wing a National Assembly, are made repeatedly, they cease to be easily re versible outcomes of strate gic concessions, even if made initially only under threat, and develop their own momentum. So rulers look for other strategies. All the GCC rulers rely on repression to a degree, although the range varies from Bahrain, where it is fairly heavy-handed, to Kuwait, where the opposition occasionally complains to the government that the police are not doing enough. States typically resort to force from desperation or clumsiness. Repression is not a particularly good general strategy because using force has costs, in money and morale. Force alienates people. Force can even create political opposition where it may not have existed. Banning groups can backfire. Where political groups are banned, apolitical groups from families to funeral societies all become charged with political importance. Still, it works often enough to be worth trying. In Bahrain, the opposition in the 1990s died down even before the accession of the new *amir*, largely because of the force the government used.

## Conclusion

It is quite possible that the GCC states will continue to enjoy substantial stability in the coming decade. After all, the years 1985 to 2000 witnessed enormous internal stability, despite the collapse of oil prices. Real instability could come about only as a result of a combination of factors, among them sustained low prices coupled with clumsy state efforts at economic reform that fall on precisely the wrong groups, visible factional breaks in the ruling family with factions then forging alliances with Islamists, or emerging private sector interests, all in the context of some regional crisis (for example, civil war in Iraq). Such combinations are not impossible, but neither are they terribly likely.

What is to be done from the American perspective? If we define our primary interests in the Gulf as safeguarding access to oil, this is a goal not likely to change much in the next 15 years. One small complication might be the increased direct pressure on the American government from Western oil companies if its role in the energy sector increases. As the energy sector privatizes, these companies will become more interested in politics (at least economic policy). As a group, the Western oil companies are important to U.S. policymakers. If Britain's experience is any guide, an extraordinarily high level of tension and difference of opinion in short-term policy goals and tactics can exist between this industry and the American government, alongside substantial harmony of interests and long-term goals. While their direct impact on politics and policy outside the energy sector is likely to be modest, the Gulf governments may (as Kuwait's did in the 1970s) tolerate or manipulate assembly opposition to these companies as a way of securing better agreements in the future.

In any event, U.S. policy should be to get along with the GCC states or to get along with the Saudis, who will then make sure the GCC states get along with us. The GCC states' need for America is not likely to change substantially in the near future. What GCC leaders will likely want is what the y want today, contradictory though it is: an American presence that is virtually in visible but offers protection from external and serious internal threats. In light of the above discussion, it follows that U.S. policy on internal opposition should be as hands-off as possible, and, to the e xtent that there is a polic y, it should be to reinforce trends toward representation rather than repression. If more democratic regimes were actually to emerge, they would probably be relatively tame, and in time the rulers would learn, as their colleagues elsewhere have, to manipulate an electoral system in a way that allows the system to vent without shattering. This outcome may not be ideal for the Gulf, or for the United States, but we can live with it, and for both sides, it is much better than most of the alternatives.

## Notes

[1] All figures taken from Population Reference Bureau, accessed at <http://www.prb.org/pubs/wpds2000/wpds2000_WesternAsia.html>.

[2] The authors are perhaps overly optimistic about the impact of education in changing Saudi outlooks from regional to national. Mai Yamani, in her study of the rising generation in Saudi Arabia, argues the opposite based on interviews with young Saudis. See Mai Yamani, *Changed Identities: The Challenge of the New Generation in Saudi Arabia* (London: Royal Institute for International Affairs, 2000). The question remains open and worth continued study.

[3] There are a number of sources on the Kingdom that detail the intrafamily struggle in the late 1950s and early 1960s. The most recent is Sarah Izraeli, *The Remaking of Saudi Arabia: The Struggle between King Saud and Crown Prince Faysal, 1953–1962* (Tel Aviv: Moshe Dayan Center for Middle Eastern and African Studies, 1997).

---

*This chapter is based on a paper that was presented at a conference on* The Middle East in Transition: The Persian Gulf, *which was held at the Institute for National Strategic Studies, National Defense University, Washington, DC, on January 21, 2000.*

Chapter 10
# Arms Control: In the Region's Future?

*Steven L. Spiegel*

This chapter analyzes regional trends in proliferation and arms control in an effort to predict what the Middle East will look like in 2015. The region clearly has changed much in the past 15 years. In the mid-1980s, Israel and the Palestine Liberation Organization (PLO) were bitter enemies trying to destroy each other. The United States was tilting toward Iraq in the Iran-Iraq War, the Cold War was very much alive, and Mikhail Gorbachev had just come to power in the Soviet Union. Anyone who had predicted in 1985 that within 5 years, the Cold War would be over, and within 6 years, the Soviet Union would collapse, would have been thought of questionable sanity. These kinds of prognostications, therefore, should always be taken with more than one grain of salt.

The changes brought about in the Middle East by the conclusion of the Cold War have been both good and bad. On the one hand, the end of U.S.-Soviet competition over the region has offered

---

*Steven L. Spiegel is professor of political science and associate director at the Burkle Center for International Relations, University of California, Los Angeles. He is the author of several books, including* Dominance and Diversity: The International Hierarchy *(1980),* The International Politics of Regions *(with Louis Cantori), and* World Politics in a New Era *(1999). Dr. Spiegel's most recent publication (with Jennifer D. Kibbe and Elizabeth G. Matthews, eds.) is* The Dynamics of Middle East Proliferation *(2001).*

an opportunity to move toward general peace accords, which, with the exception of the Egyptian-Israeli accord, had long been blocked by the superpower rivalry. Certainly the Madrid and Oslo processes were in part generated by the end of the Cold War. On the other hand, just as the superpowers are no longer limiting cooperation in the region, they also are no longer limiting conflict. During the Cold War, although the superpowers allowed plenty of conflict and even encouraged it, they did not allow one state to destroy its opponent (or itself); either the United States or the Soviet Union intervened to prevent this final, destabilizing step. If the Cold War had continued, we probably would not be as concerned about the proliferation of weapons of mass destruction (WMD) [1] as we are today.

The conventional wisdom has been to view these two aspects, the peace process and the status of weapons of mass destruction, as somehow congruent; the assumption is that if progress is made in one area, advances will occur in the other. If the peace process is successful, concurrent advances will be made in limiting the danger of weapons of mass destruction, and by contrast, if the peace process collapses, then weapons of mass destruction will proliferate.

The major argument made in this chapter is that the peace process cannot and will not prevent further proliferation, which I believe to be inevitable. The peace process can, however, help to manage that proliferation. Moreover, this is just the most significant example of a fundamental error that Americans are making in their approach to the peace process. The question is not merely one of settling particular issues but also one of creating the potential for the United States to address other concerns that deeply affect American interests, the threat of WMD proliferation most prominent among them. In other words, the peace process is not the entire house, it is just the gate—the entry point for trying to manage further problems.

It has been said that the Hollywood film industry is incapable of dealing with marriage in its pictures. It is good at depicting romance and getting people to the altar, but it does not know how to portray the normalcy of marriage. In a sense, the Arabs and Israelis, as well as the Americans in their Middle East policy, are very similar. They are focused on peace treaties as the endgame, and very little thought is given to life after the peace treaties are signed. The United States is going to be critical to the post-peace period, and especially so to any effort to manage the WMD problem. That said, stemming WMD proliferation cannot wait until the peace process concludes.

## Why WMD in the Middle East?

Why would Middle Eastern governments turn to weapons of mass destruction? The first, most basic reason is simple security. They may be afraid of somebody. However, their very act of acquiring WMD, even if they intend it only for protection, may well threaten the state they were trying to protect themselves from, causing that state to seek out WMD as well—a dynamic known as the security dilemma. And a particular difficulty in the Middle East is the additional characteristic of overlapping problems, which tends to multiply the security dilemma. If a country takes action vis-à-vis another country, it may open a Pandora's box. Thus, Iran may make moves in response to its principal worry, Iraq, but the Gulf states, Israel, Egypt, and others are concerned about what Iran does. Similarly, although proliferation moves by Pakistan and India in the late 1990s were clearly aimed at each other, they also worried Tehran. And Israel may be concerned about a situation in Lebanon, but how it responds may pose problems for other Arab states in the region. Thus, because there are so many overlapping power balances in the Middle East involving Arabs, Persians, Israelis, Turks, the Gulf states, and the countries of the Eastern Mediterranean and the Maghreb, it is not just protective weapons that proliferate, but also the security dilemma itself.

Second, weapons of mass destruction, particularly chemical and biological weapons, are cheaper than a large arsenal of conventional weapons. Despite the recent rise of oil prices, the oil bonanza is over for many of these states. Middle Eastern governments have less money and thus are buying fewer conventional weapons. Weapons of mass destruction, therefore, represent an inexpensive way to shore up their security. Not for no reason are biological and chemical weapons called the "poor man's nuke." Moreover, not only are they cheaper, but also they are easier and require less technological sophistication to produce. And in the irony that is WMD logic, many proposed forms of counterproliferation (defenses against WMD) can act as incentives for states to develop biological weapons (which, to date, cannot be defended against) and use unconventional means of delivery.

Finally, for several states, WMD actually serve a deterrent function. Some states see the value of WMD in preventing the United States or a regional power from exercising coercive diplomacy or taking particular actions. For example, would the United States have acted the way it did in the Persian Gulf War or in the Kosovo crisis if Iraqi WMD capabilities were known at the time or if Yugoslavia had had WMD? To some states, then, this category of weapons may represent an affordable, feasible way to at least partially even out the balance of power, even when they have no thought of actually using them.

There are also several non-security-related reasons for acquiring WMD. Nuclear weapons in particular have long been seen as a surefire way of gaining national prestige. As a spokesperson for the Indian Bharatiya Janata Party put it in 1993, "[n]uclear weapons will give us prestige, power, standing. An Indian will talk straight and walk straight when we have the bomb."[2] And for many Middle Eastern governments, the prestige afforded by WMD is critical in the all-important task of keeping up with Israel. The drive to acquire WMD capability has also been fueled by the ambition of scientists trying to prove their ability and by the need of leaders to score points or create distractions in domestic political battles.[3] All three of these elements were certainly factors in Iraqi (and to some extent Iranian) WMD development.

## WMD Capabilities in 2015

In trying to make any kind of prediction about the Middle East in 2015, the next thing to consider is which states will have WMD capability by then. Because this book takes the long view and is looking at 2015 rather than 2005 or 2010, a prediction is easier.

*Iran's* WMD capabilities and intentions are the topic of intense debate in the United States, Israel, and Europe. Much of the discussion focuses on *when*, not *whether*, it will acquire nuclear capability, and the answer has been phrased in terms of 3, 5, or 7 years. Within this framework, it is not difficult to predict that Iran will have a viable WMD force within 15 years. In its August 2000 semiannual report to Congress on foreign countries' efforts to acquire WMD-related technology, the Central Intelligence Agency (CIA) declared that Iran "remains one of the most active countries seeking to acquire WMD . . . technology from abroad," and noted that it is developing production capabilities in every WMD category: nuclear, chemical, and biological, as well as missiles.[4]

Iran continues to seek missile development assistance from China, North Korea, and Russia.[5] In addition to already being able to produce its own Scud short-range ballistic missiles, Tehran conducted its first successful test of the Shahab-3 medium-range ballistic missile (MRBM) in July 2000. The Shahab-3, based on North Korea's No Dong MRBM upgraded with Russian technology, has a range of 1,300 to 1,500 kilometers (810–940 miles) and thus enables Iran to hit both Israel and Saudi Arabia.[6] Israeli and American officials have expressed concern that the successful Shahab-3 test means that Iran will move on to completing the Shahab-4, expected to have a range of 2,000 kilometers (1,250 miles), and the Shahab-5, estimated to have an intercontinental range of 5,500 kilometers (3,400 miles). Experts differ in their estimates of when Iran will be ready to test its first intercontinental ballistic missile capable of hitting the United States. Israeli officials claim that the Shahab-5 will be ready in 2005;[7] the CIA 1999 National Intelligence Estimate predicted that Iran could test a missile capable of hitting the United States by 2010; other experts believe Iran has less than an even chance of testing such a missile by 2015.[8]

Iran has made limited progress in the nuclear area. Despite Iranian claims that it is solely interested in nuclear technology to strengthen its civilian energy program, intelligence analysts generally agree that Iran is trying to develop a nuclear weapons capability. It is trying to negotiate with several sources, particularly in Russia, for the purchase of whole facilities, such as a uranium conversion facility, which could be used to produce the fissile material needed for a nuclear weapon. Moreover, in addition to its efforts to complete several new nuclear reactors, ostensibly for civilian use, CIA unclassified reports say that "Tehran continues to seek fissile material and technology for weapons development and has set up an elaborate system of military and civilian organizations to support its effort."[9] Iran ratified the Non-Proliferation Treaty (NPT) in 1970, and the International Atomic Energy Agency (IAEA) has reported that it has found no evidence of weapons development in declared facilities in Iran. However, the IAEA only inspects Iran's small research reactors and conducts only informal walk-throughs of its other sites.[10] In addition, as many skeptics readily point out, the IAEA never found anything awry in Iraq before 1990 either. The United States has attempted to restrain Iran's efforts by encouraging an international consensus against nuclear cooperation with Iran. The United States also has pressured Russia, the only nuclear supplier assisting Iran, by focusing on specific Russian firms engaged in missile and nuclear development cooperation with Iran. So far, however, these efforts have met with limited success.

Iran has had an active chemical weapons program since being the victim of several Iraqi chemical attacks early in the Iran-Iraq war. Tehran is thought to have increased its efforts to build a self-supporting chemical weapons (CW) infrastructure in the early 1990s when the United Nations (UN) discovered substantial Iraqi progress with advanced agents such as VX gas. Iran is estimated to have an inventory of several thousand tons of various agents, including blister, blood, and choking agents, and its production capacity is estimated at as much as 1,000 tons a year. Although Iran ratified the Chemical Weapons Convention, under which it will be obligated to eliminate its chemical weapons program over a period of years, the CIA has noted that Tehran continues to seek production technology, training, expertise, and chemicals that could be used as precursor agents from both Russia and China—indicating its plans to maintain and improve its CW capability.[11]

Iran also began a biological warfare (BW) program during the Iran-Iraq war, which is now believed to be in the advanced research and development phase. Although little confirmed information is available on Iran's BW program, it is believed to have weaponized both live agents and toxins for artillery and bombs. Iran is also judged to be able to support an independent BW program with little foreign assistance (although it is receiving some foreign expertise, especially from Russia). Tehran has ratified the Biological Weapons Convention, but it "continues to seek considerable dual-use biotechnical materials, equipment, and expertise from abroad ... ostensibly for civilian uses."[12] In sum, then, Iran clearly will have at least a minimal WMD force by 2015.

*Iraq* has not permitted UNSCOM inspections since mid-1998, and most analysts assume that Iraq is developing whatever it can. Even before the UN inspectors left Iraq in December 1998, the information they had been able to gather about its WMD capabilities was incomplete. Iraq is known to have rebuilt many of its key chemical facilities since 1991, albeit in the inspection-acceptable guise of industrial and commercial plants. However, as with its various bio-technical research facilities, much of the technology is dual-use and could be converted for weapons development relatively quickly. Moreover, Iraqi scientists still possess knowledge of chemical weapons production, and Saddam Husayn is thought to retain a range of precursor chemicals, production equipment, filled munitions, and program documentation. For example, according to Iraq's own production figures, the equipment the country is known to possess could produce 350 liters of weapons-grade anthrax per week.[13] In addition, an Iraqi Air Force document found by the United Nations Special Commission in July 1998 and later seized by Baghdad indicated that Iraq had not consumed as many chemical weapons during the Iran-Iraq war as it had claimed, raising the possibility that as many as 6,000 CW munitions remain hidden. [14]

On the missile front, the U.S. Department of State reported in September 1999 that Iraq had refused to credibly account for over 40 Scud biological and conventional warheads, 7 Iraqi-produced Scuds, and truckloads of Scud components. Moreover, Iraq continues to work on the short-range missiles that it is allowed to possess. It completed a set of eight tests of its Al Samoud ballistic missile in June 2000. Although the Samoud's range is less than 150 kilometers (95 miles), which does not violate UN-imposed restrictions, experts have pointed out that it nonetheless provides Iraq with valuable practice in ballistic missile technology, which could be adapted to longer-range missiles as soon as sanctions are lifted. [15]

Even on the nuclear issue, not all information is known. UN inspections found evidence of two potential weapons designs, a neutron initiator, explosives and triggering technology, plutonium processing technology, centrifuge technology, calutron enrichment technology, and experiments with chemical separation technology. What remains unknown is whether Baghdad managed to conceal a high-speed centrifuge program; whether it made any progress on a radiological weapon; whether it is continuing to develop a missile warhead capable of carrying a nuclear device; and the whereabouts of a "substantial number" of UN-declared nuclear weapons components and research equipment that were never recovered. Thus, although the UN believes the Iraqi nuclear program has been largely disabled, it warns that Iraq retains substantial technology as well as a clandestine purchasing network that it has used since 1990 to import prohibited weapons components. U.S. experts believe that, despite the sanctions regime, Iraq has an ongoing research and development nuclear program. [16]

In 15 years, Iraq clearly will have some form of WMD capability, if not a full complement. On the political side of the equation, Saddam Husayn, who has been in power 15 years, may still be in power 15 years from now. Unless he is replaced by a government with a different strategy, the safe assumption is that Iraq will be militarily stronger and will remain a significant threat to its neighbors.

*Libya* remains a significant proliferation concern, particularly in the area of chemical weapons. Libya has been producing small amounts of chemical weapons since the early 1980s, and even though its main plant at Rabta has not been operating at full strength, it has nonetheless produced at least 100 metric tons of blister and nerve agents. Of even greater concern are the ongoing construction of a major underground chemical weapons plant near T arhunah and the speed with which Tripoli renewed its contacts with sources of expertise, parts, and precursor chemicals in Western Europe as soon as UN sanctions against the country were lifted in April 1999. Although Libya's ability to deliver any chemical weapon so far remains limited to its aging Scud-B missiles (with a range of 310 kilometers, or 196 miles), it continually has tried to obtain ballistic missile-related equipment, technology, materials, and expertise from foreign sources.[17] Libya is not likely to obtain a WMD capability without substantial foreign assistance.

*Syria* has also focused primarily on missiles and chemical weapons and is considerably further along than Libya in both categories. Syria is believed to have around 200 Scud-B missiles, possibly with chemical warheads. It has also deployed the longer-range North Korean Scud-C missiles, which have ranges of up to 600 kilometers (374 miles), thus rendering Syria capable of reaching targets throughout Israel from much deeper within its own territory. Syria is estimated to have 50 to 80 Scud-C missiles and is now able to build both the B and C variants in their entirety. Damascus has been developing its chemical weapons arsenal since the 1970s and is thought capable of producing several hundred tons of CW agents per year. Its current stockpiles have been estimated at "several thousand aerial bombs, filled mostly with sarin," and between 50 to 100 ballistic missile warheads. Intelligence analysts also believe that Syria is actively seeking to manufacture the more powerful VX gas.[18]

The Syrian and Libyan capabilities arguably may be easier to control than the Iranian and Iraqi capabilities because of their location and size and because of some indications that both countries are moving in a somewhat more moderate direction.

*Israel* clearly possesses the most advanced WMD in the region. Israel is estimated to have 50 Jericho I missiles (with a range of up to 640 kilometers, or 400 miles) deployed and to have developed the Jericho II, with an increased range of up to 1,440 kilometers (900 miles), enabling it to reach almost the entire Arab world (although how many are deployed is unclear). Israel has also been working on extending the range of the Jericho II to 2,000 kilometers and on developing submarine-launched cruise missiles, which would give it a second-strike capability. Israel reportedly carried out its first test launches of Popeye Turbo cruise missiles (which are capable of carrying nuclear warheads) from its Dolphin class submarines in May 2000. [19] Specific information is scarce on biological and chemical weapons, but U.S. experts include Israel on the list of nations with stocks of both. Estimates of Israel's nuclear arsenal range from 60 to 300, with most assessments falling somewhere between 100 and 200. [20]

Given developments elsewhere in the Middle East, these forces will have to increase in capability and effectiveness if Israel is to retain its position of perceived superiority since WMD probably will continue to proliferate even with the successful conclusion of peace treaties. Unless Israel's security can be assured by outside powers, particularly the United States, Israel is likely to believe that these weapons are even more central to its security after it has returned additional territory. Maintaining a deterrent against WMD will be complex; not only will Israel be trying to deter several potential aggressors in a multipolar situation, but also weapons of mass destruction leave less room for error than conventional weapons. Pursuing advantages such as a second-strike capability—whether in the form of submarine-launched missiles, anti-missile defense, or other new technology—is extremely expensive. Therefore, although Israel will be stronger in absolute terms in 15 years than it is now, it also could actually be more vulnerable in terms of both its military security and its economic stability, relative to weapons developments elsewhere in the region.

*Egypt,* the wild card in all of these calculations, was the first country in the Middle East to obtain chemical weapons training and materiel. It was also the first to use chemical weapons (in the Yemeni civil war in the early 1960s). [21] Cairo is thought to have a current stockpile of mustard gas and phosgene (the agents it used in Yemen) and to be producing VX gas. Egypt also has had long-running cooperation with North Korea on ballistic missiles, has approximately 100 Scud-B missiles, and is thought to be working on the medium-range Scud-C. [22] However, Cairo has not been a player militarily in the area of nuclear weapons, having chosen diplomatic means to try to affect the nuclear balance in the region. It has called for a nuclear-free zone in the Middle East since 1974, urging all countries to sign the NPT. It added to this effort in April 1990, calling for the Middle East to be WMD-free, and in April 1996, hosting the signing of the declaration of the African nuclear weapons-free zone.[23]

If all conditions remain the same, particularly with Israel's presumed capabilities, or if Israel obtains a true long-range nuclear strike capability, Cairo may not be content to stay in this moderately passive role over the next 15 years. Because of its unconventional approach, however, Egypt's behavior is the most uncertain, problematic, and difficult to predict in terms of its WMD capacity. Cairo may remain content to voice major diplomatic protests but to do very little, although doing little may work against Egypt's desire to be a lead state in the region.

## Factors Affecting Proliferation

Although the peace process will not solve the proliferation problem, it can help stem it by defusing incentives for conflict and increasing the possibility of cooperation between regional states to help manage new perils. Accommodations between states would also enable the United States to exercise greater leadership in attempting to thwart the effects of proliferation. Another factor is the possibility of moderation, coup, or revolution in Iraq and Iran, which might limit the danger from either. Clearly, forces are at work in Iran in favor of moderating some policies (if not those regarding security and WMD acquisition), and those forces are reinforced by 70 percent of the population under 30 where President Khatami's support is strongest. Gradually, and quite possibly by 2015, the Iranian WMD problem may be solved through a change of government. In Iraq, the only possibility of internal change may be by a coup, a dim prospect so long as Saddam maintains his iron grip. In any event, his successor may share his ideas about the utility of WMD systems. Iraq is, therefore, a more dangerous proliferation prospect because it lacks the possibility of a long-term positive trend that may be present in Iran.

More potential factors could fuel WMD proliferation in the Middle East than could dampen it. One of the most potent stems from the very nature of technological advances—they inevitably trickle down to less advanced powers. So improvements in satellite targeting and weather models, cheap cruise missiles, drones, and aircraft con versions will all have a potentially lethal impact by increasing e very state's destructive capability. On the missile level, hardened or mobile launch facilities, large numbers of spur systems, and rapid launch ability with minimal warning indicators will all contribute to the declining prospects for controlling WMD proliferation. Advanced computer modeling and simulation technology, reduced testing requirements, and the availability of strike aircraft with some stealth features will further exacerbate the situation.

The next generation of chemical weapons not only will be more effective, but it also probably will be more stable than the ones Iraq used before 1990, which will give states increased confidence in working with them. Every major power in the Middle East will have the required technology base to rapidly manufacture advanced biological weapons by 2010. The most dramatic improvements are likely to come in genetic engineering, weaponizing infectious agents such as Ebola, and rapid conversion of civilian pharmaceutical fermentation and other dual-use facilities. As the American experience with Sudan suggests, it is very difficult to distinguish pharmaceutical plants from those involved in weapons production. The U.S. bombardment of a suspect Sudanese pharmaceutical plant in 1998 in retaliation for the terrorist attacks on the U.S. embassies in K enya and Tanzania is still being debated, with many experts claiming that it was a harmless installation. Finally, there will be more sophisticated co vert delivery systems and possible terrorist devices.

Beyond the risks of technological advancements, factors favoring increased proliferation include the availability of outside technical assistance; rising regional rivalries and military insecurities; lessening U.S. involvement and political/economic assistance in, and military disengagement from, the region; the rising belief that the United States cannot safeguard the security and stability in the region; the inability to contain competing Iranian and Iraqi WMD ambitions; the political fallout from the Indian and Pakistani nuclear tests; and the perception of an increasing Israeli WMD capability. A breakdown in the Arab-Israeli peace process only accelerates these trends. Indeed, most of the developments in the past 5 years have been in the wrong direction.

## What Will Rampant WMD Proliferation in the Middle East Be Like?

These technological developments, and the clear possibility of many more, strongly suggest we will have a WMD-equipped Middle East in 2015, even with the successful completion of agreements on all outstanding issues between the Arabs and Israelis. What would this Middle East be like? Some political scientists argue that countries that acquire WMD become more cautious. In the case of India and Pakistan, for example, some analysts have argued that the two were deterred from war in the Kashmir crisis of 1990 by each side's knowledge that the other was nuclear weapons-capable. [24] The ultimate logic of this position is that WMD should be dispensed like prophylactics against war.[25] Given the history and complexity of both South Asia and the Middle East, however, assuming that hostilities would end and that a newfound caution would ensue just because these states have acquired WMD would be reckless indeed.

In addition, there is the problem of overlapping concerns. For example, Israel alone could be engaged in a variety of confrontations by 2015 with countries that possess WMD, including Iran, Iraq, Syria, and possibly even Libya. The peace process is critical in this situation because it could remove the spark to the conflict and limit the intensity and diversity of these confrontations. Complicating the situation even further is the possibility that these overlapping interests would induce new countries to acquire WMD. In the Gulf, for example, with Iran and Iraq both developing WMD capabilities, Saudi Arabia may also feel impelled to enter the WMD competition.

Predictions are also complicated by the proclivity of Middle East governments toward switching alliances. Libya and Iran were both once close to the United States and Britain. Before 1973, Egypt was a major Soviet client. The West—including the United States—has both befriended and opposed Iraq and Iran. The PLO is Israel's most bitter foe and potential partner for peace. In trying to predict what the WMD balance will look like in 2015, we must consider the impermanent nature of relations in the Middle East.

Assuming that Iraq, Iran, and Israel will all have a full WMD complement by 2015, and that several other key states, particularly Egypt, Libya, Syria, and Algeria, will have smaller arsenals of biological and/or chemical weapons, the region could be a highly unstable, multipolar system. The countries of the area would have to prepare for several adversaries at once. To make matters worse, although Israel will probably have a second-strike capability by then, none of the other states probably would be able to develop the stabilizing sort of second-strike capability that characterized the Cold War. Regional governments also will have to deal with the problem of collateral damage. The Palestinians and Jordanians, for instance, warn that if an adversary decided to attack Israel, it could inadvertently hit Jordan or Palestine instead because of poor targeting, weapons failure, or inclement weather.

One way to alleviate the multi-polar problem is for the United States to provide some sort of guarantee to potential target states that would help deter potential aggressors from employing these weapons. However, Americans would have to confront the implications of accepting this new responsibility of contributing to the region's stability in this way.

Even though nuclear weapons generally are more useful to states for deterrence, prestige, or political bargaining purposes than for their actual warfighting capability (because of the potential for mutual destruction if they are employed), the incentive could still exist to use them in a clandestine fashion. Indeed, the issue of WMD terrorism is the greatest threat we face from the proliferation of these weapons. The capability already exists to make biological and chemical weapons that can be delivered in a suitcase. However ineptly handled, the Tokyo subway bombing by the Aum Shinrikyo sect in March 1995 demonstrated that a WMD attack against a civilian installation is possible. These weapons can be delivered by ship, truck, or plane. Transnational terrorists such as Osama bin Laden have operated globally out of several different places. Because of this global and regional threat, by 2015 the United States will be critical to regional stability by promoting the status quo and enforcing a disincentive to WMD acquisition and use. Washington may not be able to prevent countries from acquiring these weapons, but it is likely to become a major factor in the new deterrence equation in the area.

However, while the terrorist use of WMD may well increase as a threat to the United States by 2015, this threat is likely to be even greater in the Middle East. An extremist group or a dissatisfied government could use a clandestine weapon to inflict serious damage on the population of a perceived enemy. The leaders of Iran or Iraq might conclude that they could devastate the other party, for example, or someone might seek to destroy Israel. The perpetrator of the attack could well remain anonymous because the list of potential candidates could include either several possible governments or independent nongovernmental terrorist "operators." Neither advanced anti-missile systems nor a second-strike capacity would be effective against this kind of hidden threat. Therefore, in terms of regional trends, the danger of a WMD terrorist attack is likely to be the greatest peril the Middle East would face by 2015.

To confront the Middle East proliferation problem effectively then, the following factors must be taken into account:
- No combination of arms control, deterrence, and active or passive counterproliferation is on the horizon that can fully secure the region, any state in the region, or Western power projection forces.
- Theater missile defense will be meaningless without radical improvements in defense against air attacks, cruise missiles, and unconventional means of delivery.
- There is no present prospect that any combination of measures will be able to defend against biological warfare.

These are severe problems, and no easy answers are in sight. But the terrible challenges posed by Middle East proliferation will be even greater if the Arab-Israeli peace process fails and the attention of the parties is diverted onto specific territorial and emotional issues in dispute. The proliferation challenge also will be greater if no regional security system is developed; if the multilateral Arms Control and Regional Security (ACRS) process, suspended since 1995, is not resurrected; if Iran remains outside the regional diplomatic context; if Iraq remains a pariah under Saddam Husayn; and if international efforts to prevent WMD acquisition break down.

## Is Arms Control in the Region's Future?

Given these problems, is arms control a means of controlling, or at least ameliorating, the problem of WMD proliferation in the Middle East? The most important experiment in this area was the multilateral ACRS process, which began as a consequence of the Madrid conference in 1992. Until it stalled in 1995, it had a stunning series of successes, including regional plenary meetings and expert workshops with participation by Arabs and Israelis. The process ended in 1995 with a dispute between Egypt and Israel over when and how the Israeli nuclear force would be discussed. Israel sought an arms control process in which the issue of nuclear weapons (and by extension the Israeli nuclear force) would be addressed after an extensive series of discussions and agreements on conventional forces. Cairo wanted to begin discussions about a regional nuclear-free zone. Israel believed that even to raise the subject was to move down a slippery slope that inevitably would lead to pressure on the subject. Egyptian officials were convinced that unless the nuclear issue was discussed, any other arms control agenda would only weaken Israel's insecurity without even addressing its own concerns.

The U.S. Government at first failed to comprehend the depth of the division. After all, Israel and Egypt had agreed to limit military spending, reduce conventional arms stockpiles, prevent a conventional arms race, promote cooperation in the peaceful uses of outer space, and adopt confidence- and security-building measures that would increase transparency and openness and reduce the risk of surprise attack. These goals were to be accomplished by developing regional institutional arrangements to enhance security and the process of arms control. Unfortunately, the agreement was never approved because of the Egyptian-Israeli dispute over the nuclear issue. Israel proposed a broad statement that favored the establishment in the region of a mutually verifiable WMD-free zone. Egypt countered with language that WMD were the greatest threat to regional security and that all parties would, by signing, adhere in the near future to the NPT (which Israel has refused to sign for fear its nuclear deterrent would be compromised). Israel refused. The United States suggested bridging language—a WMD-free zone in the region with these weapons described as a "grave threat to security"—but both parties rejected the compromise. This failure, accompanied by the collapse of the Arab-Israeli peace process, devastated prospects for controlling regional WMD proliferation.

Some examples of past Arab-Israeli arms cooperation are worth considering in thinking through steps toward proliferation peace in 2015. Arab governments and Israel have concluded several major accords that serve as models for global peacekeeping efforts. These include the disengagement agreements made between Israel and Egypt and Israel and Syria after the October 1973 war; the thinning out of forces between Israel and Egypt; the Sinai multilateral force that reinforces the

Egyptian-Israeli peace treaty; and the Jordanian-Israeli working agreements, many of which preceded the Jordanian-Israeli peace treaty. Almost no violations of these treaties have occurred.

This brings us back to regional security, which is itself a means of limiting proliferation by lowering the temperature of regional conflicts and broadening the instruments for resolving them. Regional security would decrease the incentives for WMD development and increase cooperation between the local parties. Of all the regions of the world, the Middle East is the least developed in terms of region-wide institutions. Not only is there no NATO, European Union, or Organization of American States, there are no serious bilateral relationships as exist between the United States and Canada, Germany and France, Norway and Sweden, or even Japan and China. There are no formal mechanisms for discussing these issues and very little in the way of informal mechanisms.

The United States could help make the region a safer, less WMD-dominated zone in 2015 by:

- continuing efforts to dissuade the parties from developing or acquiring WMD (although a dubious prospect at best)
- restricting access to technology and WMD through export controls and other tools
- promoting global arms control, trying to reinforce the NPT, the biological and chemical weapons conventions, the Missile Technology Control Regime, and other international efforts designed to stabilize arms races
- applying sanctions and international pressure to punish violators and encourage governments that help them to stop
- supporting diplomatic initiatives such as for peace settlements, economic incentives, and financial and military assistance, any of which efforts could help convince countries that costs of possible proliferation outweigh the tangible available benefits of not doing so
- rewarding restraint to reinforce the belief that WMD acquisition is unnecessary for prestige and security.

In the end, the most effective means of thwarting proliferators and decreasing the value of proliferation may well be the need to consider the provision of U.S. security guarantees (for example, a nuclear umbrella), increased military assistance, and closer security alliances with the United States to preclude efforts by friendly governments to obtain WMD. This assumes that leaders who believed that the United States would attack them if they used WMD against their neighbors would be more reluctant to develop and use them. By 2015, this may be a false assumption.

## Notes

[1] *Weapons of mass destruction* as defined here include nuclear, chemical, and biological weapons, as well as their delivery systems.

[2] Quoted in George Perkovich, "Think Again: Nuclear Proliferation," *Foreign Policy* 91 (Fall 1998), 14.

[3] Ibid.; Scott D. Sagan, "Why Do States Build Nuclear Weapons?" *International Security* 21, no. 1–3 (Winter 1996–1997).

[4] "Unclassified Report to Congress on the Acquisition of Technology Relating to Weapons of Mass Destruction and Advanced Conventional Munitions, 1 July Through 31 December 1999," Central Intelligence Agency, August 2000.

[5] Anthony H. Cordesman, "Weapons of Mass Destruction in the Middle East, " (Washington, DC: Center for Strategic and International Studies, July 2000), 41–51.

[6] Andrew Koch and Steve Rodan, "Concern as test boosts Iranian missile development," *Jane's Defence Weekly*, July 26, 2000; Barry Rubin, "Shihab 3 test: The Iranian nuclear threat should not be overestimated," *Jerusalem Post*, July 17, 2000.

[7] Ibid.

[8] Cordesman, 64 and 51, respectively.

[9] "Unclassified Report to Congress"; Cordesman, 57–64.

[10] Cordesman, 57.

[11] "Unclassified Report to Congress"; "Iran: Chemical Weapons," Federation of American Scientists report, September 24, 2000, accessed at <http://www.fas.org>; Cordesman, 51–54.

[12] Cordesman, 54–55; "Iran: Biological Weapons," Federation of American Scientists report, September 24, 2000, accessed at <http://www.fas.org>.

[13] "Iraq: Biological Weapons—Current Capabilities," Federation of American Scientists report, September 24, 2000, accessed at <http://www.fas.org>.

[14] "Unclassified Report to Congress"; Cordesman, 72.

[15] Steven Lee Myers, "Flight Tests Show Iraq has Resumed a Missile Program," *The New York Times*, July 1, 2000, A1.

[16] Cordesman, 77–78.

[17] "Unclassified Report to Congress"; Cordesman, 16–18.

[18] "Syria—Special Weapons," Federation of American Scientists report, September 24, 2000, accessed at <http://www.fas.org>; Cordesman, 35–41.

[19] "Israel," Federation of American Scientists report, September 24, 2000, accessed at <http://www.fas.org>.

[20] Cordesman, 23–30; "Israel—Special Weapons," Federation of American Scientists report, September 24, 2000, accessed at <http://www.fas.org>.

[21] E.J. Hogendoorn, "A Chemical Weapons Atlas," *Bulletin of the Atomic Scientists* 53, no. 5 (September/October 1997), 35.

[22] Cordesman, 19–22.

[23] Ibid., 21.

[24] Devin T. Hagerty, "Nuclear Deterrence in South Asia: The 1990 Indo-Pakistani Crisis," *International Security* 20, no. 3 (Winter 1995–1996), 79–114.

[25] Kenneth N. Waltz, "More May Be Better," in Scott D. Sagan and Kenneth N. Waltz, *The Spread of Nuclear Weapons: A Debate* (New York: W.W. Norton, 1995); John J. Weltman, "Nuclear Devolution and World Order," *World Politics* 32, no. 2 (January 1980), 169–193; John J. Mearsheimer, "The Case for a Ukrainian Nuclear Deterrent, " *Foreign Affairs* 72, no. 3 (Summer 1993), 50–66.

---

*This chapter is based on a paper that was prepared for a conference on* The Middle East in Transition, *which was held at the Institute for National Strategic Studies, National Defense University, Washington, DC, on November 5, 1999.*

Chapter 11
# Conclusion: Three Parts of the Whole

*Judith S. Yaphe*

Fifteen years ago, in 1985, the key issues driving U.S. policy in the Middle East included curbing Iranian efforts to export its revolution; countering the growing menace of international terrorism in Lebanon and by state sponsors such as Libya, Iran, and Syria; and limiting the damage to shipping, access to oil, and stability posed by the Iraq-Iran w ar. To this latter end, the United States offered assistance to Iraq, increased its military presence and operations in the Persian Gulf, and tried to engage Arabs and Israelis in entering talks similar to those that produced the Israeli-Egyptian agreement in 1979. The Iraqi opening was short-lived and counterproductive, reflagging of Gulf oil tankers led to more extensive and dangerous engagement by U.S. forces in the region, and peace talks between Arabs and Israelis went nowhere. International terrorism—including the taking of W estern hostages in Lebanon and terrorist attacks in the Gulf and Europe—continued unabated.

---

*Judith S. Yaphe is senior research professor and Middle East project director in the Institute for National Str ategic Studies at the National Defense Univer sity. Previously, she was a senior analyst on Middle Eastern and Persian Gulf issues in the Office of Near Eastern and South Asian Analysis, Directorate of I ntelligence, CIA. Dr. Yaphe teaches Middle East regional studies in the Industrial College of the Armed Forces and Goucher College.*

In the year 2000, some of the key issues driving U.S. policy were maintaining sanctions on Iraq and Iran, dealing with high oil prices and energy shortages, moving the Israeli-Palestinian-Syrian peace process forward and then trying to contain the *al-Aqsa intifada,* which brought the process to a dead stop in September, and pursuing investigations of terrorism against American military targets in Saudi Arabia and Yemen. Perhaps because it was a presidential election year in the United States, no progress was made on the peace process, and no policy was clearly pursued regarding Iran or Iraq.

Both old and new American administrations struggled with defining an Iraq policy. Is it a new set of smart sanctions plus downsized inspections for weapons of mass destruction (WMD) plus military operations plus regime change? Or is it old sanctions and inspections in the spirit of the United Nations Special Commission and military operations writ broadly but no regime change? Despite efforts to formulate less antagonistic approaches to Tehran, appeal to the rising reformist elements, and end the Iran-Libya Sanctions Act imposed by Congress, policy remains restricted by legislative mandate and focused on issues of Iranian support, such as international terrorism, opposition to the Arab-Israeli peace process, and acquisition of WMD. Perhaps the most difficult development was the clear and direct linkage made for the first time by Arab leaders and publics between U.S. policy toward the region, including Iraq, and the failed peace process.

What will drive U.S. policy in the Middle East in 2015? Will it still be the Arab-Israeli peace process and the fate of Jerusalem? Will it be refugees, secure borders, and settlements? Will it be belligerent governments armed with cheap WMD-armed missiles? Will Iraq still be led by a Saddam-like figure, and, if so, who will be more isolated by the myth of sanctions—Baghdad or Washington? Will Iran have a secular government? There were no singular policy remedies that could have been applied coherently and consistently in 1985 or 2000 to the many complicated issues that confronted U.S policymakers. Moreover, there are not likely to be any in 2015. Resources may be fewer, countries now rich in oil may be poor, while those with water will possess *the* coveted liquid regional resource. Democratic institutions may litter the Gulf region, North Africa, and the Levant rather than the authoritarian regimes that prevail nearly everywhere today. The region may be a nuclear-free zone. The region may be less stable, less affluent, less autocratic. It may be more liberal politically, more privatized economically, more tolerant socially.

The answers are more easily discerned, again, if one considers the parts of the whole: the Maghreb (North Africa), the Mashreq (the Levant), and the Khalij (the Persian or Arabian Gulf). In this concluding chapter, we will examine the parts and consider what could happen to change our judgments or assumptions about the regional factors that will shape U.S. strategic policy or policies in 2015.

## The Maghreb: Forecasting Trends, Predicting Woe

The countries that comprise the Maghreb—Egypt, Libya, Algeria, Morocco, Tunisia, and Mauritania—will face many of the same problems in 2015 as they did in 2000. Most European and regional experts see little risk of a military or security threat between the northern and southern edges of the Mediterranean. The greater threat to regional security and stability comes from economic and domestic political imbalances. Issues of political and economic stability and regional security will be affected by the relationship between civilian and military institutions, economic benefits or liabilities from entering the new European Union (EU) free-trade zone, and the tension between Islamist and secularist.

*Egypt: The Most Promising and Intransigent.* In the year 2000, Cairo had improved its economy and quelled much of the opposition motivated by Islamists. Political decompression was evident; there seemed little hope of meaningful political reform, and the government maintained a vigilant watch on any signs of liberal deviation.[1] The military had long since transitioned from small, highly politicized, coup-prone units to a large, more professional, less politicized force. By 2015, military leaders will still be an important part of any ruling coalition and, along with prominent businessmen, will be key in determining political succession. Both will be worried more about upsetting domestic political stability and social peace than implementing significant reforms. Egypt will still need foreign investment and an end to capital flight, and the Islamist opposition could benefit from government failures to raise living standards or create new jobs. Egyptians in 2000 had not looked beyond the peace process and, given the tenacity of Arab-Israeli confrontations, Egyptians probably will remain incapable of planning the issues as they will stand in 2015. The generation coming to power in 2015 probably will be less interested in Arab nationalism or pan-Arabism and more concerned about local and self-interest. Its relations with the United States will be tactical and not strategic. Egypt will not desire ending a long-standing strategic friendship that, by 2015, may be more positive publicly than it was in 2000. Egypt, which prides itself on being the oldest country in the world, is likely by 2015 to be more liberal, more privatized, and more stable, especially if given relief for foreign debts. Its political leaders will still be in search of a regional leadership role. What Egypt will not be is changed.

*Algeria: Less Promising Trends.* By 2015, the population of Algeria will have increased by one-third, but the government's ability to produce jobs and a stable economy will not have improved. Its populist political traditions and revolutionary generation will be long gone, but its Kafkaesque political system is likely to be there. Inability to change is rooted in both the government and military. The rising generation in civil society and the dominant military institution will not remember the war for national liberation or care about broader Middle Eastern issues. Military power in politics might even wane as leaders lose legitimacy. Regionalism (that is, regions within Algeria) will be key to identify and to mobilize popular support. By 2015, the majority of Algerians will have been born in the 1980s and 1990s and witnessed years of reduced economic expectations. Then, as now, the poor and unemployed will most likely want jobs and a strong-man ruler, not democracy and not Islamic activism. In this context, ideological distinctions will be superficial, and demands for political reform will be weak. Algeria could experience more violence and weakening of central political authority and institutions. Insulated from Middle East issues, such as Arab-Israeli relations, Algeria will look north and west for validation rather than toward the Arab East.

*Morocco: Guarded Optimism.* Moroccan optimism in 2000 reflected hopes in an improving economy, coalition government, and a new king, Muhammad VI. Moroccans had raised expectations of political reform, including perhaps a limited monarchy and expanded power to the parliament, and new markets and jobs under greater economic cooperation with the European Union. Muhammad VI faces formidable challenges: an economy based on traditional agriculture, institutionalized corruption, large foreign debt, high rates of unemployment and illiteracy, a youth bulge with

50 percent of the population under the age of 30, and little prospect of improvement in the standard of living for the foreseeable future. Despite high expectations, the new king has shown so far no indication of relinquishing control over the instruments of state power (for example, justice, interior, foreign affairs ministries, and the military) nor of ending the corruption that pervaded his father's government. Unless the government can ease poverty, raise the standard of living and literacy rates, improve health care, and ensure social justice, Morocco faces an uncertain future in 2015.

*Libya: Bleak Prospects.* Libya was not included in our case studies because of the limited contact and lack of critical issues between Tripoli and Washington since the resolution of the Pan Am 103 bombing case. Libya in 2000 has neither political nor governmental institutions. Even the military lacks institutional structure. Decisionmaking is controlled by Muammar Qadhafi and an informal network of personal advisers, and none of them are likely to be around in 2015. The mystique of Arab nationalism is important to Qadhafi but will not survive him or last until 2015. Qadhafi is incapable of reforming Libya. Libya without Qadhafi will revert to local issues and tribal politics. At best, by 2015 the rising generation of technocrats, professionals, and other university-educated Libyans will have taken over and created a new state. At worst, Islamist and tribal elements will govern, and Libya without oil (approximately half of its reserves are depleted) could revert to a sandbox to be squabbled over by Tunisia, Egypt, and Algeria.

*When Europe sneezes, North Africa catches a cold.* An issue of critical importance to the economic health of the North African states is their relationship with their Mediterranean neighbors: Spain, France, Italy, Greece, and Turkey in particular. These countries have been especially supportive of the NATO Mediterranean initiative, which is focused on creating an economic and security dialogue with at least six regional states: Israel, Egypt, Jordan, Morocco, Tunisia, and Mauritania.[2] The Europeans do not see a security threat from the southern Mediterranean countries. They show little concern over Libya, Egypt, or even Algeria's potential acquisition or possession of WMD systems or long-range missiles. Rather, they worry about limiting the flows of cheap labor and illegal immigration to Europe while they preserve their economic dominance in the free trade zone that will be established by 2010.

More importantly, the root causes that have weakened Maghreb governments and strengthened their erstwhile Islamist opponents remain unchecked. In 2015, poverty, unemployment and underemployment, lack of housing, official corruption, and a sense of moral as well as military weakness will continue to attract the middle class, urban, educated Maghrebian as well as his poorer, rural cousin. Assuming that the region sees some economic growth over the next decade, what will be the impact of closer economic links to the European Union when, for example, Egypt, Morocco, and perhaps Algeria join the free trade zone in 2007? Some North African businessmen, scholars, and policymakers see the economic links of their countries to Europe in the form of trade, investment, labor flows, and remittances as helping the North African economies and political systems to remain stable. Others, however, warn that partnership in a free trade zone between the North African countries and Europe could prove more beneficial to European exports while weakening native industries in the Maghreb.[3] Maghrebian expectations are high, but European and Arab scholars note that the benefits are more likely to flow to Europe's advantage and come at a high price for North Africa in loss of jobs, failure of businesses unable to compete with cheaper European goods, and the shutting out of North African labor.

What might this all mean for the United States? In the Maghreb, America has not played a direct security or economic role, preferring to follow the lead and interests of Europe. This is unlikely to change by 2015.

## The Mashreq: After the Peace, Who Will We Be?

Trends in the Mashreq region—Israel, Jordan, Syria, and the Palestinian Authority—focus more on identity, legitimacy, and security than on purely economic issues, although demographics is key to problems plaguing this region as well as the Maghreb. Identity and political legitimacy are complicated in this region by the newness of the states, uncertainties of borders, and movements of refugee populations in countries that have been in a virtual state of war since Israel was created in 1948. In the years preceding 2000, with the prospect of peace at hand, these states asked: After peace, how will we benefit, and who will we be? Will we manage peace the same way we managed war? What will be the impact on the disparate elements that exist within our fragile societies, which have been bound together to a large extent by the external threat to our security? How will the Palestinians move from their actual and imagined role as ungovernable revolutionaries to being governed? How will Israel go from living in a perpetual state of hostility to one of no war or even peace? How will both of these societies hold themselves together if the threat of "the other" is removed? These issues go to the very foundations of these states and their national identity. They also apply to a lesser extent to Syria, Lebanon, and Jordan—all who have undergone significant political changes in the past year. In 2000, the question shifted from "Ho w do we live with peace?" to "How long can we live at war with each other and ourselves?"

Israel will remain the strongest and most dominant military and economic power in the region over the next 15 years. Crisis or change in its neighbors will not threaten its security. Israelis ask two questions every time there is a change in the region: Is it good for the Jews, and whom can we trust? Future answers will reflect the deep changes that Israeli society has been experiencing. Indeed, Israelis divide over whether and how to deal with the Arabs, but the arguments are even more fervent between the Sephardim (Jews who emigrated from the Arab world) and Ashkenazim (Jews who emigrated from Europe); between the Orthodox and non-Orthodox religious groups; between religious and secular Jews; between the remnant who remain loyal to Zionist ideals (a diminishing number) and the new émigrés (the Russians and those from Arab lands) who squabble over the economic and social benefits but are not enamored with f ighting for occupied territory. If Israel is still a country under siege in 2015, the siege will come from inside, and not outside, this small state. For the first time in Jewish history, Israel may have no active, militant adversary. It will have, however, Jewish citizens who question whether one can be an Israeli and not a Jew, an Israeli and not a Zionist. The motto "F or Us," which characterized the generation of the founders, will have been replaced by "For Me."

When polled on their views of national security in 1998, on the 50th anniversary of the Jewish state, one-third of the Israeli respondents answered that they were hawks and did not trust Arabs, one-third identified themselves as doves and did not trust Arabs, and one-third said they were neither hawk nor dove and did not trust Arabs. Will this have changed by 2015? Israel today has a young population, most who have not fought in an Arab-Israeli war, many who will not have fought even in Lebanon, few who directly experienced the Holocaust, and some—the Russian Jews in particular—who know little of Zionism. By 2020, one-third of Israel's population could be Arab, if current demographic trends continue. The question of who is and what it means to be an Israeli will not have been resolved.

Whether Israel has resolved its differences with its Arab neighbors by 2015, it will need to reconcile imbalances within its social and political fabric by correcting disparities between Israeli Jew and Israeli Arab, immigrant and native-born, religious and secular. It also will need to resolve the fissures in its political parties that have threatened the stability of nearly every government since independence. The Israeli political "center" will shift by 2015, but it is not clear in what direction or on what issues. A bi-national state does not seem likely from the vantage of 2000, although two states could coexist, albeit uneasily, by 2015. The hopes of Palestinian Arab moderates and Israeli Jewish liberals may be dashed if the current trend of rising extremism continues among Islamist and Jewish radicals.

By 2015 there will be a Palestinian state, but no one can predict what form it will take or what status it will hold vis-à-vis Israel, the Arabs states, or, most importantly, the Palestinians themselves. The Palestinian Authority is in transition from statelessness to nation building and self-rule. Palestinians need to focus on writing a constitution and establishing a legitimate, transparent, accountable government and a vibrant civil society. If there is no change in the style of autocratic rule now governing the Palestinians, scholars and analysts warn, then a Palestinian state will be on the defensive and unable to make the compromises necessary to achieve a final peace agreement with Israel.

The key issue now is Arafat. He will not be the key issue in 2015, but how Palestinians handle the transition of authority from him to a successor or series of successors will be key. Arafat is not a man of institutions, and Palestinians need stable and strong political institutions to give a new state credibility and legitimacy. Arafat's style is authoritarian and autocratic, much the same as that of the rulers in Jordan, Egypt, and Tunisia. Palestinian society today is a complicated amalgam; it is those who stayed in the Occupied Territories, participated in the *intifada* of the 1990s and were marginalized by Diaspora Palestinians on their return with Arafat from Tunis in 1994. It is also those who accompanied Arafat home from the Tunisian Diaspora and hold a monopoly on power and political positions. They control the security services, the b ureaucracy, and b usiness concessions in the private sector. The real danger for the future health of the nascent state will be the consequences of the growing alienation of the Palestinians who remained in the Occupied T erritories during the long years of exile and the fact that the exiled Palestinians relate to the Israelis and the peace process in ways different from local Palestinian elites. Finally, like all the other re gional states, the P alestinians face a serious demographic dilemma. The population of the W est Bank and Gaza grew 50 percent from the 1980s through the 1990s, with 20 percent of the population in the 15- to 24-year-old age bracket. This is a dangerous youth bulge for the early 21$^{st}$ century in a non-country comprised of refugees and school dropouts who cannot find work and demand social services.

Jordan and Syria in 2000 are in transition from the generation dominated by strong-willed rulers, such as King Hussein and Hafez al-Asad, to their young and politically untested sons. Those transitions should have been long completed by 2015, but there is the possibility that the once turbulent history of both countries could repeat itself in the coming years. Both countries share pastoral, Bedouin roots but are in the rapid process of becoming urbanized. Both have been ruled for long periods by authoritarian and hierarchical regimes, whether hereditary kingship or extended families. Both face challenges from the large Palestinian refugee communities that they shelter and Islamist militants who, though banned, are never far from the surface of both societies. Moreover, both ha ve survived to 2000 because of the infor - mal social contracts for ged by tradition, po wer, and tribal or institutional loyalties. In particular, Jordan and its Hashimite rulers ha ve honored their social contract with the ruled—peasants, Bedouin, merchants, and Palestinians—and all have benefited. King Hussein and his grandfather, King Abdullah, addressed peasant grie vances by dealing with absentee landlords, served merchant interests by creating a state-guided capitalism, and assisted homeless Palestinian refugees in Jordan by providing legal documentation and passports.

Jordan and its rulers will survive through 2015 if they continue in the same vein, but the small and vulnerable country will face many challenges in that timeframe. Some challenges will include the result of disengagement from the Palestine Authority and Syria because of the peace treaty with Israel or because of reengagement with Iraq.

Others will reflect demands for democratization—especially more political and press freedom. Finally, King Abdullah may face a succession crisis similar to that created by his father when he passed over his brother, the long-recognized successor Crown Prince Hassan, for his son. Abdullah will probably have less conflict with the Palestinians, in part because of his acceptance that Palestinians will remain in Jordan despite peace with Israel. Echoing the basic problems facing the other Arab states in the region, the greatest risk to Jordanian stability through 2015 will lie in the state's inability to provide for the economic well being of its citizens. What could go wrong with this basically up-beat analysis? The variables are failure of the peace process, especially between Israel and Syria, a dramatic change in the government of Israel, and water woes.

Syria is a dangerous place. Syrians crave more exposure to the West and upward mobility, but the path around peace to those goals is uncertain. With the coming of Bashar al-Asad to power, many analysts of Syrian politics have tried to paint an optimistic picture of Syria after peace and beyond its self-conscious pan-Arabism. They describe Syria in 2015 behaving like a state, and not an Arab state. Several factors, however, threaten Syrian stability, including the need for economic restructuring, depleted resources (water and oil), a rapidly growing population, a weak education system, unemployment, and a rising foreign debt. Half the population is under the age of 15 years, the social welfare safety net is disappearing, and Syria is being bypassed by the global revolution. Syria also lacks the source of cheap weapons and strategic balance that the Cold War provided. It has chemical weapons capability and missiles able to reach Israel but realizes that it cannot face Israel alone in a military confrontation. The Bashar al-Asad government will be faced with demands for reform and an end to corruption, and it will be less able to exert the kind of control over society that Hafez al-Asad did.

Given its domestic and external difficulties—which are not likely to be resolved easily or soon—will Syria be able to cope through 2015? Much will depend on the outcome of the negotiations with Israel. The longer peace is on hold, the less chance there will be for reform in Syria. Two scenarios are possible. In the best-case scenario, peace reigns, Bashar consolidates his power, and his rivals are "neutralized." Bashar, who is more attuned to change and modernization, will focus on "monied" interests rather than sectarian ones, whether Alawite or *asabiyah* (based on tribalism or Arabism). Political reform will be gradual and not threaten power bases, and there will be a slow decline in authoritarianism. In the worst-case scenario, there is no peace with Israel, and powerful Ba'th Party members and military barons rule Syria. Sectarianism and Islamic activism are on the rise, with half of Syria veiled and radicalized. Syrians will face bleak economic prospects, and the country will be e ven more isolated than it is currently . And, finally, terrorism will increase.

What might this all mean for the United States? Israeli society is torn by the collapse of the peace process and united against a threat perceived as overwhelming. Both Palestinians and Israelis see that for the first time in 50 years of conflict, their basic assumptions about legitimacy and national destiny are at odds with the reality of peace. Palestinians and Syrians, like Israelis, are clearly more worried about the impact of alarming trends on societies already rent by uncertainty . Palestinians and Israelis worry that their fragile societies will be at war with themselves if steps are not taken soon to end palace corruption and official mismanagement and open up society and civil institutions. All look to the United States to act "now" to mediate peace between Damascus, the P alestinians, and Israel or risk failure. W ithout Hafez al-Asad and Arafat, no one may be powerful enough to promote a deal, and the potential for ci vil unrest in Syria will gro w. Should America try to force all sides to the bargaining table without preliminary preparedness on their parts to negotiate on the critical issues—refugees, settlements, borders, Jerusalem, water—then we may be doomed to a perpetual state of war between Israeli and Palestinian, Jew and Muslim. Israel will demand a heavy price from the United States for its "cooperation" in a peace settlement, whether in security arrangements, money for new developments, or constant and unquestioning support in confrontations at the United Nations and with regional governments. Syria and the Palestinians will also make security demands on Americans, perhaps as simple as manning monitoring stations on the Golan, in Jerusalem, and along the uneasy borders between Israel, Palestine, and Lebanon.

## The Khalij: It's the Economy, ya Shaykh

Any consideration of future trends in the Persian Gulf is dominated by thoughts of the present—oil and Saddam Husayn. Iran, Iraq, and the smaller Arab states that compose the Gulf Cooperation Council (Saudi Arabia, K uwait, Bahrain, Qatar, the United Arab Emirates [UAE], and Oman) will continue for the foreseeable future to depend on oil and gas revenues to fuel their economic aspirations and political ambitions. Each has a unique set of factors shaping their current and future needs, policies and relationships, and divergent political systems, yet each faces similar challenges. Over the next decade, these societies will be shaped by how wisely or unwisely they allocate their economic and social treasures. The shared concerns outweigh the differences.

*Their economies are based on oil and gas.* Iraq, Saudi Arabia, Kuwait, and the UAE, in particular, have had the luxury of v ast wealth, seemingly limitless budgets, and small populations enjoying the unearned fruits of the oil economy . In 2000, their needs could be met at the same time there was sufficient money to cover all manner of purchases. This was true even of Iraq under sanctions, which earned an estimated $18 billion in oil revenue during the 1999–2000 oil boom.

*Their demographics reflect similar, skewed trends that if unchanged will put at risk futur e domestic well being.* All of the countries have high birth and fertility rates, lo w infant mortality, and populations that are more than 50 percent under the age of 18 or 20 years. More importantly, all ha ve youth b ulges in the 15- to 30-year -old range, where unemployment is high for populations that are relatively well educated and used to enjoying the "rights" of a welfare state—free education and health care, high salaries, easy employment, and the safety net of the e xtended family.

*Their populations are "post-historical."* In all the countries, the bulk of the population does not remember "the time before"—before the Islamic revolution, before Saddam Husayn, or before oil. The results of this trend are diminished vision and increasingly unmet expectations.

*They find it easier to blame "the other" for national woes than to accept responsibility for their decisions.* Foreign-imposed economic sanctions, neo-colonialist conspiracies, or unfair competition in capturing a lar ger oil market share are responsible for our po verty, lack of jobs, and high rate of un- and under-employment. Our own lack of skills, corruption, or unrestrained greed for wealth or weapons of mass destruction, or unwillingness to cooperate in controlling oil pricing and production to stabilize supply and demand to our benefit—these factors have nothing to do with why we are poor or weak or behind the West in development.

Looking toward 2015, some important trends and indicators of stability emerge. Iraq's history of a violent and exclusive political culture will shape its future as it has its past. Iraq's history before Saddam is littered with violent coups by military officers and political thugs. Saddam has refined the practice of terror and reliance on an inner circle comprised of family, clan, tribe, and revolutionary stalwarts to a new degree not previously seen in Iraq, but the country has been dominated by a Sunni elite with power centralized in Baghdad and challenged by rebellious Kurds and occasionally intemperate Shia since 1920. Saddam in 2000 rules in various guises—as republican shaykh and as grand patriarch, as party leader and tribal chief. What will the Iraq of 2015 resemble? Except for Saddam and the concentric circles of family, security, and military forces that protect him, Iraq has no other political or governmental institutions that could provide leadership at this time. The Ba'th Party has been marginalized by the cult of personality; it is devoid of intellectuals, ideology, or loyalists. The Peoples' Assembly is irrelevant. The middle class has all but disappeared. Iraq is a polarized country—Kurds and Arabs, Sunnis and Shias. The population has grown to 22 million—up 3 million since the end of the war—with 40 percent born since 1989. Education standards have declined dramatically. What will the future hold for a country impoverished by Saddam, sanctions, and the isolation of a generation of children?

Of the three succession scenarios outlined in chapter 8, the most likely is Saddam or a son continuing in power. In 2015 Saddam would be 79 years old. If alive, he would probably be ruling in tandem with his second son Qusay, already virtually designated as the prime candidate to succeed Saddam. He or a successor from the military—Iraq's military has a long history of coup plotting—would be very much like Saddam because of schooling by Saddam and Iraqi history. He would be oppressive and authoritarian. The succession would be bloody, and there would be a risk of civil war. The least likely scenario is political change engineered by the exiled opposition with U.S. help. They, too, are *not* inherently democratic. Some scholars and analysts describe them as highly authoritarian and undemocratic, their leaders divided by deep and abiding personal animosities. Others describe the opposition as anarchic, more interested in destroying each other than in removing Saddam. While the United States in theory would prefer a republic of Iraq, where Iraqis freely chose their leaders in open elections, foreswore interest in regional hegemony or weapons of mass destruction, and enjoyed an open, unsanctioned economy, reality is likely to be different. For those who worry that Iraq without a strong central authority figure will slip into anarchy, warlordism, or civil war, then American interests will seem to be best served by *Anyone But Saddam*. A new leader, most probably a general, would need U.S. backing to remove sanctions and improve the economy, thereby legitimizing his rule. Here the United States could be pivotal in perception and reality. If Americans can help turn around Iraq's economy, then Iraqis may accept the United States and whatever political leadership provides economic security and political stability. For Iraqis, the ability to feed and educate their children is far more important than voting in free elections.

*Iran is undergoing a profound social transition that may have significant political repercussions by 2015.* Like Iraq, the majority of today's Iranian population is in the 15- to 30-year-old bracket. They did not participate in the revolution or the war with Iraq and are, for the most part, alienated from the political system. They came of age in a period of hardship, war, and sanctions; they worry about the lack of jobs, housing, and a decent standard of living. They are better educated than their parents, with women having made the most significant advances in literacy. At the same time, the generation that made the revolution is dying off, and those leaders remaining are aging—President Khatami was elected in 2001 to his second term as president and cannot run again; Supreme Leader Khamenei is 63 and apparently in ill health. Both are likely to be gone by 2015.

The tremendous pressure for economic and social reform evinced by the reformist victories of 1997 and 2001 will not necessarily translate into demands for political liberalization and full-scale Western-style democracy. Most of the generation that is coming of age cares little for politics. Few supported the students' brief protest last summer, and none will take to the streets to change the regime. Iran's political factions—Islamic leftists favoring political liberalization, Islamic centrists focusing their attentions on economic reform, and conservatives seeing any demands for change as threatening the system of clerical rule—have been locked in a power struggle since the death of Ayatollah Khomeini in 1989. The deadlock is likely to continue through

2015. Three possible scenarios suggest themselves: the reformists gain or seize power and the conservatives bow to the inevitable and change course; the conservatives crack down on Iran's reformers at the same time that they offer dramatic economic reforms and Iran becomes a police state (the Tienanmen model); and, finally and most likely, the current factional stalemate continues. Change in Iran is not inevitable. Stalemate can be a permanent condition, especially if Iranians lack the enthusiasm necessary for another revolution. They are probably not willing to risk a lot for change.

The implications of stasis are important for U.S. and regional security policies. Iran's leaders share a consensus on foreign and defense policy. They will continue their moderate course in foreign affairs, especially in the Gulf and with Europe. Full normalization of relations between Iran and Saudi Arabia will not result in full security cooperation. Iran's leaders want to reduce their security concerns; they do not want a return to the hostilities of the 1980s. Their interest is in ending economic sanctions and removing U.S. military presence in the Gulf. They would like America to unfreeze Iranian assets, settle all claims still pending against Iran, and sell spare parts for aircraft. Even though few Iranians were alive in the Mossadegh era, the coup is a vivid memory rankling Iranian national pride. Most Iranians would like the United States to apologize for its role or, at least, express remorse much as Khatami did in acknowledging Iran's misguided actions in taking U.S. diplomats hostage in 1979. Most Iranians probably do not know how they would gain from relations with America, but the United States could offer cooperation against Iraq, on creating a new and stable government in Afghanistan, and for the beleaguered Shia of South Lebanon. Most Iranians are isolated from the real diplomatic world; they know little of the Arab-Israeli peace process or issues surrounding WMD proliferation. Until the *al-Aqsa intifada* began, these remained issues for elite debate. The optimal trend for U.S.-Iranian relations looking toward 2015 is one of constructive engagement, especially if the reformists consolidate their power and harmonized policies with Europe. U.S. sanctions policy and other "sticks" will not change the course of Iranian decisionmaking on supporting international terrorism, opposing the peace process, or ending its quest for weapons of mass destruction, especially nuclear. But it could defuse these issues and make them more negotiable by 2015.

The GCC states may now be enjoying the best of all possible times. Oil prices are up, succession in most of the states is not an issue, and the neighborhood bullies—Iraq and Iran—are not threatening regional security or stability. By 2015, there are not likely to be signif icant changes in the kind of governance now ruling; individual rulers will have been replaced by family members as determined by family consensus. Democratic institutions and transparency in government—reforms limply sought by some reformists—will have made only minimal incursions into the traditional political arrangements that govern these small societies.

Like the other states in the region, Saudi Arabia and its small neighbors will face daunting demographic challenges over the next 15 years. Their populations are likely to double—as will the demands on the economic infrastructure for jobs, housing, and the kinds of subventions that the oil-rich Gulf Arabs have grown accustomed to as their right. Some predictable trends include a decreased dependence on expatriate labor and a limited increase in economic privatization. As in political reform, ruling family members will impose limits on economic reform so that their interests are protected at the expense of private sector development and non-royal participation in decisionmaking. The Saudi ruling f amily, if it is to survi ve, may ha ve to redefine who is a royal—there are now approximately 15,000 princes and princesses drawing down on the government dole. Cutting the more distaff members off could have dangerous repercussions by encouraging political factionalism in a society known for consensus and family solidarity. Labor issues will be more important than Islamist issues, including the current debate on the presence of foreign troops. Gulf Arabs will be better educated and more interested in national than tribal issues. (Arab scholars would probably agree openly and disagree privately with this statement.) Most scholars agreed that Islamic activism is *not* a trend.

Gulf Arab prosperity and complacency will depend on stable oil prices, seamless political succession, and reduced regional tensions. Right now, the trends are positi ve. Several indicators could warn of shifts in the social and economic fabric of the GCC states:

- *Women:* Will they be inte grated into political and economic life or isolated even more by advances in telecommuting technology? Will the debate be framed as an economic issue by

businesses and families or as a moral issue by conservative *'alims* (religious scholars)?
- *Fiscal policy:* Can the oil-rich Arabs learn to live within a budget? Can they get a hold on spending, whether oil revenues are up or down, and account for economic decisions?
- *Investment:* Will the Saudis, Kuwaitis, Emirians, and Qataris—the "oil haves"—invest their wealth abroad or in their own countries?
- *Family politics:* If the ruling families and their elite allies split over issues of political power or economic spoils, then society will fracture, too. Will the traditional ties that bind these fragile societies together hold in the face of economic adversity or social disarray?

What might this all mean for the United States? Iraq, Iran, and the GCC states differ in their political systems, styles of decisionmaking, and tactical means to resolve security problems. The academic experts seem convinced that all will muddle through 2015 in much the same way that they have survived the last 15 years: decisions will be made opaquely and with apparent consensus by family, clan, or factions; they will spend money on pet projects (whether Saddam on weapons systems or the Gulf Arabs on hawks and horses) without regard to fiscal realities; they will blame the "outside" for their economic woes and inability to cooperate with one another. They will use the U.S. military presence as a form of insurance while they pursue self-interest and balance of power. This includes the Iranians, who have benefited from American condemnation of Saddam, UNSCOM inspections, and UN-imposed sanctions on Iraq; and the Gulf Arabs, who occasionally deplore our overt presence but know that they could not move closer to Iran or Iraq without it. One underlying theme repeatedly raised by analysts and deferred by scholars was the issue of weapons of mass destruction. It is an issue on which most are reluctant to voice a judgment.

## What Could Go Wrong with These Assumptions?

Trying to predict a vision of the Middle East in 2015 is as difficult today as predicting the year 2000 was in 1985 or estimating the future of Iran in 1990 as seen from 1978. Who could have guessed that the Soviet Empire would collapse, the Cold War would end, and one Arab Muslim country would invade two of its neighbors? Who predicted the fall of the Shah? Many may have wished it, but none "predicted" it in academe or government.

The trends described in these chapters reflect an appreciation of demography, the natural laws of economics, history, and the determination of human nature, or in this case governments, to pursue policies and courses of actions regardless of their logic or potential consequences. It is much harder to think about what could go wrong with the analysis. The most obvious unpredictable factors include a coup, an unexpected succession, or a border skirmish that escalates to war. Other developments, however, can have unpredictable and unplanned consequences. For example, the growing military and economic cooperation between Israel and Turkey could by 2015 have produced an alliance between Iran, Greece, Syria, and Armenia. *Intifada* without end could bring about a new Arab-Islamist nexus linking Iran, Iraq, Syria, Jordan, and Egypt against Israel. Globalization, seen as an effort by the new imperialists of the West to keep the East isolated and marginalized, may have connected Gulf Arabs and Maghrebian Berbers to the wonders of the Web, but its ability to effect change is almost certainly overrated.

## Notes

[1] In June 2000, Saad al-Din Ibrahim, a prominent Egyptian scholar whose work focused on human rights and civil liberties, was sentenced to 7 years at hard labor for alleged misuse of foreign funds (grants to his study center from the European Union) and for defaming Egypt. He was released in 2002.

[2] Algeria is included in some discussions.

[3] See Judith S. Yaphe, "Do No Harm: Thoughts on NATO's Mediterranean Initiative," *Mediterranean Quarterly* 10, no. 4 (Fall 1999), 56–71. One of the most comprehensive studies was produced by the RAND Corporation for the Italian government; see F. Stephen Larrabee, et al., *NATO's Mediterranean Initiative: Policy Issues and Dilemmas*, DDR–1699–IMD (Santa Monica, CA: RAND, 1998). The study assumes that any new security threats to NATO members will come from the southern periphery of the alliance—the Balkans, the Mediterranean, the Caucasus—and that the Barcelona Process as well as the proliferation of weapons of mass destruction, drug traficking, and terrorism will force NATO to play a more active role in the region. Simon Serfaty warns that Europe is preoccupied with threats from North African and other Middle Eastern immigrant communities who threaten to carry their homeland battles and terrorism to the European mainland. See Serfaty, "Algeria Unhinged: What next? Who care? Who leads?" *Survival* 38, no. 4 (Winter 1996–1997), 137–153.

Postscript
# Israel-Turkey: Strategic Relationship or Temporary Alliance?

*Alan Makovsky*

Although Turkey and Israel had informal relations since the 1950s, the relationship assumed a new and public dimension in the 1990s when military leaders of both countries began a series of cooperative exercises and agreements. By the year 2000, the relationship had expanded to include joint training and military exercises, co-production of missile systems, Israeli upgrades of T urkey's U.S. origin aircraft, and intelligence sharing on topics of mutual concern. Both governments are pro-Western, anti-Islamist, and highly compatible in military in ventories. They share common suspicions of Syria and Iran and common ambitions to develop trade and commercial contacts into Central Asia' s new energy markets. Even if there were to be peace between Israel and Syria or T urkey and Syria (from our v antage point a remote prospect), these relations are likely to have expanded further by 2015.

---

*Alan Makovsky is senior fellow and director of the Turkish Research Program at the Washington Institute for Near East P olicy. He pr eviously served in the Department of State as special adviser to the special Middle East coor dinator, political adviser at Operation* Provide Comfort, *and division chief for Southern Europe in the Office of Western Europe and Canadian Affairs, Directorate of Intelligence, CIA. He is the author of* New Directions in Turkish Foreign Policy *(forthcoming).*

Establishing close ties with Israel was a bold initiative for Turkey. A long-time supporter of Arab positions on the peace process, Turkey's move had the aura of a major switching of sides in the Arab-Israeli peace process. This was not quite the case. The 1993 Oslo agreement, especially the Palestine Liberation Organization (PLO) recognition of Israel, freed Ankara to pursue relations with Israel without criticism from the PLO. The Turks' declarative policy on the peace process remains pro-Palestinian—Turkey recognized the "State of Palestine" in 1988 but has played no substantive role in the Israeli-Palestinian equation. At the same time, Ankara's declining relations with the Arab world and Iran facilitated its growing ties with Israel.

*Israel and Turkey cooperate for strategic reasons*, and the proper designation for their relationship is "strategic relationship," not "alliance." Neither side is obligated to go to war if the other is attacked, and it is difficult to imagine any circumstances in which either would do so. The strategy is based on two common needs; the most important is the military-security dimension, and the second is economic. Of the two dozen agreements signed since 1993, the key ones have covered military cooperation and training, defense-industrial cooperation, and a free-trade agreement, all signed in 1996. Both sides have benefited:

- *Israel* gets access to Turkish air space to train its pilots for long-range missions; enhances its ability to collect intelligence against arch-foes Syria, Iraq, and Iran; expands its arms sales opportunities; eases its regional isolation; and burnishes its credentials as a partner for the Muslim-majority states of the former Soviet Union. Israel has upgraded Turkish F–4 and F–5s, and Israeli press reports indicate other military deals are in the works.
- *Turkey* sharpens its military know-how through joint training and close cooperation with the Israeli military; boosts its intelligence-gathering against hostile and potentially hostile neighbors; and, most important, gains access to sophisticated arms and materiel that can flow unimpeded by supporters of Greek, Armenian, Kurdish, and human rights advocates—issues that make West European states and the United States uncertain arms partners for Ankara. The Turks also anticipate that over time, close ties with Israel will boost their standing with the U.S. Congress.

The initial impetus for Ankara to build close ties with Israel was to strengthen its deterrence against Syria, which borders both Turkey and Israel and long supported the anti-Turkish Kurdish separatist movement, the Kurdish People's Party (PKK), and other anti-Turkish terrorist groups. Turkey largely achieved this objective in October 1998 when Damascus expelled PKK leader Abdullah Ocalan under threat of attack. It is widely believed that Syrian President Asad feared a fight with Turkey would bring in Israel as well and thus decided that surrender of Ocalan was the wiser course. As for the economic dimension, trade grew steadily in the 1990s, especially with the 1997 bilateral free-trade agreement. Trade volume, which was $90 million in 1989, grew to $900 million in 1999—a ten-fold increase. In 1999, Israel emerged as Turkey's leading export market in the Middle East. Israel is also considering a major purchase of water from Turkey.

*Turkey and Israel have divergent views on some significant regional security issues.* Turkey prefers an integrated Iraq and a strong central government, and it would even be content if Saddam Husayn were to reassert Iraq's rule over the northern, predominantly Kurdish provinces that are above the 36th parallel (out of deference to Washington, Ankara does not say so publicly). Israel prefers a weak, fragmented, even broken Iraq, all of which are anathemas to Turkey. Ankara fears the emergence of a Kurdish state, which Israel in the past has encouraged. Israel sees Iran as an existential threat. Turkey, despite ideological differences and often tense relations with Tehran, does not.

The military and economic dimensions of Turkish-Israeli cooperation are likely to remain vibrant. There are, in fact, few impediments. Most of the criticism has come from the countries bordering Turkey and that feel most directly threatened—Iran, Iraq, and Syria. Regional and Islamic objections, such as those orchestrated by Iran at the Organization of the Islamic Conference meeting in Tehran in December 1997, have been less intense than generally portrayed. [1] Predictions that Turkish-Israeli ties would fragment the region, spawning menacing counter-alliances, for example between Greece, Armenia, Iran, or Syria, have not come to pass.

*There are limits on the nature of relations* and areas where expectations from the other side must be kept within bounds. Neither side will defend the other on issues that isolate it from the international mainstream. Israel will not defend Turkey's Kurdish policies, and Turkey will not defend Israel's settlement policies or other controversial aspects of Israeli policies toward the Palestinians. The two sides generally do not criticize one another on these issues, or , when they do so, it is in a muted w ay. The American Jewish establishment's interest in Turkey has increased in recent years, with American and Israeli Jewish groups making of ficial visits to T urkey, where they often meet with senior of ficials. However, it is doubtful that this will translate into significantly greater support for T urkey in Congress any time soon, particularly regarding weapons sales. Over time, Turkey's ties with Israel, if the y prove durable, are lik ely to create positive associations for T urkey in the minds of pro-Israel Congressmen and executive branch officials alike. Ties with Israel were initiated primarily by the T urkish military, rather than by the ci vilian leadership for strategic reasons, and not in response to popular sentiment. Given Islamist sentiment in T urkey, a significant minority of Turkey's population is al ways likely to be critical of T urkish-Israeli relations. Israel's role in rescue ef forts following the August 1999 earthquake gained some popular support for the relationship. The considerable anti-Arab feeling among the T urkish establishment also helps sustain ties with Israel.

Regarding the peace process, T urkey would like to see an Israeli-Palestinian peace agreement, which would enhance the legitimacy of ties with Israel among the still significant pro-Palestinian segment of the population. T urkey has misgi vings, however, about the Israeli-Syrian peace track. D eterrence against Syria was the original focus and glue of T urkish-Israeli relations. Ankara w orries about the loss of the Israeli factor as a deterrent on Syrian actions against Turkey. An Israeli-Syrian peace could upset the status quo, where Syria is weak and isolated and Ankara relati vely secure. Although the T urks have been encouraged by a decline in Syrian support for anti-T urkish terrorism since the expulsion of Ocalan, they harbor a deep mistrust of the Syrians that is unlik ely to dissipate soon. T urkey also w orries that Israel, with American backing, will try to bar gain away Turkish water by suggesting that Syria be compensated for Golan waters with water from the Euphrates;[2] that Syria will be removed from the U.S. statesponsors of terrorism list merely for cutting ties with anti-Israel terrorists, without ha ving to tak e similar action re garding anti-Turkish terrorists; that peace with Israel will allow Syria to redeploy its forces to its northern border; that the United States will build close ties with

Syria, as it did with Egypt and Jordan following their peace treaties with Israel; and that Israel might give precedence to relations with Syria over its relations with T urkey.

Israeli-Turkish ties in 2000 are strong and multdimensional. They are likely to withstand Syrian peacemaking with both Israel and Turkey. For some observ ers, Turkish-Israeli relations are a lik ely pacesetter for Muslim normalization with Israel. Indeed, in a world of Middle East comprehensive peace, it is quite possible that Israeli-Turkish relations could form the core of a ne w type of re gional co-operation featuring agreements on security , trade, and w ater. For others, the Israeli-Turkish marriage of con venience could spawn reactive regional alliances intended to counter real or imagined intentions in Ankara and Israel and to punish the United States for its close ties to both.

## Notes

[1] Turkey's Prime Minister Erbakan left the Islamic summit after the second day of criticism. A few weeks later, Iran's foreign minister was in Ankara for talks on improving trade and diplomatic ties.

[2] In early 1996, Israeli Prime Minister Shimon Peres publicly proposed this to Ankara's chagrin.

*This chapter is based on a paper that was presented at a conference on* The Middle East in Transition, *which was held at the Institute for National Strategic Studies, National Defense University, Washington, DC, on January 21, 2000.*

# About the Editor

Judith S. Yaphe is senior research professor and Middle East project director in the Institute for National Strategic Studies at the National Defense University. Previously, she was a senior analyst on Middle Eastern and Persian Gulf issues in the Office of Near Eastern and South Asian Analysis, Directorate of Intelligence, CIA. Dr. Yaphe teaches Middle East regional studies in the Industrial College of the Armed Forces and Goucher College.

Printed in Great Britain
by Amazon.co.uk, Ltd.,
Marston Gate.